RECORD AND FILM PRODUCER JOE BOYD was born in Boston in 1942 and graduated from Harvard in 1964. He went on to produce Pink Floyd, Nick Drake, Fairport Convention, REM and many others. He produced the documentary *Jimi Hendrix* and the film *Scandal*. In 1980 he started Hannibal Records and ran it for 20 years.

White Bicycles, an anthology of Joe Boyd's record production in the 1960s, is available from Fledg'ling Records.

Joe Boyd's website is located at www.joeboyd.co.uk.

praise for *White Bicycles*

'As a memoir of the enchanted '60s, *White Bicycles* is among the elite. It isn't just that Boyd was among the era's movers and shakers, he has a rare recall of events... and a fluid, engaging style. The book bristles with evocative anecdotes... exhilarating' *Observer Music Monthly*

'One of the most lucid and insightful music autobiographies I've read' Michel Faber, *Guardian*

'Terrific... This engaging and readable book is an important addition to the history of its time' Hanif Kureishi, *New Statesman*

'A rock memoir that shuns the usual '60s clichés... while providing insightful character studies of Brit-folk's future stars... refreshing and cleverly observed' *Uncut*

'Among the musical anecdotes are thoughtful observations on the era... Boyd remains a true believer, for whom it was a joy to have been alive in that permissive dawn. At 40 years' distance, his prose still conveys the hues of the sunrise with startling vividness' Nigel Williamson, *The Times*

'Impossible to put down' *Q*

'Boyd is one of that select group of rock luminaries, like John Peel, or the American producer Rick Rubin, who didn't have to pick up a guitar to shape the evolution of entire genres of music. And this book is the perfect literary echo of a lifetime's subtle facilitation... Boyd's pages abound with astute observations and fascinating personal detail... a transport of delight' *Independent on Sunday*

'A vivid eye-witness account... pulses with the mad enthusiasms of its period and its author'
Robert Sandall, *Sunday Times*

'Boyd's account far exceeds the breadth of most rose-tinted ruminations... detailed and lucid... A wise, thoughtful and engrossing account, *White Bicycles* is one of the best 1960s essays of recent years' *Scotsman*

'Boyd writes in a dry, assured style about remarkable times, and he achieves the goal of any music book: to make the reader want to check out the music he writes about'
Will Hodgkinson, *Guardian Guide*

'Reading Boyd's cracking account of the Sixties, you wonder if his life since hasn't been one long disappointment... It's a colourful story, beautifully told... You are left relieved that such a central figure wrote this exceptional memoir' Mark Ellen, *Observer*

'A fascinating book overflowing with entertaining and insightful musical anecdotes' *Morning Star*

'Compulsive quirky detail, rare sanity and razor sharp recall... puts it in the same bracket as Simon Napier Bell's *Black Vinyl White Powder* or Julian Cope's *Head On*. A delight' *The List*

'Packed full of funny, telling anecdotes and wry, insightful observation, it takes us on a fantastic musical adventure'
fRoots

white bicycles

making music in the 1960s

Joe Boyd

SERPENT'S TAIL

A complete catalogue record for this book can be obtained from the British Library on request

First published in 2006 by Serpent's Tail,
an imprint of Profile Books Ltd
3A Exmouth House
Pine Street
Exmouth Market
London EC1R 0JH
www.serpentstail.com

The cover design is by Nigel Waymouth and Sheridan Wall.

The cover photograph was taken at the 1965 Newport Folk Festival by Jim Floyd and includes Eric Von Schmidt (beard), Joe Boyd (hat), Tom Rush, Geoff and Maria Muldaur.

The candy-stripe script is from the first UFO poster in January of 1967 by Hapshash & The Coloured Coat (Nigel Waymouth and Michael English).

Designed and typeset by Sue Lamble

Printed in the United States

ISBN 1 85242 910 0
ISBN 978 1 85242 910 2

10 9 8 7 6 5 4

acknowledgements

MANY FRIENDS HAVE GIVEN ME support, encouragement and advice. I owe a huge debt in particular to Lucy Bailey, who edited the final drafts with unerring eye and whose unsparing critiques improved it immeasurably. The book's shape and scope are largely the result of advice from Melissa North and Pierre Hodgson, for which I am very grateful. After some early setbacks, Deborah Rogers' belief and support gave me the energy to stick with it. A thoughtful response to the first draft from Rose Simpson made it clear what I needed to improve in the second. The musicians and colleagues without whom there would be no story to tell will, I trust, find their acknowledgements in the text that follows.

In memory of my grandmother, Mary Boxall Boyd,
who taught me to listen.

Saturday sun came early one morning
In a sky so clear and blue
Saturday sun came without warning
So no one knew what to do.
Saturday sun brought people and faces
That didn't seem much in their day
But when I remembered those people and places
They were really too good in their way.
In their way
In their way
Saturday sun won't come and see me today.

Think about stories with reason and rhyme
Circling through your brain.
And think about people in their season and time
Returning again and again
And again
And again
And Saturday's sun has turned to Sunday's rain.

So Sunday sat in the Saturday sun
And wept for a day gone by.

Nick Drake

prologue

THE SIXTIES BEGAN in the summer of 1956, ended in October of 1973 and peaked just before dawn on 1 July, 1967 during a set by Tomorrow at the UFO Club in London.

John Hopkins and I had launched the weekly UFO events at an Irish dance hall in Tottenham Court Road just before Christmas 1966, and they had quickly become the hub of psychedelic London. By April, our resident attraction, Pink Floyd, had outgrown us, so I was always on the lookout for new groups. I saw Tomorrow at Blaises one night and thought they were pretty good. When they made their UFO debut on 19 May it was love at first sight between them and our audience. Steve Howe, later to make his name and fortune with Yes, played guitar, while Twink, a key figure in the genesis of punk, was the drummer. I don't know what became of Junior, the bass player, but his mad-eyed, don't-give-a-fuck presence in a string vest was a key element in their appeal. Lead singer Keith West had a solo hit that summer with 'Excerpt From A Teenage Opera, Part 1' ('Grocer Jack, Grocer Jack, please come back...') and did his best to maintain a pop-star presence while around him the group was morphing into something quite different. 'My White Bicycle', a tribute to the free transport provided by Amsterdam's revolutionary *provos*, was their new theme song, while Howe's solos got longer and Twink's drumming ever wilder.

A month or two earlier, I would never have gone to Blaises and Tomorrow would barely have heard of UFO. Everything was accelerating that spring: new drugs, clothes, music and clubs. The psychedelic underground and the pop scene were starting to overlap. UFO crowds were bigger each week, and it was getting hard to maintain the original atmosphere. It was also difficult to ignore the increased attention from the police: the longer the queues, the more customers were getting frisked and busted.

Hoppy ran UFO's light tower, playing records between shows, putting on Kurosawa samurai films at 3 a.m. and troubleshooting around the club while I stayed near the entrance and trousered the money. When plainclothes policemen asked to have a look around, I would state our policy: no search warrant, no entry. (There was nothing to prevent them from merging with the crowds and paying their way in, of course; UFO's ads often touted a 'spot the fuzz' competition.) As for Mr Gannon, our landlord at the Blarney Club, he felt the case of whiskey delivered to Goodge Street police station every Christmas should take care of them well enough.

A few weeks before Tomorrow's return visit on 30 June, a uniformed bobby turned up, asking to be allowed in to collect clothes left behind by a man being held in custody. This made sense: half an hour earlier, a naked guy had bolted past me up the stairs and disappeared into the night. Hoppy and I agreed that an exception could be made, so I told the audience we were going to let the fuzz in to look for the clothes and turn on the overhead lights (murmurs and booing). As the crowd spread out in a wide circle, some garments could be seen scattered around the floor. The young bobby seemed to blush as he glanced at the crowd, a vivid cross-section of 'London Freak' *circa* May 1967: long hair on the boys, flowered dresses on the girls, Arabian or Indian shirts, a few kaftans, jeans, even a few white shirts and khaki slacks. Many were tripping; most were laughing or grinning.

The laughter grew as it became clear that the bobby's hastily gathered armful contained more than was required to make his prisoner decent: two or three pairs of underpants (gender undetermined), a couple of shirts, a bra, several socks, etc. As he made his way to the door, the working-class constable regarded us with amazement, not hatred. We, in turn, regretted that he could not grasp why we took drugs and danced in the lights, lived for the moment and regarded our fellow man with benign tolerance, even love. That was the theory, anyway. Tested, it would come undone in the ensuing years, even as the bobby's mates donned kaftans, rolled joints and joined the crowds at festivals.

The first man I knew to take hallucinogens was Eric Von Schmidt. (You can see Eric's photo on one of the record jackets beside Sally Grossman on the cover of *Bringing It All Back Home* and hear Dylan blurt, 'I learned this song from Ric Von Schmidt' on his eponymous first LP.) Mail-order packages of peyote buds from Moore's Orchid Farm in Texas arrived periodically at the Von Schmidt apartment near Harvard Square. He would cook them up in a pot and invite friends over to drink the soup. They would stack some LPs on the record player – Ali Akbar Khan, Lord Buckley, Chopin, the Swan Silvertones, Lightning Hopkins – then drink the potion and try not to be sick. If you couldn't keep it down you weren't, in Eric's view, calm enough ('centred' had not yet been used in this context) to deserve the high. It was an experience meant for an intellectual and spiritual elite, not the masses (although he certainly would never have put it that way).

The market is too efficient, of course, to limit transcendence to people who can stomach peyote. Down the street from Eric's flat in 1962 was the laboratory of Professor Timothy Leary, who advertised in the Harvard *Crimson* for volunteers to take LSD at a dollar an hour and was determined to become the Johnny Appleseed of hallucinogens. By 1967, pure, powerful LSD tabs were still available while adulterated, amphetamine-laced concoctions were starting to be widely distributed. Few bothered about how elevated the experience might be.

In June that year, a *News of the World* reporter tipped off Scotland Yard about a 'drugs-and-sex orgy' at Keith Richards' place and was rewarded with a ringside seat at the raid. It has become the stuff of legend: Mars bars, threesomes, Marianne Faithfull naked under a fur rug, etc., a symbol of out-of-control decadence. The media stopped winking and grinning about 'Swinging London' and started wallowing in horror stories about teenagers being led astray. *Sgt Pepper* was the world's soundtrack that month and powerful Establishment figures were horrified by the implications of influential pop stars' open fondness for drugs.

For the UFO audience, the Stones' bust represented the sinister collusion of circulation-seeking editors, treacherous grasses and killjoy drug squads. Jagger and Richards may have been wealthy superstars, but they were counterculture heroes, too. Hoppy had also been busted that spring (after a plainclothes man reached, conjuror-like, behind his sofa and pulled out an evidentiary plum) and had just been sentenced to eight months in Wormwood Scrubs. Ads and editorials in the *International Times*, posters around UFO and graffiti in Notting Hill Gate reminded everyone of the injustice. A bucket was circulated at the club, the money going to a legal defence fund for drug busts.

One Friday, just before Tomorrow took the stage, I found myself in conversation with Twink and a few others. Hoppy's jailing outraged us and the behaviour of the *News of the World* seemed like the last straw. We decided to close the club after the first set and parade through the West End, finishing off with a protest in front of the *News of the World* building in Fleet Street. The West End at 1 a.m. on a Friday night was nothing like as busy as it is today, but there were quite a few 'normals' about, and they gaped as we rounded Piccadilly and headed for Leicester Square, then down through Covent Garden towards Fleet Street. Our destination was a letdown: the *News of the World* building was dark and silent. Firebrands among us started planning a blockade of the Sunday paper and an assault on their vans the next night.

The long walk in the night air, the hostile stares from the 'straights' and the threats from the police had energized everyone, so the club was packed and buzzing when Tomorrow hit the stage about 4 a.m. The unity of spirit between audience and musicians was tremendous: Twink had been at the head of our two-hundred-strong column. Tearing into 'White Bicycle', they had never sounded tighter. At some point Skip from The Pretty Things took over on drums as Twink grabbed the microphone and plunged into the audience. Howe's playing moved to another level of intensity, sending the dancers leaping into the cones of light as Twink crawled along the floor, hugging people and chanting 'Revolution, revolution'. Everyone was high – on chemicals or adrenalin or both. You really did believe in that moment that 'when the mode of music changes, the walls of the city shake'. The tide of history was with us and music was the key.

The bill for this glorious moment was presented a

month later. The *News of the World* may not have known who we were before that weekend, but they certainly did afterwards. The fruits of their plotting burst forth on the last Sunday in July: beneath a grainy, out-of-focus shot of a bare-breasted girl, the front page screamed that she was fifteen years old and that the photograph had been taken at the 'hippy vice den' known as UFO. Our normally stoic landlord buckled under police pressure and evicted us.

A recording may preserve elements of a great musical moment, but bottling the energy of social and cultural forces is impossible. Without realizing it, we had started on a downhill slope that was mirrored in New York and San Francisco. The *agape* spirit of '67 evaporated in the heat of ugly drugs, violence, commercialism and police pressure. In Amsterdam, people began stealing and repainting the white bicycles.

There was music still to be made on the way down, of course; and on the way up, I had heard wonders.

chapter 1

WHEN I WAS ELEVEN, we became the last family on our street in Princeton, New Jersey, to get a TV set: now we could watch Sid Caesar in *Your Show of Shows*, *The Ed Sullivan Show* and baseball games. A year later, in the autumn of 1954, my brother Warwick and I discovered the real reason we needed it: *Bob Horn's WFIL-TV Bandstand*, beamed out of Philadelphia every afternoon after school.

Horn was a large man with the false bonhomie of a used-car salesman. He wore amply cut suits with wide ties and swept his hair back from a high forehead. Like Alan Freed and other middle-aged hustlers in the early 1950s, he provided a link between rhythm and blues and the growing teenage audiences for rock'n'roll. *Bandstand* had a simple formula: students from local high schools dancing to records; a ritual reading of the charts; 'roll-call'; groups lip-synching their latest record; and the occasional interview with a singer plugging a local appearance. The production was cheap: two static cameras, maybe three. The playlist was full of doo-wop by groups like the Cleftones, the Five Keys, the Flamingos, Frankie Lymon & the Teenagers, the Five Satins, etc., and up-tempo R&B by Fats Domino, Little Richard and Chuck Berry. Chuck Willis and 'The Stroll' became a favourite: the kids would line up across the studio

– boys on one side, girls on the other – and take turns sashaying and spinning down the aisle.

Revelations exploded out of the TV set daily: no New Jersey radio station played music like this, at least not before we had to start our homework in the evening. The years 1954 to 1956 were the great cusp, when black music was discovered by white teenagers and sold millions of records. The horrified guardians of the nation's morals feared the underclass world it represented and the miscegenation implied in its rhythms; major record labels hated it because they didn't understand it, putting them at a disadvantage with buccaneering independents like Ahmet Ertegun of Atlantic, the Chess brothers, Lew Chudd of Imperial, Morris Levy of Roulette and George Goldner of Gone.

The world revealed every afternoon fascinated us. I had a crush on a duck-tail-hairdo'd girl from South Philadelphia named Arlene, who wore sleeveless blouses and tight black skirts. During one roll-call, Horn asked a boy named Vinny to explain the diagonal bandage across his cheek. In the deepest of Delaware Valley accents (the home city is 'Phiwy' and you dance on the 'flaw') he said: '*Wew*, uh, *Bawb*, I ran into a *daw*.' The next morning in my seventh-grade classroom we felt very worldly speculating about the length and type of blade responsible for Vinny's wound.

We were respectable middle-class kids. There were a few DA haircuts and raised collars in our class, but they weren't really serious, at least not Philly-serious. Princeton kids would never perfect the dance steps and clothing styles paraded on *Bandstand*. The bourgeoisie can only borrow its culture from below and above – and America never did have much of an 'above'. The sullen insouciance of the Italian kids was intimidating enough, but we had no hope of matching the swagger of the vocal quintets as they walked onstage, or the shake of the head that freed their processed hair to tumble over their foreheads, or the snap of the fingers as they crossed their feet preparatory to an elegant spin as they ooohed and waahed behind the lead singer.

Horn delegated the chart countdown and the interviews to a rota of regular girls, always blonde and built. They were calm and professional while making announcements from the tacky podium (no waving to friends or giggling) and completely at home interviewing dangerous-looking pompadoured black men in sharkskin suits. It was not lost on us that these were probably the only occasions on American TV in 1955 when white girls and black men could be seen in such close physical proximity (*Bandstand* dancers being almost entirely white, of course).

At the close of every programme the charisma-free Horn would thank the guests, the technicians and his producer, Ernie Mamarella. We loved the name Mamarella. I would like to think we caught its curvaceous resonance, but it probably just sounded funny.

One afternoon early in the summer of 1956, we were stunned to see a small unremarkable man in Horn's place. He followed all the show's rituals without once mentioning the host's name. At 4.30 he simply said, 'This is Ernie Mamarella saying so long until tomorrow.' Speculation began on the school bus the next morning and continued between classes. After lunch, a group of us were talking in the hallway when Pat Fischer, a clever black girl with reddish pigtails, overheard our conversation. 'If you want to know what happened to Bob Horn, you better get yourselves a copy of the *Philadelphia Inquirer*,' she said, and disappeared into science class.

After school, one of us went to the news-stand while the rest grabbed a booth at the local luncheonette. We examined each page until we came to the headline reading

'Disc Jockey on Morals Charge'. The position atop the podium could be earned, it seemed, by visits to a motel with Bob. Horn was accused of statutory rape and contributing to the delinquency of a minor.

Sixteen years later I was living in Los Angeles and running the music department of Warner Brothers Films. Ted Ashley, the company president, asked me to 'take a lunch meeting' with some famous TV producers who were pitching a series of music films. When I heard their names, I could barely contain my eagerness. In an Italian restaurant in Hollywood, I asked Ernie Mamarella about that day.

News of Horn's arrest had arrived late in the morning, he said, leaving him no option but to fill in. Afterwards, the station bosses announced they were pulling the show. He pleaded and cajoled, pointing to its minuscule budget and remarkable ratings. They agreed to give him until noon the following day to find the most clean-cut, above-suspicion, white-bread, all-American disc jockey in God's creation. Mamarella told me he drove all over Greater Philadelphia that night interviewing one leering, seedy, unshaven DJ after another. He was on the point of giving up when someone suggested a late-night jock in Reading, an hour north-west of the city. He arrived about two in the morning as Dick Clark – the other half of my 1972 lunch date – was spinning records for local insomniacs.

For Americans, the denouement of this story lies at the heart of our popular culture. Clark, his white shirt collar outside his blazer, his smile as bright as a toothpaste commercial, started work the next day. Within six months, the network was pumping the show into every market in America. Arlene, Vinny and their friends became teen icons. For the next three decades, *American Bandstand* beamed an ever blander version of popular music into millions of homes, making hits, creating stars and homogenizing the dance steps and fashions of American youth.

The WFIL-TV studios were in North Philadelphia, a few blocks from the now derelict station where express trains used to stop before turning west towards Chicago and St Louis. Alighting passengers descended an iron staircase to the then-noisy immigrant streets below. Clark and Mamarella told how they rented an office above a barber shop opposite that stairway. Brill Building men in snap-brimmed hats and dark suits would catch the 11 o'clock from New York and join them for lunch at the coffee shop next door, bringing briefcases stuffed with cash or contracts giving Dick Clark Productions a share in the publishing rights to the B-side of a new single. That afternoon, their records would be played to millions of teenagers across America. In those days, 'payola' was considered just good business. (It still is, but the methodology is more subtle.) The smart money – the big money – was on white stars and safe music.

In a used bookstore in Albuquerque, New Mexico, many years after my encounter with Clark and Mamarella, I came across a fevered but well-sourced history of the events of the summer of 1956 written by Stanley Blitz, a fan of Horn's. Clark, he claims, had been waiting in the wings at WFIL radio, not out in Reading, and the rape and drunk-driving charges that cost Horn his job were a set-up. WFIL-TV was part of the media empire of Walter Annenberg, later Nixon's ambassador to London, and Mrs Annenberg evidently hated the kind of music Horn played. The deeply religious station manager was also revolted by Horn and his hipster ways. By the time he was found not guilty of molesting the girl, Horn was a forgotten man in Philadelphia, although not by the many *Bandstand* 'regulars' who wrote to Blitz of how much they loved him and how the show had lost its soul with Clark.

My brother and I were appalled by Dick Clark from his first day on air. Before long, prefab rockers like Fabian and Frankie Avalon started edging out the doo-wop groups. In a year or two, the rock'n'roll era was over, replaced by chirpy corporate pop. Like most non-conforming kids, we began to look further afield for our musical adventures.

chapter 2

THERE IS A *NAÏF* SKETCH from the 1820s of apprentices at a New York market watching black kids 'dancing for eels' on overturned stall tables. The white boys lean forward, fascinated by the exuberance of the dancers. Warwick and I and a few of our friends were like the boys in that old drawing, leaning towards a culture we sensed held clues for us about escaping the confines of our middle-class upbringing and becoming male sexual beings. For Christmas one year, my maternal grandmother – a woman who didn't know Louis Armstrong from Louis Napoleon – accidentally gave me one of the great compilation LPs of all time, RCA Victor's *Encyclopedia of Jazz*, with tracks by King Oliver, Duke Ellington and Sleepy John Estes. From its first spin, we were completely hypnotized by it.

When Warwick and I began listening to old blues and jazz records, the fraternal fighting that had marked our childhood ceased. Fellow obsessive Geoff Muldaur moved to Princeton soon after and the three of us would spend long afternoons exploring singers, soloists or genres by playing every relevant track in our collections. The artists appeared in our imaginations like disembodied spirits in front of the hi-fi speakers as we listened.

When I returned to Princeton at the end of the 1960

summer holidays prior to my first semester at Harvard, Warwick and Geoff were full of excitement. They had discovered a Philadelphia radio station with a late-night jazz and blues show hosted by Chris Albertson. *We were not alone!* The revelation on the previous week's broadcast was that Lonnie Johnson was alive and well and working as a cook in a Philadelphia hotel.

That weekend we played track after track from Johnson's long discography. Born in New Orleans at the turn of the century, he came up the Mississippi to St Louis and began a career as a crooning blues singer. His music evolved from country blues in the 1920s to an urbane Chicago style in the '30s and slick ballads in the late '40s. He was a brilliant and versatile guitarist who recorded duets with white jazz star Eddie Lang and cut dazzling solos with Louis Armstrong's and Duke Ellington's orchestras. Listening to his seemingly numberless recordings, we tried to absorb the notion that he was just an hour and a half down US Highway 1, living in obscurity.

A borrowed phone directory revealed *Johnson, Lonnie* at a North Philadelphia address, the blackest area of the city. We dialled the number. 'Is this Lonnie Johnson? The Lonnie Johnson who recorded "Blue Ghost Blues" in 1938? Yes? Would you come to Princeton and play a concert next week? Yes, I think we can manage fifty dollars.'

We looked at each other in amazement: we had booked Lonnie Johnson! We commandeered a neighbour's large living room and ordered our friends to attend and bring a dollar each for the kitty. When the day came, we borrowed Geoff's father's Rambler and headed for Philly. Outside a downtown hotel, a neatly dressed grey-haired man stood by the kerb with a guitar case and a small amplifier.

Lonnie seemed as pleased to see us as we were to see him. He told of returning from a European tour in 1951 to find that his girlfriend had run off with his money, guitars and record collection. Rock'n'roll was coming in and he didn't have the energy to fight it; he hadn't played a gig in eight years. When we reached rural Pennsylvania, Lonnie marvelled at the fireflies in the summer twilight, the trees and green lawns; it had been years since he had been out of the city. He answered our eager questions and laughed gently. When we ogled a girl walking beside the road he added to our teenage lexicon of essential phrases by warning us to beware 'the fuzzy monster that causes all the trouble'.

When we got to Princeton, the room was full. No one had the faintest idea who he was, but as soon as he picked up his guitar all were entranced. At first Lonnie brushed off requests for blues and sang standards like 'I Cover The Waterfront' and 'Red Sails In The Sunset'. 'White people always think Negroes just play the blues. I can sing anything.' There was a beautiful black girl sitting on the floor by his chair and he started singing to her, flirting shyly. As the evening went on and everyone relaxed, the music grew more intense and Lonnie began playing his old blues. Our friends and their parents edged closer to Lonnie's chair in the middle of the room; none of them had ever heard anything like it.

We collected $100 for him and he was so pleased he took the train home to save us the drive. The following year he would start performing in coffee houses for the young white audiences he met for the first time that night in Princeton. He made a few LPs for Prestige Records, was reunited with Ellington at a New York Town Hall concert, moved to Toronto, where he had the support of some devoted fans, and died in 1970 having added yet another chapter to his remarkable fifty-year career.

For me the experience meant more than just the music

and the man: we had imagined something and made it happen so everyone could hear. It was the perfect sequel to the moment a few months earlier when, on a baseball field at Pomfret, my Connecticut boarding school, I had been forced to conclude that I would never star for my beloved Pittsburgh Pirates. Events of the spring season – a lowly .143 batting average, for example – meant that on the Friday before Spring Dance Weekend I was catching fly balls in the outfield while Saturday's starters took batting practice. My girlfriend wouldn't even get to see me play! As I pondered this depressing fact, someone in a nearby dorm turned on a radio and the new Fats Domino single, 'Walking To New Orleans', echoed across the field.

In that instant, I made a connection that had previously eluded me. It now seems obvious that jazz and blues begat rock'n'roll, but there wasn't much literature on the subject in those days. Warwick, Geoff and I saw our listening sessions as nerdish and unsexy and not to be discussed in front of outsiders. At parties, like normal teenagers, we jitterbugged to the fast ones and insinuated our knees hopefully between girls' legs during the slow ones. The contemporary and the historic seemed unrelated. But that spring afternoon, all was suddenly clear: *Fats Domino is descended from Jelly Roll Morton. Rock'n'roll is the blues! Popular music is the same stuff I listen to in my room all the time, only newer. I can be a record producer!*

Why a record producer? I had grown up listening to my other grandmother play the piano. Mary Boxall Boyd studied in Vienna with Theodor Leschitizky and assisted Artur Schnabel in pre-First World War Berlin. In the radio transcriptions that remain, she can be heard playing emotional versions of Mozart that sound like Beethoven and Chopin Nocturnes dripping with *ritardandos*: a true Victorian. From age three, I would sit under her grand piano while she practised. She viewed me as a soulmate, the other musical spirit in the family. Despite her Cincinnati upbringing, she thought of herself as a European *manquée*. She had returned to America twice to marry, and both marriages had turned out badly. (Mitigated, of course, by the second having produced my father.) She felt marooned in a cultural wasteland and drew me into viewing myself in the same light.

I took lessons from her until I was thirteen, but never thought of myself as a musician. Listening, however, became part of my being. I had a confident opinion on anything I heard. I loved my parents' 78s of Marlene Dietrich and Bing Crosby and seized on both rock'n'roll and pre-war jazz and blues when I turned twelve. In the spring of 1960, I had just finished reading Sam Charters' *The Country Blues*, in which Ralph Peer, the pioneering producer who travelled the South recording blues and country singers for the Bluebird label, was portrayed in epic terms. In that *Eureka!* moment, it was clear to me that producing records was not only something I could picture myself doing – *listening for a living!* – but it would make the Pomfret School starting nine jealous and impress girls. From that day on, I had no doubts: I would be a record producer.

chapter 3

ONE PREJUDICE WARWICK, GEOFF and I claimed to share was a contempt for white blues singers. What could be more ridiculous? When I returned to Harvard in early 1962 after a semester off working for a record company in Los Angeles, I walked into the Café Yana one evening and who should be on stage, singing Lonnie's 'Mr Jelly Roll Baker', but Geoff! I was astounded. His voice was full of the timbres and signature decorations of our vocal heroes: Johnson, Claude Jeter of the Swan Silvertones, Don Redman of McKinney's Cotton Pickers. I was so shocked it took me half the set to realize he was actually very good. It was a betrayal, but a forgivable one.

The following autumn I took the meagre profits of my record distribution enterprise (wholesaling small blues and folk labels around Boston; the warehouse was under my dormitory bed) and booked one of the newly rediscovered rural blues legends, Sleepy John Estes. I rented the wood-panelled dining room at Harvard's Eliot House: my first concert promotion. Warwick and Geoff demanded to get in on the act. Eager to re-create the vivid drive with Lonnie Johnson, we planned to pick up Estes and his harmonica player Hammy Nixon on Friday night at the Cornell Folk Festival in Ithaca, New York (their first appearance in front of a white audience), and drive back to Cambridge on Saturday. My vehicle being an unreliable old banger, I blew most of the potential profits renting a car for the occasion.

We got lost on the Cornell campus and by the time we arrived the show – a double bill of Estes and Doc Watson – was over. At the post-gig party, the two men – both blind – sang old hymns shared by the white and black communities of the rural South. We noticed a dark-eyed beauty with a long black braid accompanying the Watson party on fiddle or keeping time with a set of bones. Geoff was too shy to talk to her, but swore he would marry her. It was the young Maria D'Amato, later Maria Muldaur, singer of 'Midnight At The Oasis', my biggest hit as a producer.

After a restless night on a faculty apartment floor, we were woken at sunrise by Sleepy John and Hammy anxious to hit the road. They were dressed in threadbare clothes, clutching cardboard suitcases held together by string. We were on the highway in a few minutes, breakfastless. As we passed through Syracuse, Hammy glanced at a clock reading 8.45 and yelled, 'Stop! There's a bar over there, and I believe these folkses open up about now.' Our hopes of hearing stories about Robert Johnson or the Beale Street Sheiks disappeared down the bottles of bourbon we were obliged to buy for each of them. They were drunk by 9.30 and out cold by ten.

I may as well have drunk a few bottles myself for all the acumen I showed when we got to Cambridge. I arranged a spot for them on the live radio broadcast that evening from Club 47 to plug the Sunday night concert. They were so amazing that the local musicians insisted on throwing a party in their honour. Eric Von Schmidt gave them each another bottle of whiskey and we invaded a large house in Newton belonging to a girl whose parents were wintering in Florida. They played for hours, people kept giving them drinks, and eventually they both passed out. At the height of the soirée, there must have been two hundred people there, the core audience I was counting on to buy tickets. By Sunday morning they had all heard their fill of Sleepy John Estes and just wanted to stay home and recuperate. All agreed it was the best party of the year but I lost a fortune – over $100.

I repeated the experiment with Big Joe Williams a few months later, but despite lessons learned, his visit was almost as stressful as Estes'. I was beginning to grasp some of the recurring themes in my life: the tension when artists from a poverty-stricken community confront the spoiled offspring of the educated middle class and the conflict between the latter's desire to hear the 'real thing' and the former's desire to be 'up to date'. Hearing traditional musicians when they first emerge from their own communities is a wonderful experience but impossible to repeat: the music is inevitably altered by the process of 'discovery'.

Around this time, I came to the notice of Joan Baez's manager and Boston's leading concert promoter, Manny Greenhill. I got only a brusque nod when our paths first crossed and flattered myself that he saw me as a young rival, so I was surprised when he rang me up and asked whether I would look after Jesse Fuller, who was coming to town for a couple of gigs and a recording session. Manny proposed paying me $25 plus expenses to keep him on time and sober. In the student economy of October 1963, particularly when the student was funding a precarious business out of his shallow pockets and waiting on tables at the Adams House cafeteria for a dollar an hour, it was too good to refuse.

When I met Fuller at the bus station, I reminded him of our earlier encounter during my semester working in Los Angeles for his previous label, Contemporary Records.

Jesse was famous for 'San Francisco Bay Blues' – a part of virtually every young folkie's repertoire – and drew a good crowd at Club 47. After he opened for Bob Dylan at the Brandeis Folk Festival on Saturday, I took him to a recording session with producer Paul Rothchild for Prestige – an entire LP in one Sunday afternoon session. I helped Paul keep track of the takes and gave him some tips on Jesse's repertoire, which I knew backwards by then. I also solved the problem of a squeak in his foot-operated bass contraption by greasing the pedal with oil from a can of tuna – the only lubricant to be found on a quiet Sunday in pre-mall Boston. Paul mentioned my resourcefulness to Greenhill.

In January, as I contemplated my impending mid-year graduation from Harvard, I paid a call on Manny. I was determined to go to Europe, the Promised Land where the music I loved was appreciated. I fantasized that I would support myself by writing articles for English jazz and blues magazines, trumping the local journalistic talent with my fresh American perspective. (I would later meet contributors to *Jazz Journal* and *Jazz Monthly* and discover that the standard pay was £5 per article.) I would hustle tours for American folk and blues artists. I would be a middleman, an *éminence grise*, a role to which I had aspired ever since I had first understood the expression. Could Manny use my services?

He heard me out, then picked up the phone and called George Wein in New York. 'Hey, George, you know that English Blues and Gospel Caravan thing you booked Brownie and Sonny for in April? Have you found a tour manager for it yet?' He put his hand over the mouthpiece and eyed me. 'Can you be in New York tomorrow morning?'

The day after my meeting with Wein, I reported for work at his New York office and set about finalizing the tour line-up and writing a press release. Basically a jazz man, George was bemused by my vehemence over the choice of sidemen and let me get on with it as long as I didn't go over budget. After a week on Warwick's sofa (he was attending Columbia) I went back to Harvard to take my final exams.

Finishing university meant I was prey to the Selective Service Organization, otherwise known as the Draft Board. I was duly summoned to meet a chartered bus in Princeton early one morning in February '64 and taken to Newark for a physical. With me were about twenty-five mostly familiar faces: some I knew from grade school, some were friends of my brother's, some had been team-mates or opponents in the summer baseball league. Most were from the Neapolitan or black communities in Princeton. I sensed I was probably the only one on the bus with a letter from his doctor about flat feet and a bad back. Years later, when visiting the Vietnam Memorial Wall in Washington, I wondered whether the inscribed names included any of my fellow passengers from that day.

After the examination, I stood in my underwear in front of a sergeant who looked at me as if I were an insect as he shot off a list of questions. I had longish hair and a bad attitude. When I said I was a 'writer', he repeated the word contemptuously as if it were a synonym for 'pimp' or 'bank robber'. He scribbled something on my form and told me to get dressed. A few weeks later, my 1Y classification arrived. It wasn't quite a 4F, but it put me at the end of the queue and freed me to pursue my life without worrying about the growing war in Vietnam. Within six months, so many freaks had shown up for their physicals tripping, claiming to be homosexual, with Dexedrine-fuelled heart rates, or applying for conscientious objector status that the army realized its aversion to 'bad apples' would leave them short of cannon fodder. Had it been the autumn rather than the spring of

1964, I would have had my head shaved and been sent straight to boot camp.

With a month and a half to kill before the start of the tour, I decided to pay my first visit to the South. Like Andalusia for Spain or Transylvania for Hungary, the American South is the source of almost all the nation's traditional musical forms. The year 1964 marked a climax of dramatic change in the region: black voters were being registered, lunch counters and buses integrated and schools forced to admit black students. The resistance by Southern whites was at its most intense. Overdue as these revolutionary changes were, I wanted to catch a glimpse of the old South before it disappeared.

The first leg of the journey involved driving Ramblin' Jack Elliott and some friends of mine to Eric Von Schmidt's winter quarters in Sarasota, Florida. Despite knowing, as all Northerners did in those days, that certain counties in Carolina and Georgia paid no property taxes thanks to the money gouged from sun-seeking Yankees, we were caught in a speed trap and needed a $75 whip-round to avoid a night in jail. We bemoan the homogenization of American culture and accents, but generations of Northern drivers would be happy to have been spared the sight of a drawling, racist, sunglass-wearing, pistol-packing Southern cop pulling them over on a lonely stretch of Georgia highway.

After some R&R on a Gulf Coast beach, I headed for Johns Island, South Carolina, where Guy Carawan was hosting a festival of local music. He took me to an Easter night 'watch service' at Moving Star Hall, a flimsy wooden box set on cement blocks. The congregation were mostly domestics who worked for white families in Charleston. They shivered in their thin clothes as the preacher opened the service in the Gullah accent unique to these islands: 'This *morning*… at *five* o'clock… the *Lord*… blessed *me*…

once again…with *SIGHT!* Praise the Lord!'

They sang hymns in their own style. The clapping is slow for the first few verses then doubles in tempo while the singing maintains the original tempo. The intensity grows and the clapping becomes faster and more syncopated until the song ends with a wild flourish – at exactly the same tempo in which it began. The Top Forty at the time was full of Motown, whose churning beat under ballad melodies was inspired by bass player James Jamerson, a Gullah who learned his music in a church not far from Moving Star Hall.

I spent the following afternoon at Guy's house with Bessie Jones, John Davis and the Georgia Sea Island Singers. Bessie was a fount of folklore, a key figure in Alan Lomax's documentation of the region's music five years earlier. The Rolling Stones learned 'This May Be The Last Time', originally a children's ring dance, from Lomax's recordings there. Carawan encouraged the preservation of local dialects and traditions, helped to register voters and organize against the developers pushing aside residents lacking deeds to their homes. There were already golf courses on nearby Hilton Island and the big money boys were eyeing Johns. By bringing attention to the music, Guy hoped to build local pride and an organization to halt the destruction of this unique culture. Many of the fishermen and farmers on these islands were descendants of runaway slaves from the Bahamas and other West Indian islands. Their ebony skins and sharp features told of African lineages undiluted by the rapacious practices of American slave owners. Guy's festival was sparsely attended but full of great singing and warm feelings from an audience of determined Southern liberals and brave local blacks.

My next stop was Albany, Georgia, where Peter deLissovoy, a friend from Harvard, was working for SNCC (the Student Non-violent Coordinating Committee). At nineteen, Pete had been kicked out of South Africa for paying an illegal visit to Albert Luthuli, the pre-Mandela anti-apartheid leader. Rather than fly back, he hitch-hiked from Johannesburg to Cairo, getting arrested as a spy in Tanganyika, becoming infected with bilharzia on the Nile and spending months in hospital after his return. He took me to a chicken dinner at a nearby church and I was struck by the gentle courage of the local people and the Northern volunteers. For two nights I slept in the bunk below Pete's in a wooden house on one of the many unpaved roads in the black district. When I asked him about the marks on the wall above my bed, he said they were bullet holes from a nocturnal drive-by a few weeks earlier.

When I was ready to leave, some of the local activists were worried that my New Jersey number plates had been visible in town for a couple of days. The implications of my meeting a cop on the highway out of town might be more unpleasant than just a speeding ticket, so they led me down dirt back roads through the red-earthed pine forests of south-western Georgia. I rejoined the highway across the state line in Alabama. (Andrew Goodman, Michael Schwerner and James Chaney were doing work similar to Pete's not far away in Mississippi; they were murdered three months later.)

New Orleans, my next stop, was – and has remained – a law unto itself: in the South but not really of it. The struggles of my friends in Carolina and Georgia seemed far away once I hit the French Quarter. I located Preservation Hall and spent the next seven evenings there.

Twenty-five years before the blues and folk booms of the sixties, there had been a Dixieland revival. As jazz moved from swing towards bebop in the late '30s, a group of white fanatics set about rescuing traditional New Orleans jazz from obscurity, much as we were trying to do for blues.

There are generally two strands to white fascination with African-rooted music. First, dance floors fill with people excited by a new way to shake their behinds. Then, as the fashion shifts and the beat changes, the intellectuals and wallflowers who have admired the music's vitality and originality move in to preserve or resurrect the form. Preservation Hall was run by Alan and Sandy Jaffe, New Yorkers who had fallen in love with New Orleans music and set up a tiny showcase for the musicians who still played in uptown funerals and parades. The Jaffes provided them with a regular payday in the French Quarter, where devotees, mainly European or Japanese, would pay homage. I stayed until the last note every night as George Lewis, Kid Howard, Kid Thomas, Percy Humphries, Billie & Dede Pierce, Alcide 'Slow Drag' Pavageau and Joe Robichaux improvised elegantly in a long-ago style.

There were some surprisingly young players in the Preservation Hall bands. New Orleans is unusual for an American city in its ability to embrace the old and new simultaneously. As in Brazil or Cuba, musicians and dancers there follow the latest fashions yet can still demonstrate skills in fifty-year-old forms, a phenomenon seldom encountered in Brixton or South Los Angeles.

I walked around the corner one evening into Bourbon Street, then not quite the drink-sodden playpen of Texas frat-boys and conventioneers it is today. Cousin Joe Pleasant, the member of the upcoming Blues and Gospel Caravan about whom I knew the least, had a regular gig there singing vaudevillian blues and telling tall stories. His signature tune was 'I Wouldn't Give A Blind Sow An Acorn, Wouldn't Give A Crippled Crab A Crutch', a wry send-up of the bragging blues form. We hit it off immediately; his help would prove invaluable in the difficult early days of the tour. After a week, I headed north to Chicago.

On the South Side I toured the declining blues clubs, most of whose customers were old and poor. The area was poised between its golden age, when it vied with Harlem for the role of capital of Black America, and the dismal last decades of the twentieth century when it spiralled down into violence and destitution. I introduced myself to Muddy Waters at Pepper's Lounge, his home base. His band included stars in their own right, such as James Cotton on harmonica and pianist Otis Spann. During the late set, a young white guitarist named Mike Bloomfield sat in and played some enthusiastic lead.

Leaving Pepper's around 2.30, I stopped to give some change to a panhandler and found myself being pushed at knife-point towards a dark doorway. My friends shouted and people came out of a fried chicken joint to chase the muggers away. A crowd gathered round to make sure I was OK and someone bought us drinks in a nearby bar. Like a down-at-the-heel unofficial chamber of commerce, they wanted our assurance that the experience wouldn't put us off coming back. The next day I headed east to pack for the start of my European adventures.

chapter 4

I PASSED THROUGH CAMBRIDGE a few days before my departure. As I was standing by a phone booth in Harvard Square with a handful of nickels in search of a bed for the night, a girl I had always fancied (a concise British term that would not enter my vocabulary until I got to London) walked by. She told me she had a new boyfriend-free apartment and I was welcome to stay. Another English verb I would soon learn was 'to pull': I thought I had just pulled Mary Vangi.

She gave me a key and a kiss and put my bag in her bedroom as I set off to hear legendary blues master Skip James at a Boston coffee house while she got ready for her waitressing job. Later, she and a friend planned to crash a post-Joan-Baez-concert party; she'd be home about one. After an exhilarating evening of music, I strode eagerly up her front steps at the appointed hour to find the sofa made up in the front room, my bag beside it and a note reading: 'Dear Joe. Sorry, change of plans. Will explain in morning. Sleep well. Love, Mary.'

When I woke to the smells of coffee and bacon, I threw on my clothes and peered into the kitchen. Mary was standing by the stove in a dressing gown looking extremely pleased with herself. The bathroom door was closed and I could hear water running. She grinned at me conspiratorially. 'Guess who's in the shower! Dylan!!' What, in the spring of 1964, when His Bobness was king of the folk world, could I say? I joined the happy one-night couple for a monosyllabic breakfast and hit the road.

By the spring of 1964, Dylan and Baez had become folk's royal couple, uniting the rival New York and Boston camps with their musical energy while becoming sexually potent icons of popular culture. Folk music had come a long way from its origin as an offshoot of left-wing politics. When Leadbelly and Woody Guthrie arrived in the '40s to lend authenticity to the 'people's music', its popularity surged. It got a bit *too* popular for the McCarthy-ites in the early '50s after Pete Seeger's Weavers got to number one with 'Goodnight Irene'. Subpoenas were issued and warnings whispered to radio and TV networks about communist influences. Folk music went into a long Eisenhower-era decline.

In 1957 the Kingston Trio found a song about a hanged killer named Tom Dula on an Appalachian field recording and their slick version topped the charts and brought folk music back from the wilderness. In the early sixties, the civil rights activism of the Kennedy era needed a better soundtrack than corporate pop; protest songs, mostly by New York-based singer-songwriters, provided it.

In Boston, things evolved differently. The spark that lit up the local scene was Joan Baez's barefoot appearance at the first Newport Folk Festival in 1959. Singing a duet with the hokey Bob Gibson, she brought the house down, triggering a boom in guitars, long hair and black turtlenecks back in Massachusetts. In my first year at Harvard, I saw her riding a Vespa with her boyfriend through the slush of the Cambridge winter, grinning wickedly with that beautiful dark mane trailing behind. She radiated sex and humour, not earnest politics. The pleasure she took in her own voice was sensual, her choice of songs based on the beauty of the melodies and the way they told of a world of wild (but often doomed) women and free-spirited, dangerous men.

The scene that flourished in the ripples of her success was full of eccentrics, visionaries and travellers. Around Harvard Square, people were always going off to or coming back from India, Mexico, North Africa, Paris, London or Japan. They soaked up Zen, flamenco guitar, Rimbaud's poetry and new ways of getting high. Everyone bought the blues and country music reissue LPs emerging in the wake of Harry Smith's masterful *Anthology of American Folk Music* compilation. In cheap apartments in old wooden houses they taught themselves a particular Appalachian banjo or fiddle style, or figured out how Bukka White tuned his National steel-bodied guitar. New Yorkers like Seeger and the Weavers gave music from all over the world – often learned from Alan Lomax's field recordings – the same chirpy strum and hearty harmonies, as if that proved all men were brothers. The Cambridge scene was drawn more to differences than to similarities.

The wildly divergent personalities and tastes of Smith and Lomax were central to the two approaches that would clash so memorably at Newport in 1965. Lomax was a bear of a man, a skirt-chaser, completely sure of himself and his theories about the inter-connectedness of music across cultures and continents. Travelling from Mississippi prison chain gang to Italian tobacco fields with his tape recorder, he had developed a thick hide and a bullying manner. Smith, on the other hand, had become a collector of recordings of traditional music almost by accident. He was a homosexual who made experimental films, spoke several Native American languages and smoked frequent joints. His vast record collection almost buckled the floor of his apartment in the Chelsea Hotel, a few express stops downtown from Lomax's sprawling West Side apartment. New York folk singers were more comfortable with the earnestness of Lomax's field recordings, while the Cambridge musicians were drawn in a context-free, almost postmodern way to the vivid personalities that shone through the commercial 78s Smith and later compilers made available. Big Bill Broonzy, Jimmy Rodgers, the Carter Family and Blind Lemon Jefferson had been stars in the 1920s and early 1930s for good reason: the artistry of their music far surpassed that of Lomax's amateurs.

Lomax viewed commercial recordings as tainted by Mammon. At a dinner party in London in the late '80s, I suggested to him that folklorists and record producers were both just professionals making a living by recording music for a targeted audience. His response was to invite me outside for a fist sandwich.

I had arrived at Harvard with the same prejudices against folk music that I had against white blues singers. I bought tickets to a Joan Baez concert that first autumn only to please a girl I had just met. But the opening act was Eric Von Schmidt, and his astonishing renditions of Blind Willie Johnson songs lured me down to Club 47 on Mount Auburn Street to hear more. I liked the raffish atmosphere of the place, the eccentric musicians and the enigmatic girls who sat along the window ledge. Despite my best intentions, I became a folkie.

The bearded Von Schmidt was a hero to the younger singers, a skilled painter of historical murals, world traveller and psychotropic adventurer. Living around Harvard Square were bluegrass virtuosi, balladeers, blues guitarists and ragtime experts. Returning after my semester working in California, I was assigned – by chance – the lower bunk in a dorm room with Tom Rush, a Von Schmidt-influenced singer who was fast becoming the pin-up boy of the local coffee-house circuit.

Von Schmidt's New York counterpart, by dint of Germanic surname and gruff-voiced blues style, was Dave Van Ronk. For me, Van Ronk had none of the lyricism of Von Schmidt and lacked his generosity of spirit. He was a hard-core communist who seemed drawn to the blues for its value as a political stance rather than the beauty of the form. Perhaps I am biased: Dave and his wife were sleeping on my sofa after an all-night poker game on 22 November, 1963. Woken by news of Kennedy's assassination, he gloated about 'chickens coming home to roost' and went back to sleep.

As the Boston scene grew and coffee houses and concerts proliferated, the business world made its presence felt. For regulars at Club 47, 'music business' meant Paul Rothchild. Rothchild had been a salesman for an independent record distributor, working the New England territory since the late 1950s. He wore a suit, carried a briefcase, and lit the odd joint while listening to jazz at home with his wife. In 1961, he made his first visit to Club 47 and soon became a regular.

Paul had receding wavy blond hair and intelligent blue eyes. He ditched the suits in favour of fringed leather jackets and jeans and was among the first in Harvard Square to sport 'fruit boots' – ankle-high numbers with a zip on the side and a rakish heel. At first he looked like the out-of-place salesman he was, but the Harvard Square aesthetic was cool, never hyper, and he soon absorbed the elite aura of many of the musicians and their friends.

Rothchild moved into a vacuum by recording Harvard Square favourites Bill Keith & Jim Rooney and the Charles River Valley Boys, pressing 500 copies of each LP and selling them to his local clients. He was out of stock within weeks and Prestige Records, a jazz outfit from New Jersey that had strayed into blues and folk, offered to buy the masters and make Paul head of their folk department. By 1963, he had moved to New York and was signing the best Cambridge talent for his new employers: Tom Rush, Eric Von Schmidt and Geoff Muldaur. Cool Cambridge wasn't sure what to make of this. There was the excitement of seeing local boys making good, but was there a hint of anti-Semitism in the *froideur* towards this spurt of ambition and acumen? Many said they didn't trust him and others openly resented his success.

By 1963 I was sharing an off-campus apartment with Geoff, now lead singer with Boston's most popular group, the Jim Kweskin Jug Band, suddenly the object of a bidding war between labels. Their New York debut was jealously scouted by Greenwich Village rivals, the Even Dozen Jug Band, whose lead singer was the mysterious beauty from the Cornell Festival, Maria D'Amato. She heard Geoff sing one verse, turned to a friend and said, 'I'm going to marry that guy.' The fact that she threw up in his lap on their first date didn't stop him swiping her from the Even Dozens and moving her into the Kweskin band as co-lead singer and into our apartment as his girlfriend. The Even Dozen broke up soon after, but its alumni went on to illustrious careers: John Sebastian with the Lovin' Spoonful, Steve Katz with Blood, Sweat & Tears, Joshua Rifkin as a classical music scholar and producer and interpreter of Scott Joplin, Stefan Grossman as a blues guitarist and teacher, David Grisman as virtuoso mandolinist and collaborator with Jerry Garcia, and Peter Siegel as a recorder of ethnic music.

The inter-city rivalry was rarely that overt. Pete Seeger's first campus concert after his refusal to testify before the House Un-American Activities Committee, for example, was at Harvard, and I remember it as one of the greatest I've seen. But the fact that the Dylan phenomenon began in New York made us doubtful about him. Just another political songwriter, we thought. His first LP confirmed our suspicions: the original songs were of no great interest and his versions of traditional material derivative. If this was the best New York could come up with, our smug superiority was secure.

On the night of the spring blizzard of 1963 there was a big party in Cambridge. Harvard Square was abuzz with visitors that week: the big folk labels – Vanguard, Elektra and Prestige – were all in town competing for local artists. I arrived late and remember seeing Joan Baez and Manny Greenhill in close conversation with Maynard Solomon from Vanguard in one corner, while Jac Holzman of Elektra plotted with Rothchild in another. The apartment was packed with guys in work shirts and jeans and girls in corduroy skirts and peasant blouses drinking jug wine from paper cups.

Looking for a place to throw my coat before heading in search of a drink, I entered one of the tiny bedrooms. I could see two girls seated on the floor and heard a guitar being strummed behind the door. As I tossed my coat in a corner, a voice began singing:

Oh where have you been, my blue-eyed son?
Oh where have you been, my darling young one?

I collapsed on to the floor as if I had been bludgeoned. For the length of the song I remained motionless, astonished, moved almost to tears. (This was a few months after the Cuban missile crisis.) No sooner had he finished 'Hard Rain' than he went straight into 'Masters Of War'. In the tiny room, Dylan's brittle strum and nasal voice enveloped you, you couldn't think of anything else. He finished the song, asked one of the girls to keep an eye on his guitar and went off to look for the bathroom. My regional scepticism about Dylan was over.

By the time he passed the toast across Mary Vangi's kitchen table a year later, Dylan had transformed folk music. It was far more now than just a soundtrack for students and liberals, it was affecting national politics and creating huge cultural waves. But while we were preoccupied with the conflict between the various 'schools', he was way ahead of us, plotting a frontal assault on the fortress of American popular music. The next time our paths crossed, at the '65 Newport Folk Festival, I would help him storm the citadel.

chapter 5

IN APRIL 1964, I MET MUDDY, Otis and Cousin Joe again in a rehearsal room in London. The line-up of the Blues and Gospel Caravan also included Chicago bass player Ransom Knowling, Muddy's drummer Willie Smith, Brownie McGhee and Sonny Terry, the Reverend Gary Davis and Sister Rosetta Tharpe. I had called the run-through to explain and rehearse my ideas for the tour. I wanted Ransom to play bass with most of them, Otis and Willie to play with Rosetta, Brownie to play guitar with Joe, Sonny to play harmonica with the Reverend Gary and so on. When I finished my speech, they looked at me blankly. Resentments and objections came at me from all sides. Muddy was upset that we hadn't brought his whole band. Rosetta didn't want a blues player like Otis backing her up. What emerged, to my naive surprise, was that they were almost complete strangers to one another.

The world of Brownie McGhee and Sonny Terry and the Reverend Gary Davis – of coffee houses, college concerts and 'folk blues' – was unknown to the Chicagoans. Brownie and Sonny had played together as a duo since leaving South Carolina and following Leadbelly on to the 1940s folk circuit. Brownie was a deft finger-picking guitarist and a warm singer with a limp, a cane and a huge girth. Underneath the practised politeness was a bitter man: years of conforming to the expectations of white audiences had taken their toll. Sonny was the genius of the rural blues harmonica and had been blind from birth. He was so gentle and deferential behind his dark glasses that it was difficult to determine what he felt about anything. Brownie and Sonny, I discovered, cordially loathed each other offstage. The one thing they agreed on was that, owing to some ancient feud, they wanted nothing to do with the Reverend Gary.

Also blind and from South Carolina, Gary's harsh persona had been formed on the back roads of the rural South as an itinerant preacher between the wars. A nephew brought him to the Bronx in the '50s, where a small band of devotees discovered his monumental skills in a long-forgotten ragtime picking style. A generation of white guitarists took lessons, often earning their schooling by arranging gigs for him. They would lead him from his Bronx tenement to the stage, making sure he ate and dressed himself properly along the way.

Gary was an alarming-looking man who took some getting used to. His chin was covered in grey stubble and he wore a battered hat and a rumpled black suit. His dark glasses slid down his nose to reveal milky sightless eyes. He horrified Rosetta and her husband/manager Russell the first morning at breakfast when, with shaking hand, he seized the sunny-side-up fried egg, lofted it over his upturned mouth (yolk all the while dribbling down the front of his shirt) and dropped it into his mouth. The edges of the white, trailing grease, protruded from his jaws as he chewed.

Tom Hoskins was delegated the task of swabbing down the front of Gary's shirt. Tom was a twenty-five-year-old Southern charmer, responsible for the detective work that had tracked down Mississippi John Hurt in the town of

Avalon the previous year. He had listened over and over to the 78s until he decoded lyrics alluding to the South Delta hamlet where he found Hurt sitting on a front stoop, exactly where the scout from Paramount Records had discovered him thirty-five years earlier. With Hurt bowing out of the tour due to illness, Tom came along to help me with the other musicians. Looking after Gary proved to be a full-time job.

Tom had none of the awkward deference of Northern blues acolytes. He quickly discovered that Gary loved a bit of marijuana in his corncob pipe along with the rough tobacco. Gary and Tom became the party animals of the tour, ready to hang out with fans, preferably female, long past the time everyone else had gone to bed. With young admirers at his feet, Gary would get out his guitar and Tom would load up the pipe and score a bottle of Scotch. The music would continue until the noise drew complaints from next door or until Tom had made sufficient eye contact with one of the girls to bring proceedings to a close.

There were no finer exponents of Gospel guitar than Sister Rosetta and Gary, but the resemblance stopped there. Born in back-country Arkansas, Rosetta toured the rural revival circuit with her mother, Katie Bell Nubin, from the time she was old enough to carry a tune. About those days, Rosetta once told me: 'By the time I was eighteen, I had my boots laced on *up to my hips*!' In the late '30s she started performing as a featured attraction with swing bands. Her jazzy electric guitar style brought her some hits in the '40s, allowing her and Russell to buy a house in Philadelphia. She wore an expensive red wig, a fur coat and high heels and had toured Europe many times. To find herself seated at breakfast next to Gary, the kind of man she had last seen thirty-five years before on the dirt roads of East Texas, was not what she had in mind when she signed on for the Blues and Gospel Caravan.

Ransom Knowling and Cousin Joe were the sophisticates of the group. Natty dressers in a tweedy style, they eyed the eccentricities of the rest with amused condescension. Willie Smith, Muddy's young drummer, was thrilled to be travelling outside the blues circuit and couldn't get enough of sightseeing and meeting fans.

The heart of the tour was Muddy, a man of gravitas and dignity. He stood tall and dressed sharp – always a snap-brim fedora, a little grey tie and a clean white shirt. His eyes were kind but they regarded me warily. Otis, Muddy's cousin, was an ageing boy. He drank and smoked heavily and wore the expression of a kid looking for ways to get up to mischief, his sad-eyed softness the opposite of Muddy's granite masculinity.

One appearance at the Newport Jazz Festival was the only time Muddy had played for white audiences in America; touring as a guest with Chris Barber and his English rhythm section in the late '50s had been his only previous European experience. Now at least he had Otis and his drummer, but Ransom, great as he was, played acoustic bass and it wasn't the same as having his own powerful modern band. Like everyone else, Muddy had cut down his set list to fit the crowded programme. The last thing anyone wanted was to spend a day off working out deviations from tried and true arrangements. We cut the rehearsal short and went back to the hotel. I was off to a bad start.

Things improved once we opened in Bristol. They needed introducing, so I provided the hyperbole in American MC-style tones. Otis tried playing a song with Rosetta at the sound check and it worked so well they added it to the show. The hall was full, the crowd queued for autographs afterwards and all my preconceptions about British enthusiasm for the blues were confirmed.

The next day on the bus, Cousin Joe read out highlights

from the Paris edition of the *Herald Tribune* and tried to stimulate a current-affairs discussion. At first, the others thought he was crazy, but he eventually won them over. Joe's morning news ritual became the catalyst for a growing warmth among performers who had been strangers a few days earlier.

Most halls were sold out, and little by little my notions were added to the show. Ransom played a number with Brownie and Sonny and accompanied Cousin Joe and Sister Rosetta for their entire sets. Willie started joining Otis for his song with Rosetta, then Brownie was persuaded to play some guitar behind Cousin Joe. The atmosphere began to feel like a friendly get-together rather than a formal concert.

They were listening as well, often standing in the wings during each other's sets: I spotted Rosetta there during Reverend Gary's rendition of 'Precious Lord'. Sonny and Gary were heard working something out one evening in a dressing room and the next night Sonny joined him on 'The Sun Is Going Down'. The cry of the harmonica added even more intensity to what was already a chilling and emotional song and brought tears to a few eyes in the audience.

In Manchester, producer Johnny Hamp – inventor of *Ready Steady Go!* and *6.5 Special* – set us up at a disused railway station with fake bales of cotton for Brownie and Sonny and a dolly to film Muddy walking down 'that lonesome railroad track'. The National Film Theatre periodically dredges up programmes from the archives of British television and screened the show a few years ago. I had never seen it and it was very affecting to watch all those great – and, by 1999, late – singers and musicians. Towards the end, when Rosetta gets the audience clapping along (mostly on the wrong, or white person's, beat), I glimpsed my twenty-one-year-old self in the background, clapping! I never clap along. It has always been against my principles of *éminence grise*-ness, but the camera doesn't lie. On the right beat, mind you.

In Liverpool Tom and I met a West Indian blues fan who gave us a matchbox filled with marijuana he said had been cured for two years with rum and molasses by Rastafarians in a cane stalk buried in the hills above Kingston, Jamaica. After the Leicester concert the following night, Tom, Gary, Otis and I smoked some in the back of the bus and every time we went over a bump or around a bend we got higher and higher. When we arrived in Sheffield, Cousin Joe had to take over the hotel check-in and guide us to our rooms.

We swung back through London for dates at Hammersmith and Croydon, then headed for the home stretch: an evening in the Brighton Dome followed by a show in Paris for French television. By this time, wary rivals had become ardent fans of each other's music. Rosetta told me that Gary was 'the deepest man I have ever met' while even the dour Russell was seen joking with Cousin Joe and Muddy.

As Paris would be an abbreviated show in front of a small studio audience, Brighton, we all felt, was the finale. There was an electric atmosphere that evening, beginning at the sound check. After each introduction, I would run to the back of the hall to listen. Otis's solo spot that night gave the audience a capsule history of boogie-woogie and barrel-house piano. Cousin Joe's anecdotes and songs were hilarious while Rosetta tore into her guitar solos and extended them for chorus after chorus, lifting the audience out of their seats with 'Didn't It Rain?'

During the intermission she asked me for an offstage microphone when Gary sang 'Precious Lord'. 'I don't want to take anything away from him,' she said. I coiled the mic cable and left it beside her in the wings as Gary came out to start the second half. When he picked out the opening chords of 'Precious Lord', Rosetta began to moan. She was back in that little country church in Arkansas with her mother, singing in a primitive style I had never heard from her. Gary lifted his head and murmured, 'Oh Lord, sing it, girl!' Her interjections seemed to transport him to another time and place, re-creating music that few white people had ever been privileged to hear.

By the time Muddy hit the stage, the Dome was levitating. When he got out his slide and started caressing the strings under 'another mule kicking in my stall' he appeared possessed, evoking the ghosts of Robert Johnson and Charlie Patton. Then he attacked 'Mojo Working', got the audience dancing in the aisles and propelled them out into the night. (In those days, theatres didn't destroy the music lingering in people's heads by playing records as soon as the show ends.)

At Orly airport tears were shed, addresses and phone numbers exchanged. Everyone wanted to do it again in the States. I felt confident it could be arranged, but the following winter I discovered how little interest it held for American concert promoters. Brighton would never be repeated. In years to come, Muddy took his (full) band around the world, recorded with Jimmy Page and got hugged onstage by Mick Jagger. Brownie, Sonny and Gary plied the folk circuit until they got too old to carry on. Rosetta kept touring even after she lost a leg. Cousin Joe went back to his bar in New Orleans and occasionally toured Europe. An era in American culture was passing and I had only the barest idea of how lucky I was to have witnessed the flash of the sunset.

The blues boom of the sixties marked the end of the natural life of the form. The British taught white Americans how to love their native music and the sudden enthusiasm of college kids seemed to be enough for most black audiences to decide it was time to move on. The black bourgeoisie was already ashamed of it and soul and Motown drew the rest away. By the end of the sixties, most blues artists were performing – if at all – for white audiences only.

In the mid-sixties, love of the blues united much of the American folk and English pop worlds. Most folk singers' repertoire included at least one song learned from a Leadbelly or Big Bill Broonzy record, while a large percentage of English pop groups started life as blues bands. Pink Floyd are named after Pink Anderson and Floyd Council, two obscure singers from rural South Carolina whose names appeared in the liner notes of a Blind Boy Fuller reissue. Every rediscovery of an old man whose name graced the labels of our treasured 78s from the '20s or '30s was greeted with huge excitement. With astonishing speed, however, blues became a cliché. By the '70s, lurching, screaming – or, worse, polite – guitar solos poured forth from bar bands and heavy metal groups and decorated over-produced singles by mainstream pop singers. Blues phrasing now permeates most popular music: the ultimate postmodern artefact, complete with quotation marks.

Thirty years after Brighton, I walked sadly away from the New Orleans Jazz & Heritage Fair. It was everything my twenty-one-year-old self might have dreamed of: 75,000 people packed into the Fairgrounds, with NPR-subscriber bags holding expertly marked programmes. America's black musical heritage was on parade across two long weekends and eight stages. But the audience was almost entirely white. The performers had learned their lessons, dropping any modernizations or slick showbiz gestures and re-creating the old-time styles the sophisticated audiences craved. On one level, it demonstrated respect for a deep culture and a rejection of shallow novelty. But removed from the soil in which it grew the music felt lifeless, like actors portraying characters who happened to be their younger selves. In two days wandering from stage to stage, I heard little I recognized as music.

The festival's big attraction, Aretha Franklin, left the 'Who's Zoomin' Who' spangles at home and sang her great sixties hits from a piano bench. For about thirty seconds, I was thrilled. But she and the audience seemed to know exactly what was coming next. Waves of self-congratulatory affection passed back and forth between them: she claiming credit for recognizing what they wanted to hear; the audience adoring themselves for being so hip as to want the 'real thing'. The music was caught in the middle, lifeless and predictable. Nothing that weekend bore any resemblance to what I heard in the town halls of England in April 1964 or on those unforgettable nights sitting a few feet from great masters who were not yet savvy enough to be anything other than real.

chapter 6

ON MY FIRST DAY AT WORK for George Wein in January 1964, I was assigned a spare desk in his Central Park West office, a large ground-floor room in an imposing building that no jazz promoter could afford today. Mid-morning, the buzzer sounded and Thelonious Monk was admitted wearing his famous black astrakhan cap, a heavy woollen overcoat and gloves. Everyone greeted him and George waved vaguely in my direction, saying, 'That's our new kid over there, Joe.' Monk turned and looked in my direction. Without taking off his coat, hat or gloves, he advanced slowly across the room. After what seemed a long time, he stood looming over me. I rose hesitantly. He took off one glove, gently clasped my hand, looked me in the eye and said softly, 'How you feeling?' Neither awaiting nor expecting a reply, he turned and started talking to Joyce Wein and I went back to phoning bass players in Chicago.

I was as excited about jazz then as I was about blues. When George invited me to work for the autumn 1964 Newport Jazz in Europe tour, I borrowed money to last the summer in London until I went back on the payroll.

The European jazz world had an aura of wealth and elegance in those days. Promoters lived expansively, their fortunes mostly inherited or earned elsewhere. I started moving in this rarefied world at the height of the post-war success of jazz. I crossed the Channel by ferry and motorcycle in early August, having spent the summer on friends' sofas and floors. Arriving in Paris after midnight, I made my way to George's home-from-home, the luxurious Hôtel Prince de Galles. The concierge regarded me with horror: I was covered in grease and my goggles were spattered with bugs. By the morning, I was scrubbed clean and ready to join this other world.

At lunchtime we walked up the street to Fouquet's on the Champs Elysées to meet Philippe Koechlin, editor of *Jazz Hot*, and tell him about the line-up of the autumn tour. It included Miles Davis, Dave Brubeck, the Charlie Parker All-stars with Sonny Stitt, JJ Johnson and Howard McGhee, Roland Kirk, Sister Rosetta Tharpe, the Original Tuxedo Brass Band from New Orleans, the George Russell Sextet and the Coleman Hawkins/Harry Edison Swing All-stars: eight bands, six different itineraries and four tour managers. I spoke a reasonable amount of French but fearful of finding something unfamiliar on my plate I ordered '*entrecôte bien cuit avec pommes frites*'. On our way back to the hotel, George put his arm on my shoulder and said, 'Kid, if you're going to work for me, you gotta learn how to eat.' Over the next three evenings, we went to Michelin-starred restaurants where George turned my palate around, ordering three courses for me with wines to match.

George had to stretch a bit to put an arm on my shoulder. He is short, stout and balding, a caricature of the cigar-chomping promoter. In fact, he plays very much against type (and doesn't smoke cigars). For a start, he is an accomplished jazz pianist. He horrified his clothier father by turning his back on the family business to pursue his musical obsessions. By the time he was thirty, he had opened the Storyville jazz club in Boston and married Joyce, not only not a Jewish girl, but black besides. His enthusiasm created the Newport Jazz Festival in the '50s and his determination brought it back to life in the sixties after beer-fuelled riots had run it out of town. This was his first attempt to establish that franchise in Europe. His motivation was part economic, part egotistical and part gastronomic. George loved nothing more than eating his way through the *Guide Michelin* from Paris to the Riviera and back and this way there was a business justification for the trip.

One of his partners in the venture had a Paris flat with a jumble of Degas, Matisse and Bonnard canvases on the walls. We went often to the Blue Note club off the Champs Elysées, where a couple of girls sat alone with champagne on ice and an empty chair extending an expensive invitation. You couldn't have dreamed up an atmosphere more remote from an English pub – or, for that matter, a New York jazz club.

When a crisis arose over the discount fares deal with Air France, George summoned me to meet him at the Carlton Hotel in Cannes. We lay on the beach phoning travel agents and promoters from red telephones on forty-foot wires while waiters brought us drinks and lunch. One evening he took me into the hills to have a drink at the Colombe d'Or in St-Paul-de-Vence. George was explaining the history of the Matisse and Picasso sketches on the wall and toasting the huge photo of the latter behind the bar when I gave him a nudge. Pablo himself was seated on the terrace in the evening sun, holding court at a table with six beautiful women and one small boy. His shirt was off, he looked powerful and bronzed and the women never took their eyes off him.

From my *hôtel particulier* near the Trocadéro I 'advanced' the tour, booking hotels and local flights and arranging press interviews. In the evenings I would zoom around Paris on the motorbike, hanging out in the Café Seine off the Boulevard St-Germain with a crowd of expat jazzmen and would-be Bohemians. Those relaxed weeks were needed to build up a credit balance: once the tour started I would rarely get more than four hours' sleep a night and found myself under constant threat of disaster.

The problems began in Berlin on the first day of the tour. The European promoters had insisted on adding Roland Kirk to the line-up, but the budget was tight and George refused to book Kirk's band as well. He packaged him on a bill with the Parker All-stars so he could share their rhythm section of Tommy Potter and Kenny Clarke. It was a great opportunity for Kirk, but he hated performing without his regular musicians. As a compromise, he was allowed to add a European pianist he had worked with before, the Catalan Tété Montoliu. We knew that Roland was blind and would be accompanied by his wife, but we didn't realize Montoliu was blind as well and would thus require *his* wife to come along too. Tour budgets were on a knife-edge and this meant more air fares, double rooms and per diems.

Roland's group assembled for the first time on the afternoon of the opening show. Potter and Clarke were old-school bop musicians. They (like George) viewed Roland's playing three saxes at once as a gimmick and they had even less use for his complicated time signatures. But Roland had spent the morning with Tété working out stripped-down adaptations of his arrangements. When they started to play them backstage, the other two just laughed. This was a one-night stand tour: 'Just name a few standards, choose your keys, and tap your foot for the tempo,' said Tommy.

The first two dates passed without incident, but mutual frustration was building. On the third day, I put Rosetta and the Tuxedo Band on a plane from Hamburg to Zurich, then flew the short hop to Bremen, where I picked up the Parker All-stars and Roland. In Zurich, we met the Hawkins/Edison group coming in from Frankfurt and I put them on a plane to Geneva, where another tour manager would meet them. I got Roland and the All-stars to the concert hall then boarded a train with Rosetta and the Tuxedos to Berne for a concert that night. Back in Zurich after the show there was a mailbox full of messages, most of them reading, 'Be sure to speak to me before you talk to anyone else…'

At the promoter's request, it had been agreed that Roland would close the show. This meant that Sonny Stitt, JJ Johnson, Howard McGhee and Walter Bishop Jr had spent the intermission making social plans with a crowd of girls. Everyone went off to party – except Kenny and Tommy. The extra $200 a week George was paying them for working with Roland was beginning to seem like chump change.

Roland cut a wild figure on stage. The tenor sax around his neck was flanked by a manzello and a stritch, reed instruments of his own invention. He was one of the first to wear African dashikis and brightly coloured hats, which, combined with his dark glasses and beard, made him look like the ceremonial priest of an exotic religion. He would bring one hand down sharply in a chopping motion to indicate a stop-chorus, where the rhythm section was supposed to lay out while he played a cappella, blowing continuous arpeggios in three-part harmony using his circular breathing technique. Kenny and Tommy had agreed to keep an eye out for this, and had even managed to respond once or twice in Berlin and Bremen, but in Zurich they sailed right through Roland's red lights.

Anger fuelled his playing and he brought the house down. The audience were on their feet clapping, demanding more. Kenny and Tommy were accustomed to leading their sightless colleagues offstage at the end of a show, but on this occasion Roland angrily pulled his arm away and said something that couldn't be heard above the din. Kenny said he took it as 'fuck off', so he and Tommy just shrugged and left the stage. Within seconds, they had on their coats and were out the back door heading for the bar, hoping for some as yet unclaimed chicks.

Roland had, of course, been trying to tell Kenny they were going to play an encore. First he turned to Tété, calmly seated at the piano, then to the empty drum kit and the spot where Tommy had been standing, announced the tune and the key and gave the downbeat. The horrified audience watched as, after a few bars, Roland and Tété realized they were alone onstage and stopped playing.

I spent the morning moving from room to room, getting different versions of the story and listening to musicians swear they would never again set foot onstage with 'those assholes'. The shuttle diplomacy finally bore fruit in the form of a rehearsal before that evening's concert in Geneva and a promise of better cooperation and understanding on both sides – plus a raise in Kenny and Tommy's bonuses to $250 a week in return for a more respectful attitude.

I understood the gap in generations and attitudes that led to the rift, but I thought both groups were great and particularly loved the playing of Sonny Stitt and Howard McGhee. I had met McGhee in Los Angeles three years earlier during my semester off from university working for Contemporary Records. Les Koenig, the label's owner, had been a Hollywood screenwriter blackballed during the McCarthyite era. When the ghost-writing work dried up, his hobby of recording jazz bands turned into a business. His roster of stars such as Art Pepper, Shelly Manne, Teddy Edwards and McGhee became a pillar of the West Coast sound. When Manne made an album of tunes from *My Fair*

Lady, he sold a quarter of a million copies and turned Contemporary into a success.

Bob Koester from the Jazz Record Mart in Chicago had suggested I look Koenig up during a summer visit to California. He invited me to stop by his office and hired me after a ten-minute conversation. It turned out he had been a student at Dartmouth when Count Basie came through to play a dance in the late '30s. He talked his way into a job as a band boy and left on their bus that night.

There was a grand piano in the corner of the shipping room in the back of Contemporary's office on Melrose Place (an innocent block of antique shops in those days). Once every week or two, I would take the cover off the piano and move it to the centre of the room. Our great engineers, Howard Holzer and Roy DuNann, plugged in microphones and transformed the area into a recording studio. A car would pull up in the alley behind the building and Philly Joe Jones or Roy Haynes would start unloading his drum kit. In these mundane surroundings, sublime music would go down on tape.

I usually worked in the front office next to the receptionist, Pat, a fount of gossip and opinion. She was having an affair with Frank Foster, Count Basie's tenor sax player and a close friend of Quincy Jones. I heard daily accounts of the hip world she moved in after hours, told in hilarious stream-of-consciousness jargon as she buffed her nails between phone calls.

Now, after three years of American coffee houses and English pubs, I was back in the jazz world. More experienced men looked after Miles and Brubeck. My junior position meant that I worked the outer portions of the tour, the fill-in dates plugging geographical and financial gaps between the weekend festivals. After the first week, I found myself travelling with Coleman Hawkins and Harry 'Sweets' Edison.

Hawkins was one of my heroes. From the first time I heard his jagged, joyous solos on the Mound City Blue Blowers sides from 1929 and saw him in the faded photos of Ma Rainey's touring vaudeville troupe, I viewed him as a paragon. Here was a man who had played with the earliest regional bands of the 1920s and ended up as an elder statesman of the tenor sax, revered by Coltrane and Rollins; a man who stood beside Ben Webster and Lester Young bridging the gap between swing and bebop. I couldn't wait to sit next to him on a long journey so I could ask about the old days – a dream as futile, it turned out, as the one we had of our drive to Boston with Sleepy John Estes.

Coleman always required a bottle of brandy in his sax case 'to cut my cold'. He locked his hotel room door every night and took the telephone off the hook. So wake-up calls went unheeded. I would sit in the lobby with Sweets, Sir Charles Thompson, Jimmy Woode and Jo Jones and wait for Coleman. No one would say anything: Coleman was beyond criticism. Hours were then spent begging for seats on flights packed with autumn business travellers and we were often forced to rush straight from airport to concert hall.

Coleman could walk more slowly than any man I ever met. When I shepherded him through an airport or a train station, I tried to concentrate on putting one foot in front of the other as carefully as possible, never taking long strides. Inevitably my attention would wander and Coleman would suddenly be twenty feet behind me. Or, on occasion, nowhere to be seen.

Changing trains in Toulouse, I was so obsessed with keeping track of Hawkins that Harry Edison walked far ahead down the platform and boarded the wrong train. He ended up in Perpignan while we played a concert in Marseille. 'Sweets' was a man of the world who spoke some French; when he rejoined us the next day in Bordeaux he seemed to have enjoyed getting away from the tour and having a quiet meal in a little restaurant with a good bottle of wine.

There was something positive for the rest of us, as well. Harry had spent the years after leaving Count Basie playing trumpet on Hollywood sound stages. He was a wonderful musician with a lovely clear tone, but he had lost some of the competitive edge that kept Coleman going. That night in Marseille, the All-stars shared the bill with the George Russell sextet. I had caught a few glimpses of them earlier in the tour and thought they were tremendous. Russell was one of the leaders of the avant-garde but retained a strong sense of melody. His recording of 'You Are My Sunshine' with Don Ellis on trumpet had impressed critics and sold a fair number of records the previous year. Ellis was an intellectual white player of great skill but little fire. For this tour, Russell hired Thad Jones to play the arrangements he had recorded with Ellis and the contrast was stunning. Jones, who normally played with mainstream big bands, tore into 'Sunshine' with a plunger mute and turned it into a show-stopper. His effect on the rest of the players – Tootie Heath, Joe Farrell, Barre Phillips and Garnett Brown – was equally dramatic; Russell's band were the surprise stars of the tour.

In Marseille I asked Jones whether he would sit in with the All-stars. He came straight from playing the most controlled arrangements with Russell to letting rip on swing classics with Hawkins. He attacked the tunes with an aggressiveness that had Coleman on his toes more than at any other time on the tour. The chase choruses and exchanges between them were stunning, getting more and more intense as the night wore on. I sat in the front row, cheering with the rest of the audience as they played encore after encore.

On a rainy night in Limoges a few days later, I was watching from the wings as the concert began. After the theme was stated a couple of times, Coleman started his solo and Sweets walked off and stood beside me. 'You know, I'm not used to all this,' he said. I asked whether he meant the travelling. 'Well, I haven't done a tour like this for quite a few years, but it isn't that, really. I'm just getting so worn out with all these missed trains and waiting around for Coleman. I think I might cut out early and head back to Los Angeles. Coleman can carry the show without me.'

I was staggered. 'You mean you're going to quit the tour?'

'Like I said, I can't really handle this disorganization. I love Coleman, but I just don't think I want another ten days of this.'

I begged him to reconsider as Coleman finished his solo. Harry walked onstage to take the next few choruses, passing Coleman shuffling off to stand beside me in the wings. We were silent for a few minutes, as I pondered how to handle the situation. All the good diplomatic sense I had brought to bear on the Roland Kirk crisis deserted me in a moment of madness. I told Coleman that Harry was ready to leave the tour because of his, Coleman's, lateness and disorganization and that I hoped he would make a renewed effort to get up in the mornings, meet the departure schedules and generally shape up.

Harry spotted us talking, quickly finished his solo and joined us. Coleman went straight to the point. 'This white boy says you're going to quit the tour because of me. Now, that isn't true, is it?' Harry gave me a look, as if to say, 'Sorry, kid.'

'Why, no, Coleman, I would never say a thing like that.'

Coleman turned to me with a look of lethal contempt. 'Never, in all my years of touring, have I heard such *dog-ass bullshit* as that! Don't you *ever* pull any shit like that on me again, you *hear*?' And with that they rejoined the band onstage. I was mortified, but Coleman's time-keeping improved and Harry stayed to the end of the tour.

Later in the tour, I spent an afternoon in Copenhagen airport buying drinks for Scandinavian Airlines agents and pleading with them to hold Stockholm and Helsinki flights so that fog-delayed musicians could make their connections. On another occasion, I had to rent a car and drive halfway across France with the drum kit strapped to the roof so that the other band could start the concert while Coleman and the All-stars caught a later train. I sped past vineyards where the road was splashed with red and through towns that reeked of new wine. When the tour finished and I collapsed in Paris, I reflected on how many occasions had found us hundreds of miles from the gig, with almost no chance of getting the musicians onstage in time. Somehow, we made every date. I concluded that from here on in everything else would be, by comparison, a breeze. It didn't quite turn out that way, of course, but it gave me the kind of confidence I needed to make my way in the music business.

chapter 7

WHEN I ARRIVED IN LONDON in the spring of '64, I was as impressed as I had hoped to be. There was a refreshing heterodoxy about categories and the pop scene seemed open to all kinds of music. The folk world was a bit more narrow-minded – witness the famous cry of 'Judas' during Dylan's UK tour in 1966 – but I found it all intriguing.

My image of British folk music was pretty limited: Ewan MacColl singing a sea shanty with his finger in his ear. That prejudice was blown away by a visit to a London pub to hear the Ian Campbell Folk Group. They performed traditional songs with slightly Weaver-ish harmonies but redeemed themselves by their exuberant rhythms, strong singing by Ian and his sister Lorna and the virtuoso fiddling of Dave Swarbrick. After I turned up at a second London show, Ian invited me to pay them a visit in Birmingham.

I stayed almost a week, sharing a pull-out sofa in Ian's front room with Swarbrick, whose snoring was as spectacular as his violin playing. (Our prickly relationship lasted for many years: he became a key member of Fairport Convention when I managed and produced them in the late sixties.) I attended rehearsals, went to gigs and helped out by taking young Ali and Robin to the park, pushing the swings for them and holding their hands as we crossed the streets. Twenty years later, they would marry their father's clear diction and nasal delivery to a reggae rhythm section and sell millions of records as UB40. (Around this time, I also met nine-year-old Chris, son of cockney singer John Foreman and later guitar player for Madness.)

Ian introduced me to a local TV producer who invited me to a pub in the middle of the architectural horror known as the Bullring to hear a local band. My initial exposure to British blues had come when a friend took me to the Central School of Art to hear The Pretty Things a few weeks earlier. I was impressed, not so much by the derivative music, but by the show. Lead singer Phil May had glossy hair reaching to his waist, pranced around the stage Jagger-style and seemed obviously queer (no one said 'gay' in those days). My friend laughed at my American naiveté and we watched as he was surrounded after the gig by girl fans. Time has given me two footnotes for this event: one, that Phil's other talent was tennis (we became friends and in the '80s he helped improve my backhand); and two, that he was always, in fact, bisexual. The Pretty Things still tour regularly and Phil's hair is a good deal shorter.

I had also visited a Soho blues club with some of my charges on a day off from the Blues and Gospel Caravan. I noticed a strange creature listening from the doorway. He had extraordinary hair, all puffed up and fluffed about and dyed blond. His trench coat was gathered mincingly at the waist and he was wearing some very odd boots. I had yet to grasp that, unlike in America where rebels all wore jeans and everyone was too uptight to play games with gender, English kids rebelled by investing a great deal of effort in eccentric fashion. I asked about the stylish listener and was told he was quite a good blues singer with an easy name to remember: Rod Stewart.

In Birmingham that night I saw a standard four-piece,

with a lead singer who played keyboard and guitar. The repertoire mixed folk songs, blues, skiffle tunes and some West Indian material. The singer was about fifteen and had the most convincing white blues voice I had ever heard. This was child prodigy Steve Winwood and the Spencer Davis Group and they were the first folk-rock band I ever heard. I left the pub resolved to put together a similar outfit in America.

When I arrived back in New York that autumn after the jazz tour, I sought out Paul Rothchild. Things had changed dramatically for him since the Jesse Fuller session a year earlier. Jac Holzman of Elektra, upset at falling behind Prestige and Vanguard in the 'hip folk label' stakes, lured Paul with a higher salary and bigger budgets. Now he had a corner office in Elektra's mid-town headquarters and was wheeling and dealing, meeting Brill Building record pluggers and going to sales conventions to talk up the new records he was producing for his rapidly expanding employers. More significantly, he was also becoming a great producer. Paul's work on the Doors albums and *Janis* later in the decade would stand among the best recordings of the era.

Over beers in an East Village bar, I recounted how teenage English girls had waited outside Muddy Waters' dressing room for an autograph; about *Melody Maker*, the paper with articles about pop, folk, jazz and blues all mixed together; and about white blues singers of ambiguous sexuality queuing up to follow the Stones into the Top Ten. And I told him about the Spencer Davis Group.

His response was to lead me across the Village to the Night Owl Café on West Third Street. From the doorway we heard the sound of Richie Havens and a bongo player echoing out into the street. There weren't many in the audience, but Paul told me that every night you could find singers there like Havens, Fred Neil or Jesse Colin Young, 'folk' artists with a pop sensibility and an electric bass or a percussionist.

Over the next few days we set about recruiting our 'folk-rock super-group'. We started with Jerry Yester, a pleasant red-haired Californian with one good LP under his belt who could play electric bass, and the former Even Dozen Jug Band harmonica star John Sebastian. After adding Joe Butler, a drummer Yester and Sebastian knew, the final piece of the puzzle was Zal Yanovsky, a voluble Canadian who wrote, sang and played lead guitar. In a McDougal Street bar, I gave them a pep talk about what was happening in England. They looked dubious, but agreed to start rehearsing. After the meeting, Yanovsky and I eyed each other curiously. 'Don't I know you from somewhere...?' Out of context, it took a minute – he had grown a Beatle mop-top – but then it came back to me.

In the summer of 1962, Warwick, Geoff and I had gone to Chicago on a blues expedition. We travelled back around the top of Lakes Michigan and Huron and, fuelled by a bottle of my mother's diet pills, drove straight through to Toronto. With nowhere to stay and almost no money, we put in a collect call to the well-travelled Tom Rush to find out about possible crash pads.

He gave us the address of Ian and Sylvia Tyson, a popular Canadian duo. Their place was dark, but the downstairs half of the duplex was buzzing with a party full of freaks. Geoff decided that Warwick and I were too square to lead the assault. 'You guys have no idea how to mumble,' he said, so we lurked in the shadows as he rang the doorbell, then conducted most of the ensuing conversation talking at his own left shoulder.

'Yeah, man, like, you dig... Chicago, you dig... ahhh, no sleep... place to crash, you dig?' all minimally articulated and barely audible. It worked. We were shown to a basement room filled with chrome and naugahyde furniture pilfered from all-night laundromats. Our host spotted our new Big Joe Williams LP and insisted on hearing it. We were cross-examined about the Chicago blues scene and Club 47. By dawn, the Dexedrines had worn off and we were starving. Zal (for it was he) led us out into neighbouring streets where we confiscated freshly delivered bread, doughnuts and milk from front steps. The next day he took us to Yonge Street and taught us to play snooker. A few days later, when we had barely enough cash left for the two tanks of gas needed to get back to New Jersey, we popped some more pills and headed home. I thought Zal was just a hospitable freak; he never let on he was a musician.

The plan was that once they got some original material together, Paul would sign the group to Elektra, finance getting them on the road and transform them into stars. As Paul's sidekick, I had his assurance that he would figure out a suitable reward. I never doubted he would deliver.

Yester and Butler's interest soon waned. Rehearsals would peter out into Sebastian, Rothchild and I getting high, listening to the latest English imports and fantasizing about having a Top Forty hit. Capitol Records had signed Fred Neil and Richie Havens was making a record for MGM. The big boys were moving into the scene and we were getting left behind.

I was still working for George. I liked the idea of being involved in the Newport Festivals the following summer, to say nothing of having a regular pay check, and I wanted to sell packages like the Blues and Gospel Caravan to colleges and concert halls. A bookers' convention was taking place in La Crosse, Wisconsin, early in January, and George decided I should go. I would stop in Chicago, visit Muddy to get him on board and try to get the idea off the ground. It was made clear to me that without some bookings my job was unlikely to last through the spring.

A couple of nights before my departure (by Greyhound bus – George's budgets were always tight) I took a seat at the Kettle of Fish on McDougal Street for the New York debut of Son House, the latest blues legend to emerge from the mists of history. I joined a table that included Sam Charters, a hero of mine for writing *The Country Blues*, about the early days of blues recording. When I told him I was going to Chicago, he said, 'Well, there's a band there you have to hear.'

'Come on, Sam, I know all about Magic Sam, Buddy Guy, Otis Rush and Junior Wells,' naming the then obscure South Side band leaders I assumed he was talking about.

'No, it's none of those. There's a band with white kids and black guys, led by a harmonica player called Paul Butterfield. You should make a point to hear them,' and he named a North Side bar where they appeared a few nights a week.

I rang Rothchild the next morning and recounted my conversation with Charters. 'I'll meet you there,' he said immediately. Someone in California had told him about a kid named Butterfield who was an amazing harmonica player. By the time I arrived at the club straight from the bus station, it was eleven o'clock and one set was already over. Paul, who had flown, was sitting in a booth with Butterfield and guitarist Elvin Bishop talking contract terms.

Listening to the second set, it was clear their music was unlike anything in Boston, New York or London. The combination of South Side veterans Sam Lay and Jerome Arnold with Bishop on guitar and Butterfield on harmonica and lead vocals was completely original. It was Chicago blues, hard edged and raw with nothing 'folk' or 'pop' about it.

I told Paul I could see only one problem. Elvin Bishop was a good rhythm player, a decent singer, a nice guy, a close friend of Butter's and a key to the group's conception and sound. But as a lead guitarist he was just not... *heroic*. I had been telling Paul about the charismatic role a young guitar player for John Mayall's Blues Breakers named Eric Clapton had in the mythology of English blues bands. To be *perfect*, the band needed a guitar hero.

I mentioned the white kid who had sat in with Muddy Waters: *he* seemed pretty intense and heroic. I hadn't been that knocked out with his playing, but in this context... I had first met Mike Bloomfield in the basement of Bob Koester's Jazz Record Mart during the Dexedrine-propelled summer trip to Chicago. Geoff, Warwick and I were rifling through Koester's collection of 78s one afternoon, taping the best ones on to my primitive Wollensak recorder, and Bloomfield sat with us for a while, chatting about blues and playing a few things on an acoustic guitar.

After the show, Paul and I took Butter down the street for a drink. We told him of our concerns about Elvin and the need for a strong lead guitarist as a foil to his harmonica solos. There was no talk of replacing Elvin, just adding another element. I asked whether he knew Bloomfield. 'Sure, I know Mike,' he said, 'he has a regular gig at a bar in Evanston. I think he's there tomorrow night.'

We picked Butterfield up the following evening in my rented car and he guided us north along Lake Shore Drive to a rowdy club with a stage behind the bar. Bloomfield was in mid-set, but during a pause Butter motioned to his harmonica and Mike beckoned him on to the stage. As they started jamming on a Freddy King instrumental, Paul and I exchanged looks. This was the magic dialectic, Butterfield and Bloomfield. It sounded like a firm of accountants but we were convinced it was the key to fame and fortune for the band and for us.

When the set ended, Mike joined us in the booth. He was a cheerful, open-faced, big-boned kid who had devoted his young life to the blues. Rothchild laid out the deal: join the Butterfield Band, sign a contract with Elektra, come to New York, make a record, be a star. Bloomfield hesitated for about ten seconds before nodding his agreement. Paul headed back to New York to draw up the contracts and I went north to try and peddle some Muddy Waters concerts.

Rothchild swung into action immediately, bringing Dylan's manager Albert Grossman to Chicago to see the group and planning the recording. Things happened very fast in 1965. When Dylan released *Bringing It All Back Home* that spring, it raised the stakes for everyone. As for the Blues and Gospel Caravan, American college bookers proved as cold as the frozen wastes of northern Wisconsin in January. George told me to take the spring off and come back in June to get ready for the Newport Festivals.

chapter 8

AFTER A WEEK HITCH-HIKING through the Scottish Highlands in the spring of 1965, I took a train from Loch Lomond into Glasgow. The grime of the city was astounding. Sooty black buildings loomed over me as I emerged from the station and the air was pungent with that peculiarly Scottish odour of coal smoke and granite. I noticed a small poster advertising the Kelvin Museum and thought consoling my eyes with some art seemed a nice idea for a damp Sunday afternoon. The Kelvin has recently won an award for forward thinking in museum management, but that Sunday I saw a stuffed bear looming over a model of the original Glasgow regional railway and some Charles Rennie Mackintosh chairs sharing space with Salvador Dali's *St John's Vision of Christ on the Cross*. It was dizzying in its amateur wackiness.

When the five o'clock bell rang, evicting the stragglers onto the shabby grass of Kelvin Park, I fell in alongside an arty-looking blonde and made a casual remark. She turned, smiled and proceeded to make friendly chat as we walked across the park. I nodded, agreeing with everything she said while in truth I couldn't understand a word. It was a good few minutes before my ears were sufficiently attuned to her Glaswegian dialect to have a coherent conversation.

The weirdness of the Kelvin Museum and the incomprehensibility of the natives delighted me. I loved the feeling that I was in a foreign place, and the more alien the better. Shuttling back and forth between Britain and America in the sixties provided endless opportunities for comparison and contrast. For a start, the British didn't seem to own anything. The most poverty-stricken folk singer in Cambridge or Greenwich Village had at least a record player and a refrigerator and many drove cars. In England, pilgrimages would be made with a newly purchased LP to the flat of someone with the means to play it. Milk bottles on the window ledge brought hurriedly inside on winter mornings were a reminder that kitchen appliances – and central heating – were rare luxuries. My purchase of a used 250cc BMW motorcycle in the spring of 1964 transformed our options. Friends would jump on 'Tamla Mobike' and we would head for Cambridge or Oxford, or venture to gigs in previously inaccessible corners of Greater London.

Dope was another area of cultural surprise. The nail-thin American single-paper grass joints were uncommon in Britain. I watched the construction of a five-paper British hash-and-tobacco spliff in wonder: the search for cardboard to be rolled into a mouthpiece; the ritual burning of the hashish block; the careful licking of papers; the LP cover on the knees for assemblage. Most liner notes I saw were dotted with hashish burns.

When I started meeting musicians, I noticed other differences between the cultures. Some British art students would form a group, then learn how to play their instruments well enough to perform the songs written by the group's strongest personality. The results might be technically unsophisticated but were often more original than those of their American counterparts, who were too close to our musical forms to do much more than accurately re-create them. Dylan, always the exception, was almost British in his unconcern with vocal grace or instrumental fluency.

I read an interview with Keith Richards once explaining how he and Mick Jagger had a single blues record between them when they first met. It was one I knew well: a Stateside four-track EP licensed from the Excello label, with Slim Harpo on one side and Lazy Lester on the other. They played it until it was so worn they could barely hear the music through the scratches. One way of looking at the Stones' sound is as a South-East London adaptation of the Excello style. If they had owned more records, their music might have been less distinctive.

By the mid-sixties, America was experiencing the 'generation gap'. Parents whose kids returned from school or college with long hair and a rebellious attitude often went into shock. Children were disowned, 'grounded', locked up, beaten, shorn, lectured, or sent to psychiatrists, military school or mental institutions. In Britain I visited pubs where earringed boys with long hair stood drinking a Sunday pint next to their dads in cloth caps. Neither seemed the least bit concerned. Americans were so unsure of their often newly won status that they could not comprehend the next generation rejecting what they had worked so hard to achieve. The British seemed to feel that little was going to change, no matter how long their child's hair grew. My egalitarian American impulses were unnerved when comedians or pundits referred to some working-class parents' reluctance for their kids to be educated 'above their station', yet much of British society seemed happy and content compared to status-anxious America.

But the defining revelation for me was the audiences. The crowds that filled Club 47 in the early sixties were not too different from those that came to the Newport Folk

Festival: middle-class college kids. And there weren't that many of them until the Dylan stone dropped in the pond. Black music of most kinds was a minority taste in white America. I took a group of friends to a gospel concert in South Boston in 1962. The audience was welcoming but amazed at our presence: white faces were virtually unknown at black venues.

In June 1964, I stood by the apron of the Hammersmith Odeon stage in London. The show that day starred the Animals with the Nashville Teens, the Swinging Blue Jeans and special guests Chuck Berry and Carl Perkins. Berry was a legend, but jail terms for statutory rape and tax evasion had placed him outside the boundaries of a mainstream American music business that was determined to be respectable and, if possible, white.

I had met the house manager during the Caravan tour and he gave me permission to take my camera to the front of the beautiful art deco auditorium and snap away. When Berry started his duck walk, kids rushed the stage and I found myself crushed between dozens of teenage girls and the orchestra pit. This was middle America's worst nightmare: white teenage girls screaming ecstatically at Chuck Berry.

I noticed a familiar silhouette in the wings, wearing his trademark hat. I had read in *Melody Maker* that he was about to start a club tour, so I blurted out, 'Hey, that's John Lee Hooker.' The girls around me started yelling, 'John Lee? John Lee? Where? Where?' I pointed towards the wings. They started chanting, 'We want John Lee, we want John Lee' and were quickly joined by half the hall – hundreds of kids. Berry looked annoyed, then resigned, beckoning him out to take a bow. People stood on chairs and yelled and cheered as Hooker gave us a wave before turning the stage back over to Berry.

In that moment, I decided I would live in England and produce music for this audience. America seemed a desert in comparison. These weren't the privileged elite, they were just kids, Animals fans. And they knew who John Lee Hooker was! No white person in America in 1964 – with the exception of me and my friends, of course – knew who John Lee Hooker was.

chapter 9

AS A MODEST CONSUMER OF DRUGS, I rarely met proper dealers. Around Harvard Square, there was a dangerous-looking source named Rick who rode a Harley-Davidson and sneered at twerps like me. In later years in the East Village, in Laurel Canyon and in Bolinas north of San Francisco, I waited at friends' pads for someone to turn up with what was billed as 'out-of-sight dope'. The door would open and in would walk Rick. By Bolinas, I had become a vaguely important record producer and was therefore allowed to dine with Rick and hear his tales of adventure. He seemed a restless man who had travelled the world in search of the perfect high, recounting tales of meandering through India with a debauched Russian diplomat in a private train carriage, visits to tribal villages in Afghanistan and close calls with Los Angeles cops.

There was less mystique about dope in England, perhaps because British police seemed less sinister, or maybe just because hashish is more compact and easier to stash than grass. When Hoppy drove me to the airport for my flight back to New York in November 1964, he handed me a joint 'to smoke on the plane'. I forgot about it until we landed at the newly named Kennedy airport, where my parents were waiting to welcome me home. I considered throwing the joint away, but after sailing unmolested through border after border during the jazz tour, with musicians carrying God knows what in their horn cases, I dismissed the idea as craven and foolish. Besides, it would be nice to have a joint to smoke in the back yard in Princeton.

Emerging from customs, I waved at the folks, then walked out of their sight towards the door. A crew-cut man in a brown suit flashed a badge and asked me to step into his office. He and a colleague started going through my bags. When they asked me to empty my pockets, I handed them the joint.

The Feds turned me down as too small a fry so I was offered to the Queens police. A detective with the retrospectively ominous name of Giuliani showed up wearing a sharkskin suit and dancing pumps: he had been getting ready for a Latin dance contest. I asked whether someone would please inform my parents. 'Parents?' I got the feeling that if they had realized my family were meeting me I might not have been stopped. Giuliani gave my father directions to the police station in Forest Hills and drove me there via the slums of Bedford – Stuyvesant. He pointed out junkies nodding on street corners, saying, 'You don't want to end up like that, do you?'

In a miraculous denouement, Giuliani and the assistant district attorney decided I was a good kid and contrived to get me off. After sitting through some 'counselling sessions' where I was assured by a pleasant man in a bow tie that whoever had given me the joint was 'an agent of the international communist conspiracy', I was brought before a judge who reviewed the documents and intoned that 'it is not in the best interests of the People of the State of New York for this fine young man to have a police record. Case dismissed'.

After the failure of the blues concert idea, I returned to

England in March 1965. Staying in a flat near Baker Street, I got caught up in a bizarre web involving Nigel Waymouth, a friend I had met during the Caravan tour, his girlfriend Sheila and a friend of hers from San Francisco named Freddie, who was overstaying his visa and violating a court order by sleeping with an under-age heiress. One morning, when Nigel and Sheila were away, five plainclothes men from the Drugs Squad burst in on us. Ever resourceful when it came to dope, Freddie managed to hide our small stash in his mouth, then ate it in a police holding cell. The fact that they couldn't have found anything – the ashtrays were scrupulously clean – didn't stop us being remanded in custody for twelve days on a charge of 'possession of dangerous drugs'.

I hoped I would be able to deal with my fortnight in Brixton prison as one of those colourful events I could tell my grandchildren – or perhaps you, reader – about. The first few days didn't quite feel that way. I had been denied a phone call as well as bail and had to wait a day before I could even send a letter telling someone where I was. F-wing looked like the set of a Terry-Thomas movie. There was a huge window at either end with the London skyline visible in the distance. Catwalks around each floor overlooked a central area bisected by metal steps, not unlike a New York tenement fire escape. As 'untried prisoners' we each had a cell to ourselves: a cot with a mattress, sheet, blanket and pillow; a small wooden table and chair; a window just above head height, barred; a slops bucket for a toilet. On the bed lay a booklet entitled *Rules for Untried Prisoners* which contained one encouraging sentence: 'Untried prisoners shall have access to the Prison Library'. I relaxed, slightly; I would pass the time reading those classics I had skimmed at Harvard.

Climbing back to the top floor the next morning after

the disgusting breakfast, I approached my Landing Officer. He was a dead ringer for the prison guard in *A Clockwork Orange*: small and neat, with a carefully trimmed moustache and a short-person-in-uniform's domineering glint in his eyes.

'I'd like to go to the library now, please, sir.'

'You'd like to *what*?'

'The library. It says in the rules that I can go to the library.'

'I know what it says in the bloody RULES! It says you shall have ACCESS! It doesn't say WHEN! It doesn't say HOW! That is for ME to determine! Now get back in your cell!'

An hour later, my disconsolate reverie – in which I pondered the logistics and physical demands of twelve days of thrice-daily masturbation – was interrupted by the opening of the cell door window.

'You the one wanted the BOOKS?' shouted the LO, peering in and frowning. He shoved about twenty volumes through the slot – paperbacks and hardbacks of all descriptions and conditions, including George Orwell's Homage to Catalonia, Dickens' Pickwick Papers and an H. G. Wells novel called Tono Bungay.

My relationship with the LO continued in this vein. One day the cell doors were opened and we were each given a bucket of soapy water and a hard-bristled brush and told to clean our tables. I was on my knees scrubbing away when a pair of shiny black shoes entered my field of vision. I looked up to see a scowling LO. 'What do you think *you're* doing?' he demanded.

'Washing my table, sir, as ordered.'

'Well, put some *muscle* into it!' I redoubled my efforts, scrubbing faster and harder.

'Oh, that's absolutely *useless*, that is. Here, give me that brush.'

The next thing I knew, the LO was down on his knees attacking my table, turning it over and digging the grime out of the corners. Finally, he tossed the brush into the bucket, got back on his feet and turned on his heel. '*That's* the way to clean a table, son.' I guess he had a crush on me.

Cops and Robbers in 1965 England was still a kind of Ealing Comedy: crimes rarely involved firearms. The denizens of F-Wing were losers in a game they had been playing against the cops. In queues for exercise or food, the constant questions were 'What you in for, mate?', followed by 'What you reckon you'll get?' When Freddie and I responded with 'Suspicion of drug possession' and 'We're innocent, we'll get off' they would burst into laughter, offering: 'Listen, mate, they wouldn't have you in here if they had any intention of letting you off. You're living in dreamland, you are.'

The only obvious hard men on view were a sullen group of Maltese pimps who never talked to anyone. The innocent mood was confirmed by an encounter I had one day with a trusty cleaning the walkway in front of my cell. After the ritual exchange of information, he added that he was the 'Surrey Phantom'. Asked to enlarge on this, he recounted his tale.

Married with a kid, he would commute daily to Farnham, a drive of 20 miles through the Surrey countryside. He got to know the route so well that he could tell when houses were unoccupied. One day he stopped at an isolated farm to have a look around. Finding an open window, he was off down the road with the TV and the silverware a few minutes later. A fence encouraged him to come back with more goods. Over the next two years, he quit his job (without telling the wife) and would spend his days plundering the countryside. The rash of burglaries with similar MOs sparked a local press outcry about a 'Surrey

Phantom'. He was finally stopped for speeding with an embarrassing number of other people's appliances in his boot, covered with his by now familiar fingerprints.

The night before being sent up to London for arraignment, he grew uneasy when his jailers refused him the supper they were dishing out to the other prisoners. His alarm increased when he was taken from his cell and frog-marched to a back room. There he was confronted not with truncheon-wielding uglies but an empty chair at the head of a crowded table. There was steak and two veg on his plate, a glass of wine and a dozen policemen from surrounding towns who wanted to meet the Phantom before he was swallowed by the criminal justice system.

Another inmate was an American from St Augustine, Florida, organizer of orgies for the cross-dressers among that city's police force and politicians. One night, with the head of the Vice Squad in a Merry Widow and high heels, they were raided by a rival police unit. He fled out the back window and was given get-out-of-town money by interested parties. He went first to New York and then to London, where his funds ran out, leaving him unable to meet his room service and taxi bills. He marvelled at the gentleness of his experience with British justice and seemed to be quite enjoying himself in F-Wing.

My letters eventually produced a visit from a solicitor. Freddie grew resigned and fatalistic; he knew they were determined to convict him. When the trial was postponed to allow one of the detectives to give evidence elsewhere, my solicitor got me out on bail. No such joy for Freddie: with his expired visa, he had no right to be in England at all.

It was a gorgeous April day when I emerged from Marlborough Street magistrates' court. On Regent Street, a bus marked 'Highgate' caught my eye and I thought of *Tono Bungay*. The lead character in Wells's tale repairs to the famous cemetery when he gets depressed, sits on a knoll and gazes down the hill where the gravestones blur in the fog with the chimneys of Kentish Town. My first act of liberty would be to try to locate that spot.

Sure enough, there was a grassy rise near the entrance beside an oak tree. Looking down the hill through the now (since the smokeless fuel regulations of the 1940s) fog-free air of London, I could just about conjure up a blurred line between gravestones and chimneys. I lay there for a while, looking at the sky and revelling in my fragile freedom. As I rose to leave, I noticed the row of gravestones in front of me, all from the 1890s, just before Wells had written the book. The names on the middle two stones, with first and last transposed, were those of the two main characters in *Tono Bungay*. I caught the downhill bus feeling revived and reconnected to the world.

When the case came to trial it was the judge this time who seemed impressed with my Harvard background and gentlemanly demeanour. The Crown tried their best to convict, producing a ruddy-faced, sweating (through his lies) chemist from Scotland Yard who claimed the bowl where Freddie kept his loose tobacco contained two grams of cannabis resin. They were out to get Freddie and they did: three months in Brixton followed by deportation. In my case, the prosecution produced an unposted letter to a girlfriend with references to 'getting high' and to my bust at Kennedy. I stoutly insisted that in America 'high' referred to alcohol and the judge suppressed mention of my US case on the grounds that it was hearsay evidence. Charges dismissed; two blunders and still no police record. My freedom of movement remained intact through sheer luck and the kindness of strangers.

Not long after, three bobbies approached a car on a back street near Shepherd's Bush. When they asked the driver for identification, his companion pulled out a shotgun and killed all three. The criminal fraternity were as horrified as the police: the desperate gunmen could find no shelter. One surrendered quickly, the other was found weeks later, starving in rugged Derbyshire woodlands. As both villains and police feared, this event signalled the end of Terry-Thomas time in Britain. Crime became progressively more violent, criminals and police harsher and more aggressive with each other. No more steak and wine for the Phantom.

A middle-class kid dabbling in drugs today stands about as much chance of getting busted as he does of flying to the moon. The drug laws of Britain and America are enforced almost exclusively against the underclasses. In the sixties, the authorities were genuinely rattled by 'respectable' kids using drugs: it seemed to represent the end of civilization as they knew it. Now that stockbrokers snort coke, millions of kids take ecstasy every weekend and society continues to function 'normally', they can concentrate on the ever dangerous poor, using drug laws as another means of intimidation and retribution.

The shift from grass, hash and acid to coke, smack, crack and crystal meth has brought in a hard and dangerous world with huge amounts of money at stake both for the dealers and for the gigantic drug squads. Turning policemen away at the doors of UFO was our own Ealing Comedy. Reality on the narcotics front line today is more like something directed by Paul Verhoeven.

chapter 10

WHY DOES ENGLAND HATE its own folk music? Fashionable girls at Madrid discotheques squeal with delight when the DJ puts on a *Sevillanas* at midnight and they dance it with grace and enthusiasm. Irishmen sit happily for hours in a country pub listening to fiddlers and accordion players. A sophisticated Roman won't turn up his nose at a tarantella. Abba's Benny Andersson appears at Swedish folk festivals with his accordion and has produced recordings of traditional *polskas*. In England, the mere thought of a morris dance team or an unaccompanied ballad singer sends most natives running for cover.

I think it goes back to 1066. 'Received pronunciation' derives from Norman French, the language of court until the fifteenth century, while regional accents are the vestiges of pre-Conquest Celtic and Anglo-Saxon tongues. The great Norman cathedrals were shunned by the natives until the authorities tore down their simple stone chapels and forced them into York Minster and the others at sword-point. England, at some visceral level, remains a colonial society, with the inheritors of Norman power lording it over their uncouth subjects. The upwardly mobile take on 'Norman' characteristics while the lower orders are taught to be ashamed of their roots. If the conquered tribes had been 'coloured', this pattern would be easier to perceive. In Spain, Portugal, Hungary and Sweden – and even in France – rich and poor speak with roughly the same accent and eat the same sort of food. But not in England.

Then there is the dominance of African rhythms. From the turn-of-the-century cakewalk and tango crazes to contemporary enthusiasms for everything from house to salsa, the social dances of modern Europe all come from Africa via the Americas. English folk music may often be bawdy, but it lacks the African-influenced rhythms contemporary culture associates with sexuality. Ironically, the term 'morris dance' probably comes from 'Moorish dance': sailors from English slaving ships showing the folks back home how Africans danced.

I was led farther into the mysteries of English folk music by Roy Guest, the man coordinating the Blues and Gospel Caravan for its British promoters. Roy was a plump, jocular man with wounded, sad eyes. His father had been a director of Guest, Keen and Nettelfold before it was nationalized and incorporated into British Steel. As a young man building a railway in Turkey, Roy's father had horrified his family by marrying an Anatolian Greek woman. He came to regret this union and, after a divorce, tried to pretend it had never produced a son.

In the early sixties Roy opened the legendary Howff in Edinburgh, a key venue in the early Festival 'fringe'. He married Jill Doyle (sister of musician Davey Graham) but they soon arrived at an open arrangement. Her paramour, the Scottish folk singer Archie Fisher (now a presenter for BBC Scotland), came back to their third-floor flat on Bristow Place one night, found Jill's bedroom door locked and a strange coat in the hallway, walked to the front window and jumped out. His fall was broken by her MG, conveniently parked outside with the top down and loaded with cushions. Archie only broke his arm, but the tabloids published photos of the squashed roadster amid lurid speculations about the *ménage-à-combien*? Roy's father wrote requesting that he no longer use the family name.

Roy moved to London and joined the Harold Davison Agency, where he developed a 'folk and blues' division. He and his mother – who wore black shawls and looked as if she had just stepped out of a village in Asia Minor – lived in adjacent flats near Cecil Sharp House, the centre of folk activities in London in the early sixties. In the spring of 1965, I returned to England to help Roy with a UK tour by the Reverend Gary Davis and Ramblin' Jack Elliott, filling the gap in my calendar and bank account until the Newport Festival preparations began in June. After Brixton Prison, I needed a place to stay, so Roy introduced me to Topic Records' producer Bill Leader, who offered me his sofa.

During my winter in New York, I had attended a few recording sessions with Paul Rothchild, keeping the track listings, running errands and absorbing as much as I possibly could. Bill now became my mentor, and it would be hard to imagine a teacher more different from Rothchild. Paul's records today sound expertly made: rich, full and three-dimensional. The same claims cannot always be made for Bill's, but the performances are natural and spontaneous and the sound stands up well. In his Camden Town flat or a musician's home, he would set up his two-track Revox, place the microphones in the liveliest room, nail blankets over the windows and make the musicians comfortable. His obvious love of the music and concern for the artists was something I never forgot. The hundreds of LPs Bill produced, from the '50s through the '70s, provide the backbone of any CD collection of British traditional music.

We set off for Tyneside one day in Bill's Humber Super Snipe. I helped carry the equipment, kept track sheets and even snapped the cover photograph for an album by the Fisher Family, Scots living in Northumberland. Brother Archie being the one who had jumped from Roy Guest's window, I was curious to hear his account. He shrugged and said, 'I just had to get out of there and the window was closer than the door.' The music was beautiful and the hospitality helped to prepare me for what I would encounter when I got to Scotland.

Travellers of both sexes in the early sixties thought nothing of hitch-hiking. Bill dropped me on the North Road outside Newcastle and a car stopped almost immediately. On the map I spotted a side road cutting across the lowland hills between the two main highways to Edinburgh with a village called Yarrow halfway along. The red line sported a green shadow, indicating 'scenic', so at Galashiels I made a song-inspired detour. A Boston folk singer named Robert L. Jones (whom I would invite that autumn to take over my job with George Wein and who would still be organizing George's festivals and tours thirty-five years later) used to sing 'The Dewy Dens O' Yarrow', a cheerful ditty with an eventful storyline. A Laird's daughter elopes; her three brothers give chase; her hero kills two of the brothers but is treacherously slain from behind by the third; she rides back to the castle and lays her lover's body at her father's feet; then she kills herself.

I sat on a rock in the sunshine contentedly eating an apple until a small white van pulled up. It had a wonderful meaty smell; the driver was delivering school lunches in the valley. As we approached Yarrow, I asked whether he knew the song. 'Och, aye,' he said, and pointed to some ruins overlooking the town. 'There's the castle where the laird lived and yon hill over there' – pointing to a beautiful sweep of upland beyond the town – 'that's where the killing took place. She rode back this way,' and he pointed to a worn trail through the grass. 'It happened in the eleventh century.' I thought about all the fuss in Princeton when Warwick found a 185-year-old cannon ball from the Revolutionary War.

On the outskirts of Edinburgh, I got out Bill's scrap of paper with the phone number of singer Dolina MacLennan and her husband George Brown. Not only did they offer to put me up, they used my arrival as an excuse for a party. Moreover, they lived in Roy's old flat so I could lean out of the window and gauge the drama of Archie's leap. The party was going strong until ten minutes to ten, when the men all rose and headed for the door. 'It's closing time, Joe,' one said. I asked why, with a table full of ales and stouts, we had to worry about Scotland's licensing laws. 'That doesnae matter, Joe, it's *closing time*!' We all trooped out, leaving the ladies to put a dent in the remaining bottles.

The sign on the pub across the road reads The Forrest Bar, but it is universally known as Sandy Bell's. While I was taking in this famous outpost for writers, musicians, politicians, artists and Scottish Nationalists, two of our party placed ritual orders for rounds of heavy. As I contemplated the pair of pint glasses in front of me, the man on my right, Hamish Henderson, enquired whether I was familiar with single malts. My ignorance was rewarded with doubles of Laphroaig and Talisker.

Henderson was a remarkable man. The last Pictish speaker on the planet, he ran the School of Scottish Studies at Edinburgh University and had travelled the Highlands collecting songs and stories and documenting the disappearing dialects and ways of life of the most remote glens and islands. I had made a small start on my beverage collection when the landlord slapped his heavy palm on the bar: 'Drink up, drink up. Time, gentlemen, please!'

After choking down the doubles and the pints, I could

barely walk. Hamish and I fell behind on the way back to the flat and he helped me up the dark stairway. On the second landing, he pinned me against the wall, muttering, 'Let's have a kiss of ye, lad.' I found a second wind of sobriety and scrambled up the stairs.

After a circuit of the Highlands that ended at the Kelvin Museum, I was joined by Warwick for a trip to the '65 Padstow May Day celebrations in Cornwall. In this ancient ritual, two 'hobby-horse' teams circulate through the fishing village for twenty-four hours, playing and singing a fertility-rite song. The 'horse' dances and twirls and tries to catch girls under the skirts of his costume. Every house and pub in Padstow receives this pagan serenade. The melody worms its way into your brain and you become addicted, listening out for it when you stray out of range.

The local economy may have been meagre, but the villagers had little use for tourists or publicity. Non-Cornish singers were grudgingly welcomed but a camera crew was dragged out of their hotel room and thrown – equipment and all – off the end of the dock. When the tide went out, a 16mm camera was revealed in the mud, waves lapping gently over it.

May Day 1965 in Padstow represented a high-water mark for the English traditional folk revival. The town was full of great singers: the Watersons, Martin Carthy, Luke Kelly of the Dubliners, Cyril Tawney, Maddy Prior, Louis Killen and Annie Briggs all camped out on a hill above the town. Word spread of a private gig the following night in a tiny pub down the road. It would be guest-list only, and furious lobbying began to make sure one secured an invite. There was a real sense that day of glamour and exclusiveness among these mostly unaccompanied traditional singers. The session was memorable: all had wonderful voices, a store of great songs and a vivid feeling for the past of rural England.

The Watersons and Annie Briggs were the superstars. The former were a real family: two sisters, a brother and a cousin with the rich blend that comes only from genetically matched vocal cords (Bee Gees, Carter Family, Everly Brothers, Crowded House, for example). With rough manners and strong Yorkshire accents, they effortlessly communicated authenticity, yet their harmonies drew as much from their own rich imaginations as from any deep-rooted Yorkshire tradition. Within a couple of years of their first appearances, they were the most popular turn on the folk club circuit. I was enthralled by Norma Waterson's voice: it had the soulfulness of a gospel singer's, yet was devoid of any Afro-American phrasing or texture. She wasn't a conventional beauty, but I found her alluring.

Annie Briggs looked a bit like Patti Smith, with the same slim build, dishevelled brown hair and stubborn stare. She hitch-hiked to gigs and would disappear for weeks at a time. Her 'act' consisted of ancient ballads sung starkly with no accompaniment. She and Bert Jansch represented the tortured-genius category in the British folk world, but Annie seemed uncontrived, while I was never sure about Bert. She had no stage patter and in company was shy to the point of invisibility. (Sandy Denny's 'The Pond And The Stream' conveys an awed impression of Briggs.) Like Smith, she retired in her prime to raise a family, then reappeared in the '90s, powers intact. But in contrast to Patti's reverentially awaited comeback, when Annie returned there were few venues or audiences for an unaccompanied ballad singer.

My brother and I spent a week after Padstow driving around the West Country. On one occasion we arrived at a medieval Welsh landmark called Tretower Court just as it was closing. The caretaker was so pleased to have foreign visitors that he gave us a private hour-long tour of the building. Aside from his explanation of the advantages of molten lead over boiling oil for scalding attackers either side of a battering ram (you can peel it off the bodies and reuse it), the most memorable moment was coming upon the huge door to the dining room. Gigantic oak beams were held together by three iron cross-bars. Two were beautifully smooth while the third was badly rusted. No need to guess which were forged in the twelfth century and which came from a modern foundry.

Further inspired by a Watersons recording session in Bill's kitchen, I set off for Hull, where the three siblings lived together in a crowded flat. I think Norma was more bemused than excited by my attentions, but I spent a happy week with her, surrounded by song. She had warned me of her 'serious' boyfriend but refused to reveal more than that he was a singer who travelled a lot. One night, just before closing at the group's folk club in the Ring o' Bells pub, a handsome and well-known singer walked in unannounced and I saw the blood drain from Norma's face. I whispered to her to give me a front-door key and a fifteen-minute head start and I would be on the road before they got back. I got the most adoring look I had had all week.

Half an hour later, I was standing beneath the orange motorway lighting with my thumb out hoping for a London-bound lorry. Finding a Yank by the roadside in darkest Yorkshire was entertaining enough, but as the night wore on and I climbed into my fourth truck, I started embellishing the tale in order to keep both the drivers and myself awake. Dawn found me on the A1 just north of London telling a gripped cockney that I had been chased out of Hull by a jealous boyfriend wielding a butcher's knife. He was sufficiently impressed to treat me to breakfast in a café hidden in a cul-de-sac filled with bare-knuckle fighters and other East End hard men finishing off their night with a fry-up.

Back at Bill's, Bert Lloyd paid a call and we all went out for a curry. A. L. Lloyd was a short, round man, with immense eyebrows and a perpetual expression of delight and surprise. If a bio-pic had been made of his life, Ralph Richardson would have been perfect casting. He told us tales of collecting music in Albania, Bulgaria and the farther reaches of the Soviet Union. That lunch excited dreams of travelling the world to record music, undaunted by the fact that I hadn't produced anything in English yet. Bert sang in a thin high tenor with a wide grin: sea shanties, ribald ditties, war songs and tragic love ballads. His whole being exuded a delight in the melodies and lyrics he had collected from farmers, tinkers and old ladies the length of Britain. Although he was considered joint founder of the British traditional folk movement along with Ewan MacColl, I had difficulty imagining the two as cohorts. MacColl always seemed terribly self-important and rigid; Bert had an ego, but never appeared to take himself too seriously. He was endlessly helpful to young singers and, in later years, when Fairport Convention began to amplify traditional music, he gave them valuable advice and support.

I wasn't keen on singer-songwriters in those days, but their ranks were growing. People spoke of a girl named Sandy Denny with a powerful voice. I heard her sing early on and wrote her off as too American-sounding, which, considering how I came to love and mourn Sandy and her music, shows how narrow minded I was in 1965.

Equally parochial was my attitude towards the British school of guitar virtuosi. I thought the likes of Bert Jansch and John Renbourn were just emulating American noodlers such as John Fahey and Sandy Bull and unworthy of much attention. But the modernizing trail that led through Pentangle, Fairport Convention and Richard Thompson to Kate Rusby began with an elusive guitarist I never heard perform live, Davey Graham. Being in and out of rehab did not prevent Graham from revolutionizing English folk music with a series of albums that combined blues and hillbilly techniques, jazz chords and traditional melodies. Renbourn and Jansch, along with John Martyn, Donovan, Roy Harper and Robin Williamson, studied these records closely. And while I never entirely embraced the genre, I worked successfully with many of its adherents.

My enthusiasm for traditional music, combined with these trips to the hinterlands, marked me down as an eccentric to many of my London friends, most of whom had never ventured north of Watford. In later years, when I would hand out copies of new releases on my Hannibal label, I would get effusive thanks for Cubanismo, Taj Mahal and Virginia Rodrigues CDs, and tight little smiles and nods for the Richard Thompson and Fairport Convention reissues or the Mercury Prize-nominated CD by Norma Waterson. In February 2000, Taj Mahal came to London to receive a 'Lifetime Achievement Award' from *Folk on Two*, BBC Radio's lone outlet for traditional music. The folk-averse love Taj as a paragon of blues authenticity, but that night he was hitting my arm and making faces of astonished delight as the Copper Family from Sussex sang their unaccompanied harmonies. Taj recognized soulful music when he heard it. For the grand finale, when the Coppers were joined by the remaining Watersons, John Tams, Eliza Carthy, Kate Rusby and the rest of the English folk establishment, you couldn't keep Taj in his seat. He quickly learned the chorus and his gruff baritone boomed out amid the English voices on 'Thousands Or More', a song traceable to seventeenth-century Hampshire. Afterwards, he and Bob Copper swapped record-collecting anecdotes: it came as no surprise that the rural Englishman had sent away for 78s by Sleepy John Estes, Big Bill Broonzy and Sister Rosetta

Tharpe in the 1940s. It seemed perfectly reasonable to Taj, and his grin testified to the pleasure that evening's music gave him. Perhaps it's easier for foreigners.

chapter 11

THE SUMMER OF 1965 didn't see me much farther along in my ambitions to become a record producer, but working in Newport, Rhode Island, as production manager of the Jazz and Folk Festivals wasn't so bad. We had offices in one of the robber-baron mansions that line Newport's rocky sea coast and cruised around in immense Oldsmobile convertibles loaned by a local auto dealer. The cars smelled of fake leather, but the radios had powerful speakers and I flipped contentedly between R&B and the Top Forty while exploring short cuts to the festival site north of town. The opening of the Jamestown Bridge that year had begun Newport's transformation from a hard-to-reach aristocratic resort into a crowded tourist centre. Soaring property values would eventually turn Festival Field into a tract of mock-clapboard housing.

The airwaves may have been full of Byrds, Dylan and Sonny & Cher, but the Jazz Festival line-up spoke of a genre at its peak: Dizzy Gillespie, the Modern Jazz Quartet, John Coltrane, Thelonious Monk, Duke Ellington, Earl Hines, Frank Sinatra (with orchestra conducted by Quincy Jones), Count Basie, Oscar Peterson, Herbie Mann, Dave Brubeck, Buddy Rich, Illinois Jacquet, Miles Davis, Herbie Hancock, Carmen McRae, Art Blakey, Lee Morgan, Joe Williams, Stan

Getz, Abdullah Ibrahim (then known as Dollar Brand), Lee Konitz, Wes Montgomery, Charlie Haden, Elvin Jones, Cecil Taylor, Carla Bley, Paul Bley, Memphis Slim, Bud Freeman, Muddy Waters and, bizarrely, in Thursday's opening night show, Pete Seeger. There were seven concerts spread over the 4 July weekend with tickets at $3.50 to $6.

I had a reunion with Muddy Waters on Thursday night; George had booked the whole band this time. Muddy was up for my suggestions now, so Gillespie's saxophonist James Moody joined them for the finale and battled James Cotton's harmonica for chorus after chorus.

Friday afternoon was the avant-garde show, with Archie Shepp, Cecil Taylor and the newly divorced leaders of the white contingent – Paul and Carla Bley. Paul was there with his girlfriend, Annette Peacock, later a cult figure in underground music circles. They seemed like the kind of people I had hung out with in Harvard Square a few years before – smart, hip, middle-class kids, a bit more adventurous and talented than their suburban neighbours. The innovative end of the jazz world had good energy in the summer of 1965. I had been to hear Cecil Taylor in New York in January and the club was packed. The Newport show was intense, exciting and provocative. You had the feeling that out of their collective talents would emerge something central to our culture. But the growing anger of the black militants made audiences wary of 'free jazz' and the outrage it expressed. The jazz avant-garde would soon be shunted to a siding to languish and shrink.

On Friday evening, a long, perfect summer dusk was beginning as the musicians gathered backstage. George was standing near the artists' entrance talking with Senator Claiborne Pell of Rhode Island and Elaine Lorillard, tobacco heiress and long-time backer of the Jazz Festival. They looked up as Elvin Jones, Coltrane's drummer, arrived. The

Jones brothers – Hank (the pianist), Thad (George Russell's trumpet player) and Elvin – constituted one of the most talented families in jazz, and also the most striking looking. Elvin's head was shaped like a Benin bronze, with sculpted cheekbones and the darkest of skin tones. He was wearing a black suit with a bright orange shirt and restraining a huge Dobermann on a leash. On his other arm was a tall redhead with pale white skin, a low-cut sheath dress and an expensive coat draped casually over her shoulders as she stepped delicately across the grass in stilettos. The VIPs stopped and stared, providing George's cue to bridge the gap between the worlds of politics and money and the mysterious domain of musicians. 'Hey, Elvin, baby, how's it going?'

Elvin looked over at George and grinned, then leaned down and put his arm around the neck of the dog. Like a coach having a last word with a substitute before sending him into the game, he pointed towards George. 'Ajax, go on over there and suck George Wein's cock.' The trio gaped, then quickly turned back to their chat.

The evening began with the Art Blakey Quintet with Lee Morgan on trumpet. This was not the Jazz Messengers, but I had grown up listening to those 'Orgy in Rhythm' records and loved the unique propulsion Blakey gave his bands. The group was tight and powerful, a fitting opening for a great evening.

I may have been alone in viewing Carmen McRae as filler, but I never liked her supper-club style. It seemed out of place as a preface to Miles Davis, Thelonious Monk and John Coltrane. To define what modern jazz was in 1965, you could just sit back and listen to that concert. Miles was with his legendary Quintet – Herbie Hancock, Wayne Shorter, Ron Carter and Tony Williams – yet they were eclipsed first by Monk with Charlie Rouse, Larry Gales and Ben Riley, and then by the unforgettable closing set by Coltrane, McCoy Tyner, Jimmy Garrison and Jones. These were arguably the greatest line-ups the three giants would ever have. I lay on the grass and contemplated my good fortune as chorus after chorus of 'My Favourite Things' washed over me, the stars came out and a breeze blew in off Narragansett Bay.

The next night we had limos and a military helicopter for Sinatra and Quincy Jones. The festival was a huge success. Most of the shows were sold out, but the changes that were undermining jazz would soon be felt. The smart, rebellious students who in years past had donned black turtlenecks and headed for the local hipster hang-outs would soon be strumming electric guitars and listening to Beatles, Stones, Who, Byrds and Dylan LPs. Some jazz clubs had already started programming folk singers and comedians while others would soon be taken over by rock entrepreneurs. Jazz had comfortably coexisted with R&B and rock'n'roll, but the Birth of Rock elbowed it out of the way.

chapter 12

ON MONDAY MORNING, WE BEGAN preparing for the complex logistics of the Folk Festival coming up in three weeks. Jazz musicians appeared on stage every week but many folk artists had never even used a microphone. I decided that all performers would make an advance trip to the site to be sound-checked. My self-appointed mission was to ensure that the fuzzy balances I remembered from my visit to the 1963 festival would not diminish the music this time.

In years since, I have been known to climb over fellow concert-goers and run to the sound controls when an artist of mine is performing. 'It sounded just fine before!' say my friends. Perhaps. But I know that if, for example, you bring the backing voices up just a little to create a tension between the lead voice and the sonic cushion of the chorus, or add some low frequencies so the richness of the harmonies can be felt as well as heard, the mood in the hall changes. The excitement grows, the intensity builds, performers and audience feel it, though no one can tell you why. Only when the sonic image is right can I relax and enjoy the music, and I was determined to enjoy Newport that summer. With free lodging and a few 'kin passes', I lured Paul Rothchild up to mix the sound. He owed me: the

Butterfield Band hadn't even finished recording their first album and already they were hot.

The mix of festival performers – urban folkies with record contracts, Appalachian hillbillies who had barely been out of their valleys, an advance guard of 'world music' groups twenty years ahead of their time and professional blues, gospel and country artists who rarely performed in front of middle-class audiences – were all paid the same: room and board plus $25 a day. Invitations represented an opportunity to appear before thousands of the most aware and influential kids in America, to say nothing of the worldwide media. Like knighthoods, they were seldom turned down.

The festival was run by a non-profit foundation advised by George but headed by a board of veteran New York folkies: Pete Seeger, Alan Lomax, actor/singer Theo Bikel, singer Jeanne Ritchie, musician/folklorist Ralph Rinzler and Peter Yarrow of Peter, Paul & Mary. Rules governing invitations were strict, deliberations were tortured and the April deadlines supposed to be absolute. When Yarrow tabled a motion in June that the Butterfield Band be extended a late invitation, the rest of the board were shocked.

Yarrow was the joker in the board's deck, a young man trying to live down his role in that squarest of groups. Peter, Paul & Mary were managed by Albert Grossman, a former Chicago club owner who had become folk's answer to Brian Epstein. Early photos show a pudgy crew-cut man with narrow eyes behind rimless glasses: a single-minded accountant in a seersucker suit and carefully knotted tie. Now he sported a shaggy grey mane and blue jeans. His wife Sally, whose photo graced the cover of *Bringing It All Back Home*, was young and beautiful. In a milieu with no tradition of aggressive management, Grossman had masterminded PP&M's rise and was now engineering Dylan's. To a stable of older artists such as Odetta, he had recently added the Kweskin Jug Band, as well as Butterfield. His compound in Woodstock, NY, was rumoured to contain a connoisseur's cellar of the strongest marijuana from every corner of the globe. The board of the Newport Folk Foundation, with the exception of the loyal Yarrow, loathed him.

Yarrow's request seemed like just an errand for his sinister manager, but it was undeniable that everyone was suddenly talking about Butterfield. His band was unlike any other revivalist group and multiracial besides. There may have been a feeling that it was important to invite new and exciting artists, not just the well-established ones from the coffee house and concert circuit. I was summoned to testify that it would be possible to move the group's amplifiers quickly on to the small stage at the end of the blues workshop on Saturday afternoon. (All performers had one 'workshop' performance and one set on the main stage.) In the end the well-respected Rinzler came out in favour and the racial aspect probably swayed the rest of the Board. Grossman had flexed his muscles and pulled it off for his new clients. One key element of the Newport drama was in place.

The festival extended over a four-day weekend, with concerts every evening, workshops all day Friday and Saturday and a 'New Folks' concert on Sunday afternoon. This year the crowds began arriving days in advance. A field set aside for camping was quickly full and the concerts sold out. This unique event, conceived in idealism and full of the most obscure performers from the ethnic byways of America, had become the centre of American popular culture that summer.

On Wednesday, Paul and I started shuttling artists out to the site. He made careful notes as each played a few songs, keeping a chart of mic positions, levels and equalizations. There would be no screaming feedback, no inaudible harmony parts, no booming basses; everything would be under control. Board members seemed puzzled when they stumbled across our obsessive project. Their New York wisdom held that any group worth its salt could gather around a single mic and get its music across. They revered the authentic representatives of indigenous music but were sceptical of the middle-class kids who emulated them. They sensed, correctly, that the excitement generated by the Beatles and the fascination with 'sounds' that young audiences were developing did not bode well for their approach. Bostonians, on the other hand, were conscious of wanting the right balance and the best microphones in all situations.

The day before the first concert, I met a bus arriving at the Greyhound terminal. Off it stepped a small, shy man with a tiny suitcase. He was Spokes Mashyane, the king of township *kwela*, a penny-whistle virtuoso and the best-selling artist in apartheid South Africa, who seemed dazed by the distance he had travelled. Soon he was sitting in one of the dorms amid Appalachian fiddlers and blues guitarists, amazing everyone with his joyous style on the whistle. In a nearby room, a ballad singer from North Carolina swapped verses with a Gaelic speaker from the Hebrides. Many of the Southern musicians had never shared a table, much less a dormitory, with people of a different colour.

One of the performances I was most looking forward to was by the Texas Prison Worksong group. They were life prisoners discovered by musicologist Bruce Jackson, who obtained permission to bring six of them to Newport. One of their key numbers was a cross-cutting song, where four men would stand around a tree trunk, chopping and singing in rhythm, trading verses – and axe strokes – as they brought down the tree. The sound of the chops and the rhythm of the work were integral to the song, but you could hardly plant a tree in the middle of the stage. Pete Seeger asked for a flatbed truck, chains and a chainsaw, drove off with them and their guard into the bogs of southern Rhode Island and returned with a gigantic tree stump. They could stand around it onstage, chopping and singing as if they were felling a tree in the East Texas hills.

On Friday, the workshops were packed, with crowds from one overflowing into the backstage area of another. I ran from one sound control to another, adjusting levels so as not to drown out a ballad singer from Nova Scotia with a gospel group from Carolina. In the crowds, you could hear people asking, 'Where's Dylan? Is he here yet?'

I remembered watching the close of the 1963 festival from the audience. Dylan stood arm in arm onstage with Peter, Paul & Mary, Joan Baez, Pete Seeger, the Freedom Singers and Theodore Bikel as they sang 'We Shall Overcome' while the fog rolled in off the bay. It was moving and inspiring. Young students like those in the audience had been in the Deep South that summer taking lethal risks registering voters and integrating lunch counters. When Baez invited Dylan to join her on a nationwide concert tour, his popularity surged. Then 'Blowin' In The Wind', in the facile hands of Peter, Paul & Mary, got to number one in the charts. The old guard of the folk left couldn't believe their luck: they finally had an heir to Woody Guthrie writing powerful songs against injustice, racism and war. Their dreams flowered in the idealism of the Kennedy years. The Newport Folk Festivals of '63 and '64 represented redemption, the pinnacle of the journey back from the wilderness of the 1950s.

But Dylan's new songs were not about politics. His former mentors could barely understand *what* they were about. Like the Acmeist poets in Russia in the '20s, he confused and frightened the commissars with his opacity. He was no longer outer-directed. They sensed he was slipping away from them and their New York rigidities. Already close to Von Schmidt and involved with Baez, Dylan had a new sidekick, a friend of mine from Boston named Bob Neuwirth.

The radio that month was playing 'I Got You Babe' by Sonny & Cher, 'Mr Tambourine Man' by the Byrds and 'Like A Rolling Stone' by the man himself. The first shamelessly pilfered his vocal style, thereby acknowledging what an important figure he had become. The second was a more sophisticated homage that fascinated Dylan by the way it opened for him a new vision of his own music. The third was his own challenge to the way the folk world saw him. The presence of drums, electric guitars and Al Kooper's Hammond organ on his new LP alarmed the purists who thought that once they had crowned him he would stay on their throne. He wasn't the first singer-songwriter to record with a rhythm section, but *Bringing It All Back Home*'s predecessors had been different, more… *polite.*

Dylan's whereabouts were the subject of rumours and conflicting information: he was at the Viking Hotel in a suite; he was at a private house on an island in the bay; he was still in New York; he had brought Al Kooper with him; no, Kooper wasn't here. Kooper had an aura of his own, with the cachet of coming from the world of rock'n'roll. He had played on Brill Building records! (He had been a member of the Royal Teens!)

By Friday night, there were confirmed sightings. Dylan, Kooper and road manager Victor Maimudes were at the Viking Hotel with Grossman and Neuwirth. There had been late-night rehearsals – but with whom? Among the young urban folkies, there was a ripple of excitement; speculations hung over the festival like a cloud of amphetamine gas. By

Saturday, we knew that Dylan had rehearsed with his new stable-mates, the Butterfield Band. The gauntlet *would* be thrown.

Other rumours started circulating – this time among the board and the older performers – that the pot smoke wafting around the grounds and in the dorms was coming from a particular source: Grossman! The older leftists could not accept that marijuana might be just, well, popular. In an eerie echo of their right-wing tormentors' view of communism, they felt pot had to have an evil and corrupting wellspring. Grossman was the perfect demon for the left, the moneychanger at the gates of the temple, the commercializer of folk music. Now they wanted to add drug dealer to his list of crimes.

Dylan surfaced on Saturday for the Songwriting Workshop in his familiar guise of troubadour with acoustic guitar. In years past he would have worn a denim work shirt and jeans but he and Kooper turned up in bizarre puff-sleeved polka-dot 'duelling shirts', a momentary fashion fad from a Bleeker Street boutique. In hindsight the shirts look ridiculous, but Dylan's endorsement made them mock-proof and they served as advance notice of provocation. He played his allotted half-hour and left to roars from a gigantic crowd in front of the tiny stage. This was the Folk Festival: no encores, the timetable had to be kept, and the Appalachian Fiddlers had to start on time.

The first skirmish in the battle of Newport took place later that afternoon at the Blues Workshop. Alan Lomax was introducing a strong programme of country blues, including Robert Pete Williams and Son House, to a crowd almost as large as the earlier one for Dylan. At the end it was announced that there would also be a performance by the Butterfield Band. Even without an LP on the market (Rothchild was still re-recording and remixing) people wanted to see what the fuss was about. Newport was becoming more and more a part of the world of show business and that, too, upset many on the board. The Weavers may have gone on *Make-Believe Ballroom* in 1950 to plug 'Irene', but Newport was supposed to be a world apart. Events were starting to spin out of their control.

When Son House finished, I started resetting the stage. Lomax scowled as we lugged amplifiers on to the platform and ran wires from the extra mics to the sound board. He told the audience that having heard real blues played on acoustic instruments, they would now hear some kids from Chicago try and play the blues with the help of all this equipment. As he walked offstage he passed Grossman, who muttered, 'That was a real chicken-shit introduction, Alan.' Lomax pushed Grossman out of the way. Suddenly, round one of the *kulturkampf* began, with two large grey-haired men rolling around in the dust. Sam Lay, Butterfield's burly drummer, helped pull them apart.

Word of the fight spread through the crowd and added to the charged atmosphere. The set was loud – other stages complained of the volume – but a triumph. Lomax called an emergency board meeting which convened without Yarrow (who supposedly couldn't be found) and voted to ban Grossman from the grounds. His crimes included not just the 'assault' on Lomax but being a source of drugs.

When the verdict was delivered to Wein for implementation, he reconvened the board and explained the facts of life to them. If they banned Grossman, Dylan, Peter, Paul & Mary, Kweskin, Odetta and Butterfield would leave with him. George was not sure the festival could survive the alienation of its biggest stars and the demands for ticket refunds. There was, moreover, a documentary film crew on-site (Murray Lerner's *Festival*) recording everything for posterity. With heavy hearts, the board withdrew the order.

Grossman was spared, but the old guard seethed.

That evening's highlight was the set by the Kweskin Jug Band. They had the Bostonian affection for commercial recordings of the '20s and a style amalgamating elements of ragtime, blues, jazz and country music. Their stage presence was confident, knowing and hip, full of double-entendres and dope references. Geoff and Maria had become consummate lead singers, lending their soulful technique to a wide variety of songs. Fritz Richmond, the washtub bass and jug player, was never without his deep blue granny glasses. He had explained his affection for them to Steve Allen on national TV earlier that year – 'They keep my mind quiet back here' – making him an instant cult figure for stoners from coast to coast.

Mel Lyman, their harmonica player, looked like an Okie refugee in a Walker Evans photograph. He was a fervent believer in the sacramental use of drugs of all kinds, and his quietly powerful personality dominated Jim Kweskin and caused fissures within the band. Their set climaxed in Geoff's crooning rendition of the Rudy Vallee hit, 'Sweet Sue, Just You'. The crowd adored them and the roars added to the old guard's sense of unease. Following the Jug Band, some of their veteran colleagues had trouble holding the audience's attention.

Saturday was also the night for the Texas prisoners. During Seeger's introduction, the prisoners lifted the immense chunk of wood on to the stage. After some hoeing songs and chants performed in a line, four of them gathered around the stump for the chopping song. They swung their axes in a beautiful rhythm as they sang, two diagonally across on the beat, the others on the offbeat. During the second verse, the mic cable came loose and drooped dangerously close to the path of the axes. I watched from the shadows, counting the rhythm in my head. As the nearest axe swung back, I grabbed the cable and secured it around a knob. The singers kept chopping and trading verses of elegant folk poetry, improvised against the fall of the blades. Seeger gave me an approving nod.

I suspect this incident gave rise to the myth that Seeger tried to attack the speaker cables with an axe during Dylan's performance on Sunday night. Seeger, axes, cables... somehow, in the way of legends, things got muddled up. I can say with complete assurance that this was the closest any cable came to being severed all weekend.

During the Saturday concert, Paul and I spoke to Grossman about Dylan's sound check. Since the New Folks concert took up all of Sunday afternoon, the ideal opportunity would be Sunday morning, but that would be too early for night-owl Bob. We would have to finish rehearsing the other Sunday night artists in the morning and devote the entire 5.30 to 6.30 period before the gates opened to Dylan.

On Sunday afternoon, as the parade of singer-songwriters and young folk virtuosi trooped on and off the stage, the sky began to darken. By the time Butterfield was due to go on, the clouds had opened. The stage was sheltered by the barest of cloths, designed to protect one singer with a guitar. Butterfield performed with a metal harmonica and microphone held to his mouth. We turned off the amps and covered them with a tarpaulin. The group was devastated but it was far too dangerous to play. I imagined Lomax somewhere, snorting with satisfaction.

The closing group, Mimi and Dick Fariña, had no electric instruments and were happy to go on despite the rain. They had released a popular LP that year and the crowd was eager to hear them. Mimi was Joan Baez's younger sister and Dick a charismatic Cuban Irishman with dark curly hair and an impish grin. A pal of Dylan's – and Thomas Pynchon's – he had just finished his first novel and was torn between the worlds of literature and music. His fast strum on the dulcimer, normally a delicate instrument identified with Appalachian ballads or medieval music, drove the group's unique swing. As 'Pack Up Your Sorrows' began, the crowd surged forward into the press area, now abandoned by the shelter-seeking ushers. Dick and Mimi's friends started drifting onstage with their guitars or clapping time and dancing. The images that would become rock festival clichés in the ensuing years – young girls dancing in flimsy tops made transparent by the rain; mud staining the faces of ecstatically grinning kids – made some of their earliest appearances during the Fariñas' set that afternoon. If later events had not imprinted themselves so vividly on the memories of journalists and audience, Dick and Mimi's performance would have been the defining memory of Newport 1965. Particularly since, a few months later, Dick's motorcycle sailed off the highway in Big Sur, killing him at once.

Grossman, meanwhile, was upset at Butterfield not getting his spot, and anxious about Dylan's sound check. But as we called time on the Fariñas, a rosy light bathed the western sky. Within ten minutes of the end of the concert, the downpour had ceased, a rainbow appeared following the clouds eastwards and the site glowed in soft evening colours. A car pulled up and Dylan, Maimudes and Kooper got out. The amps were dried off, the audience area cleared of stragglers, mics were positioned to Maimudes' instructions and Dylan's band took their places: Kooper and Barry Goldberg on electric keyboards, Bloomfield on guitar, Jerome Arnold on bass and Sam Lay on drums.

I joined Paul at the control board as they started the sound check. Grossman sat with us as they played through the three numbers they had rehearsed: 'Maggie's Farm', 'It Takes A Lot To Laugh, It Takes A Train To Cry' and 'Like A

Rolling Stone'. Nothing was said; we knew this was momentous. I handed Paul a fluorescent pink pen which he used to mark the levels of each channel and the equalization dials above the faders. Other artists' details were noted down on Paul's clipboard but Dylan's were in ink you could read in the dark.

Back onstage, I asked each of the musicians if they were happy with the positions and levels of their amplifiers. There were no stage monitors in those days and no direct feed of electric instruments into the sound system; a mic had to be placed in front of each amp to pick up the signal. I outlined the position of amps and microphones and the settings of the dials with the pink marker. The sound we rehearsed had to be there from the first note. When the stage was cleared and the gates opened to the public, none of us left in search of food: we were too charged up with adrenalin to be hungry.

It turned into a beautiful clear evening with delicate pastel light. As consolation for the rain-out, Butterfield was allowed to play for half an hour at seven while the crowd was still arriving. Dylan was scheduled for forty-five minutes near the end of the first half, but we knew he had only three songs prepared. Easing the anticipatory tension was a wonderful set by the Moving Star Hall Singers, whom I had heard on Johns Island a year before. The instant they finished, we rushed onstage in the dark. I went from amp to amp, checking the pink marks. When the musicians were ready, I signalled with my flashlight. The introduction was made, the lights came up and 'Maggie's Farm' blasted out into the night air.

I ran straight out to the press enclosure. By today's standards, the volume wasn't particularly high, but in 1965 it was probably the loudest thing anyone in the audience had ever heard. A buzz of shock and amazement ran through the crowd. When the song finished, there was a roar that contained many sounds. Certainly boos were included, but they weren't in a majority. There were shouts of delight and triumph and also of derision and outrage. The musicians didn't wait around to interpret it, they just plunged straight into the second song.

Someone tapped me on the shoulder. 'They're looking for you backstage.' Alan Lomax, Pete Seeger and Theo Bikel were standing by the stairs, furious. 'You've got to turn the sound down. It's far too loud.' I told them I couldn't control the sound levels from backstage and there was no walkie-talkie system.

'Where are the controls? How do you get there?' Bikel demanded. I told him to walk out to the parking lot, turn left, follow the fence to the main entrance, come back down the centre aisle and he would see it there around Row G – a journey of almost a quarter-mile. They looked daggers at me. 'I know you can get there quicker than that,' said Lomax. I admitted that I usually climbed the fence. For a brief moment we all contemplated the notion of one of these dignified and, barring Seeger, portly men doing the same. Then Lomax snarled, 'You go out there right now and you tell them the sound has got to be turned down. That's an order from the board.' OK, I said, and ran to the pile of milk crates by the lighting trailer. In a few seconds I was standing beside the sound board.

It was like being in the eye of a hurricane. All around us, people were standing up, waving their arms. Some were cheering, some booing, some arguing, some grinning like madmen. A Bloomfield guitar solo screamed through the night air. Dylan's voice took up the last verse, hurling the words out into the night air:

Now the wintertime is coming
The windows are filled with frost

Grossman, Yarrow and Rothchild were sitting behind the board, grinning like cats. I leaned over to convey the message from Lomax.

'Tell Alan the board is adequately represented at the sound controls and the board member here thinks the sound level is just right,' said Yarrow. Then he looked up at me, smiled and said, 'And tell him…' and he raised the middle finger of his left hand. Grossman and Rothchild laughed as I ran back to the fence.

As I arrived at the foot of the stairway, Bikel and Lomax were watching Seeger's back as he strode off towards the parking lot. He couldn't stand to listen any longer. His wife Toshi was weeping and being comforted by George. I gave Lomax and Bikel the message from Yarrow, minus the finger. They cursed and turned away. I went back to the press enclosure to hear the last song.

There are many accounts of what happened next. Dylan left the stage with a shrug as the crowd roared. Having heard only three songs, they wanted 'moooooooore', and some, certainly, were booing. They had been taken by surprise by the volume and aggression of the music. Some loved it, some hated it, most were amazed, astonished and energized by it. It was something we take for granted now, but utterly novel then: non-linear lyrics, an attitude of total contempt for expectation and established values, accompanied by screaming blues guitar and a powerful rhythm section, played at ear-splitting volume by young kids. The Beatles were still singing love songs in 1965 while the Stones played a sexy brand of blues-rooted pop. This was different. This was the Birth of Rock. So many taste crimes have been committed in rock's name since then that it might be questionable to count this moment as a triumph, but it certainly felt like one in July 1965.

Yarrow appeared onstage, an inane imitation of a

showbiz MC. 'Do you want to hear more?' I watched backstage as Neuwirth and Grossman ran relays to the artists' tent, trying to persuade Dylan to go back on. Finally, Yarrow announced that he would come back 'with just his guitar' (huge roar). Dylan strolled up to the mic and strapped on his harmonica neck-rig. 'Anyone got an E harp?' Only at Newport would this request be followed by a shower of half a dozen harmonicas on to the stage.

He sang 'Mr Tambourine Man' brilliantly, reclaiming the song from the shiny but shallow Byrds version and sending a signal to anyone who might be gratified by his return to acoustic moderation: there would be no 'Blowin' In The Wind' tonight. Dylan had left the didactic world of political song behind. He was singing now about his decadent, self-absorbed, brilliant internal life. He finished with 'It's All Over Now, Baby Blue', spitting the lyrics out contemptuously in the direction of the old guard.

After the intermission, fate and poor scheduling conspired to ensure that a sequence of tired, hackneyed representatives of the 'New York school' was paraded before the exhausted audience: Oscar Brand, Ronnie Gilbert, Len Chandler, and finally Peter, Paul & Mary. Even PP&M's fans seemed to sense they were watching something whose time had passed.

Backstage the atmosphere was sombre and silent, older performers in one area, younger ones in another. The significance of many watershed events is apparent only in retrospect; this was clear at the time. The old guard hung their heads in defeat while the young, far from being triumphant, were chastened. They realized that in their victory lay the death of something wonderful. The rebels were like children who had been looking for something to break and realized, as they looked at the pieces, what a beautiful thing it had been. The festival would never be the same, nor would popular music and nor would 'youth culture'. Anyone wishing to portray the history of the sixties as a journey from idealism to hedonism could place the hinge at around 9.30 on the night of 25 July, 1965.

The two camps could not even bear to discuss an alternative finale to 'We Shall Overcome', so George had to come up with something. He played piano while an odd mixture of singers tackled 'When The Saints Go Marching In'. Spokes Mashyane took a penny-whistle solo. Backstage security had dissolved: on one side of the stage was a fat Providence disc jockey doing the jerk with Joan Baez. It looked horrible, a parody of the moving finales of previous years. I spotted Pete Seeger in unlikely conversation with Mel Lyman, the first real contact between the factions. Seeger asked me to ensure that the stage lights would be turned off at the end and one mic left live on stage.

The lights went down, work lights came on at the exits and people started to file out. Mel came out and sat on the edge of the stage in the dark, pulled out a harmonica and started to play 'Rock Of Ages'. It echoed out over the emptying arena without anyone being able to see where it was coming from.

Mel was many things, not least a skilful manipulator of people. He had told the Jug Band that day he was leaving, reportedly to live in Woodstock as the Grossman compound's marijuana curator. Soon he would start his sinister 'Avatar' cult at Fort Hill in Roxbury, near Boston. But he was always a wonderful harmonica player: not a blues man like Butterfield, but an Appalachian mountain player, translating the 'high lonesome' sound of old-time vocal styles into the mouth harp. By the time he finished the first chorus of the old hymn, people backstage and in the audience had stopped wherever they were to listen. He kept playing, the melody becoming more moving with each repetition. People on both sides of the divide were crying quietly. After about ten minutes, he brought it to a close, put the mic down on the edge of the stage, got up and walked off. No one clapped. People embraced, comforting one another, then slowly gathered their belongings and went off into the night.

The old guard, I think, mostly went to bed. The rest of us gathered at a bar where Butterfield's rhythm section set up to play. As people began to dance, the sombre atmosphere evaporated. The beer flowed, the party got wilder, the dancing more frenetic, and Sam and Jerome never flagged as different singers and musicians came and went. When I left near dawn, it was still going strong. I drove back to my mansion maid's room, thinking sadly about Pete Seeger. I doubted he would ever come to sympathize with what had happened. There was no point wondering whether it was for the better. All we could do was to ride its ramifications into the future.

chapter 13

PAUL REPAID ME IN FULL for the Butterfield tip by getting me a job. I thought I had blown my chances with Elektra when I got drunk at a party and told Jac Holzman what I thought of his European set-up, but in September Paul summoned me to the office. Holzman had decided it was time to open a London office and called my bluff by offering me the job of running it.

I gave George my notice and started spending afternoons at Elektra discussing budgets, tours, distribution deals and promotion. What excited me most was a project Paul was working on, a typically Rothchild combination of creativity and pragmatism. Our abortive folk-rock group had spawned the songwriting team of Sebastian and Yanovsky, which had evolved into the Lovin' Spoonful. Before signing with the Brill Building sharks at Kama Sutra Records they threw Paul a consolation bone of four tracks. Adding out-takes from the first pass at a Butterfield album and some tracks by other Elektra artists gave Paul almost enough for an electric sequel to his successful acoustic *Blues Project* album of the year before. I volunteered to finish it off for him with the British blues band I would sign as soon as I landed in London. Holzman was worried I was treating it as a scouting job, when he wanted me to focus on promoting Judy Collins, Phil Ochs, Tom Rush and Butterfield in England. But Rothchild loved the idea so he couldn't object.

I was sitting in Holzman's office the evening before I left for London when the lights started to flicker. Jac punched the intercom: 'What are you clowns in mastering doing fucking with the power supply?' Just then I glanced out of the twenty-second-floor window towards the East River and saw an invisible hand turn off all the lights in Queens. The giant footsteps marched down the East River switching off Yorkville, Murray Hill and the Lower East Side in turn, then Brooklyn, leaving just the Pan Am building lit. It flickered, then went dark: the great New York blackout of 1965.

I spent the evening walking the crowded streets and drinking in candlelit East Village bars with a friend who had just bought a loft in the unpromising Cast Iron district – soon to be known as SoHo. Kids with flashlights directed traffic while the city partied in the most neighbourly atmosphere. When the next blackout came along a dozen years later, there was looting all over the city and people hid behind locked doors.

Once in London, I set out to find my blues band. A month of scouring West End clubs and the pages of *Melody Maker* brought me to the conclusion that the good bands were all taken. No one wanted to be Dick Rowe – the Decca A&R man who turned down the Beatles. If a band was halfway decent, they quickly got signed. In this 'tight little island', there were no American-style wide-open spaces filled with yearning unknowns avidly honing their chops.

I was beginning to regret my hubris when rescue arrived in the form of Paul Jones, lead singer with Manfred Mann. I had seen him singing 'Do Wah Diddy' on *Top of the Pops*, but beneath the matinee-idol looks was a serious music fan, with a relentless energy and charm that reminded me of fellow harmonica player John Sebastian. He had spent his own money recording a Guyanan gospel singer named Ram John Holder and wanted me to sign him to Elektra. I glossed over the fact that Ram John didn't do that much for me and changed the subject to my quest for a blues band. 'What are you wasting your time for?' he said. 'Let's put together an all-star group! Everyone would love to be on a record with Butterfield and the Spoonful!' On the back of an envelope we made up a wish list: Clapton on guitar, that was obvious; I insisted on Steve Winwood for one vocalist; Jones would play harmonica and sing a track; we agreed on a rhythm section of Jack Bruce and Ginger Baker; and Paul threw in Ben Palmer on piano to round it off.

I assumed this to be little more than a precursor of fantasy football, but two days later Paul rang to say that everyone was set except for Ginger Baker, who would be replaced by Pete York from the Spencer Davis Group. My task was to get clearances for Winwood and York from Chris Blackwell of Island Records. Thus I made my first call to the man who would become a dominant figure in my professional life for the next thirty-five years. He was friendly and cooperative, subject to the proviso that we bill his prodigy 'Stevie Anglo'.

Paul chose 'I Want To Know' by Otis Rush as his showpiece, while Steve selected 'Steppin' Out'. Clapton did not yet consider himself a singer, so we met to choose something to spotlight his guitar chops. He had in mind 'Crosscut Saw', an Albert King track that had been a regular feature of his days with John Mayall, but I suggested we look at country blues for something that could be updated to the electric group sound. We shared many enthusiasms in this area, particularly Robert Johnson. I suggested 'Standing At The Crossroads'; Eric countered with 'Traveling

Riverside Blues'. He came up with an arrangement that combined the lyrics of 'Crossroads' with a guitar lick from 'Riverside' and a modern classic was born.

We rehearsed the group (now called Eric Clapton and the Powerhouse) one rainy afternoon in mid-January and scheduled the session for a week later at the old Olympic Studios in George Street. Winwood sounded great singing 'Crossroads', and everyone was excited to be playing together for the first time. Then Holzman announced he would be coming to London that week and would therefore supervise the session. Six years after my revelation on the baseball field, I was ready to produce my first recording session and the moment was being snatched from my grasp.

When the day arrived, we all ignored Holzman and I ran things with the help of Keith Grant, the engineer who later recorded so many great Stones, Who and Zeppelin tracks. But Jac took the tapes back to New York to mix and the final result seemed somehow less interesting than what had gone down on tape. The 'Electric Blues Project' was released later that year as *What's Shakin'!*

Eric and I started meeting up to go to Marx Brothers movies. In those days he was more like a witty office colleague who liked to listen to blues than anyone's fantasy of a guitar hero: he once frightened my girlfriend by opening his door in a gorilla suit. We talked about his plan to build a group around Jack Bruce and Ginger Baker and he claimed to like the idea of signing with Elektra. But Jac hadn't been that impressed and said I could go ahead only if I didn't spend more than £400 on production – a miserly sum even in 1966. Eric rang his new manager, Robert Stigwood, from my office and passed me the phone. I could tell after a brief exchange of pleasantries that a) Stigwood had no idea what an Elektra was and b) I was totally out of my depth trying to negotiate anything with him. I sadly wished Eric the best of luck – I would have to look elsewhere for my first British signing.

Within six months, Rothchild would be in a Los Angeles studio with the Doors and I would be getting ready to record Pink Floyd in London. Neither had much to do with folk music, but in 1966 the world was changing by the week. Concepts like 'folk-rock' seemed quaint and far away.

chapter 14

IN THE SUMMER OF 1966 I had a Tuesday evening ritual for dignitaries visiting London: Chinatown for dinner at Lee Ho Fook, then a walk up Wardour Street to the Marquee for the weekly residency of The Move. John Sebastian and Zal Yanovsky, Paul Butterfield and Mike Bloomfield, Jac Holzman, Phil Ochs and a few others got this treatment. And privileged they were, for The Move in their prime were a phenomenon few Americans had the privilege of seeing.

I have fantasized about what might have happened had they made it to Monterey Pop or the Fillmore. I think American audiences would have been as astonished as they were by The Who or Hendrix. The Move were ambitious working-class kids from Birmingham with no desire to change the face of music, preach peace and love or promote altered consciousness; they just wanted to be rich and famous.

Their lead singer was the virile-looking Carl Wayne, who would end up in panto and crooning on pier-ends. He was big voiced and willing: if his manager wanted him to wear a Soho tailor's lurid fantasy of 1930s American gangster wear (and his manager did), he wore it. At the back of the stage was Bev Bevan, a working-man's drummer and precursor of Midlands powerhouses like John Bonham. The DNA of heavy metal and power pop lurked in his wrists. Ace Kefford's skeletal albino face protruded from the most outlandish of the psychedelic hoodlum outfits. He bore a curious resemblance to his San Francisco counterpart, Jack Casady of Jefferson Airplane. They were both great bass players, but none of that Californian jazzy fluency for Kefford: Ace went straight for the most powerful nail-your-*chakras*-to-the-seat-of-your-pants bass lines.

Lead guitarist Roy Wood had not yet grown his Merlin hair and beard, but had already assumed the role of shaman-in-chief. With rimless glasses and distant stare, he led the absurdly complex arrangements with nods of the head and dips of the guitar neck. Trevor Burton, the rhythm guitarist, was the innocent-looking one. He would glance at the others onstage and occasionally at the audience with a shy smile, the barest hint of a desire to please. None of the others gave evidence of any such concern.

They attacked the audience with volume and speed from the off. Their own songs, Motown B-sides, even 'Zing! Went The Strings Of My Heart' were all delivered with power, turn-on-a-dime tempo changes and rich harmonies screamed in perfect pitch by four voices, two of them usually falsetto. There were no long Frisco-style jams: the intricate arrangements foreshadowed – and overshadowed – the grandiosity of later groups like Yes.

Their music verged on psychedelia, but it was a beer-drinker's psychedelia. Wood may have taken his share of acid in later years, but initially he just incorporated sounds coming up from the underground, magpie-like, into the Move's music. They made a far superior fist of deconstructing soul tunes than did Vanilla Fudge a year later. And everything was always moving, faster and faster, more and more dazzling harmonies, arrangements and power. The confidence was overwhelming.

The Move would finish off a set with an instrumental coda to an original – 'I Can Hear The Grass Grow' perhaps. One by one they would leave the stage, instruments leaning against amps, screaming feedback until only Bevan remained, pounding out a stentorian drum solo. He would fiddle with something behind the bass drum before joining the others in the wings. The empty stage roared at the crowd in the tiny club until Bev's enormous firecracker exploded, the roadie yanked the master plug and the audience was left in smoky silence, staring dumbfounded at the stage. Mike Bloomfield and John Sebastian both told me it was the most amazing thing they had ever seen. As far as I know, there are no recordings of the original line-up's live shows. As dressing-room visitors groped for superlatives, the group would murmur incomprehensible Brummie acknowledgements, tug their forelocks and saunter out to the van for the ride back to the Celestial City.

I was desperate for them to join Butterfield, Love, the Doors and Tim Buckley in Elektra's growing stable of rock artists and thought I was getting farther with their manager Tony Secunda and producer Denny Cordell than I had with Robert Stigwood. Looking back, it seems I was little more than a shill, a naïve American bidding up their value as Cordell manoeuvred for his label deal with EMI. Just before he sacked me, I took Holzman up to Birmingham to meet them in a last throw of the dice. I wish there was a tape recording of the post-gig conversation in the cramped dressing room of the Edgbaston Mecca Ballroom among the impressed but awkward Holzman, the very earnest me, the Fagin-like Secunda, and the monosyllabic Move. The man who persuaded Jim Morrison and Arthur Lee to sign with Elektra was too far from home to make any impression on the Move.

The hits Cordell eventually produced with them were compact three-minute bits of pop with psychedelic spice tailored for the British singles market; an English producer still needed to keep his mind on the requirements of Radio Luxembourg and the BBC. In America, Country Joe & the Fish and the Grateful Dead were beginning to imagine the kind of extended tracks that would transform the shape of rock recording, but there was no place for that in the British music scene until Pink Floyd redrew the map.

Cordell and Secunda were an unlikely pair, but they enjoyed success after success from 1966 to 1968 with The Move, Procol Harum and Joe Cocker. Secunda came from South London and had knocked around the worlds of music and professional wrestling since the early sixties. He was a cartoon villain, a reptilian hustler who bragged of his time in prison but was possessed of a ready wit and sinister charm. Cordell was as dapper and cool as Secunda was fevered and scheming.

There were other pairings like this around Soho: the cockney Chris Stamp and the Bohemian aristocrat Kit Lambert managing The Who, for example. Soho that year was like the steppes in AD350, with Visigoths, Ostrogoths, Vandals and Huns queuing up to pillage, destabilize and eventually take over the Roman Empire. Lambert, Stamp and The Who were set to follow in the westward footsteps of Andrew Oldham and the Stones and Brian Epstein's Beatles; Stigwood was setting the stage for Clapton's new Cream; expatriate Jimi Hendrix was preparing for his triumphant return home under the aegis of Chas Chandler and Mike Jeffreys; and Steve Winwood's career was being masterminded by Chris Blackwell. In the coming year, the list would grow: Jethro Tull and Ten Years After with Chris Wright and Terry Ellis; Led Zeppelin with Peter Grant. The Move, in their failure to conquer America, were the exception.

America had no equivalent of these managerial hustlers. The Brill Building types who built rock'n'roll empires had little notion of how to deal with an artist who wrote his own songs and took acid. Grossman knew, but was content to lie back in Woodstock, building a studio and a Chinese restaurant and muttering gnomic pronouncements to quaking agents and record company bosses via long-distance telephone. The new British managers were willing to put in the hard graft to take America and were determined to enjoy it. The working-class barrow boys took such pleasure in the sound of their own spiels that they made for highly entertaining company. The aristocrats among them had been bred to avoid 'trade', but if one couldn't, at least it had to be *amusing*. Thugs like Grant and Don Arden resembled Lee Marvin in *Point Blank*: executives in plush offices couldn't believe anyone would be that vicious and gave in to them just to have a peaceful life. The Yank who paid the most attention to all this, of course, was David Geffen.

The brilliance of the British managers flowed from the same fount as their flaws. Like the Grade brothers who had ruled British show business since the war, they believed everyone needed a gimmick. Townshend smashing one guitar and Hendrix burning another on stage at Monterey made them overnight stars in America. Both gestures, like Bev's firecracker, were part of a British tradition of artifice. New York would never have moulded Hendrix's genius into as powerful a pop persona as London did.

When it worked, it was brilliant, but when it didn't, it could go very wrong. Secunda alienated The Move and cost them a fortune when he packaged one of their singles in a libellous cartoon about Harold Wilson. Mike Jeffreys never understood Hendrix the musician. He put him with an English rhythm section and thought that was the appeal:

'two white guys with the flashy nigger in the middle'. When Hendrix wanted to work with his black peers Billy Cox and Buddy Miles, Jeffreys' only response was to sabotage the new line-up, helping drive Jimi to the despair he was in when he died. Another ugly manifestation of the syndrome arrived a decade later with Malcolm McLaren's leering insistence that the Sex Pistols were a talent-free quartet of losers he masterminded to the top of the charts with his punk gimmick: anyone with ears could tell that Johnny Rotten was a singer of genius.

I never understood why Secunda didn't send The Move to San Francisco on spec. For all his cleverness, he couldn't grasp the changes that were transforming the American market. Cordell got it. He rode 'A Whiter Shade Of Pale' and 'With A Little Help From My Friends' into the sunset, settling in Los Angeles, forming Shelter Records and discovering Leon Russell and Tom Petty. In a melancholy footnote to their long-sundered partnership, Denny and Tony, both in their early fifties, died within days of each other in 1995: Denny in Ireland where he trained racehorses and Tony in Marin County where he published guidebooks to American national parks. They held a memorable Irish wake for Denny, full of devoted friends from all periods of his colourful life. I sometimes imagine Tony, the ex-wrestling promoter from Streatham, sitting in the Trident restaurant on the Sausalito waterfront, eating his organic salad, gazing at the sailing boats out on the bay and regretting The Move's missed chance.

chapter 15

IN MAY 1965, THE EVENING after the party in Edinburgh, George Brown took me to hear some musicians he thought I would like. We walked for a long time through cobbled streets where the only sound was our footsteps: everyone seemed quietly at home behind lace curtains. Arriving at a simple pub with sawdust on the floor and a few benches, we took our pints into an equally spartan back room where a crowd of about thirty was waiting for the music to start.

Robin Williamson and Clive Palmer, both with shaggy blond hair and wearing heavy tweeds, put down their drinks and dragged chairs to the middle of the floor. Robin was graceful and relaxed while Clive had a limp and seemed old beyond his years. They performed Scots traditional music as if it had taken a journey to the Appalachians and back via Morocco and Bulgaria, complementing each other's playing with skill and wit. Clive mostly picked the banjo while Robin sang in a soaring tenor and played violin or a guitar with its bridge lowered so the strings buzzed like a sitar.

When George introduced us after the set, Robin conversed engagingly in a lilting, heavily elocuted, burred Scots accent. His manner was somewhere between a hippy and a nineteenth-century parlour bard and he glowed with self-assurance. I was convinced I had found a star.

Six months later I was back in Britain with Holzman's grudging agreement that I could 'look around' for artists to sign to Elektra. Robin and Clive had left Edinburgh, but I eventually tracked them down to a regular Saturday gig at Clive's Incredible Folk Club in an old warehouse in downtown Glasgow. In early March '66, I dodged the drunks and the pools of puke that were prominent features of Sauchiehall Street nights, arriving at the venue only to find the door locked and a crowd outside arguing with a policeman. Hamish Imlach, a singer I had met in London, told me the club had been closed as a fire hazard and gave me a phone number along with the news that Robin and Clive were now a trio called, in honour of the padlocked club, the Incredible String Band.

The group photo on the cover of *The Hangman's Beautiful Daughter* gives an idea of the atmosphere at the cottage north of the city where I found them the following afternoon: kids and dope everywhere, flowered skirts and blouses, velvet cloaks, silk scarves and muddy shoes, all infused with the scent of patchouli. The new recruit was Mike Heron, formerly of the Edinburgh band Rock Bottom and the Deadbeats. He was short and solidly built with clumsy-seeming but effective movements, a contrast to Robin's vague ethereal grace. He teased the other two constantly, laughing and slapping his knee at the slightest provocation.

We drank tea and smoked joints for a while, then Robin and Mike played me the fruits of their new interest in composing. I was astounded: the songs were completely original, influenced by American folk and Scottish ballads, but full of flavours from the Balkans, ragtime, North Africa, music hall and William Blake. The combination of Mike's Dylan-tinged vocals and Robin's keening glissandos created harmonies both exotic and commercial. I had to have them. Fortunately, when Holzman heard an acetate of Robin's 'October Song', he said, 'Yeah, this is pretty good, go sign them.' I then had to deliberately misunderstand his instructions and add £50 to the advance to beat out Nat Joseph at Transatlantic Records for their signature.

We made the first LP one weekend in London. Clive, a true rebel who didn't care a fig for my ambitions, left soon afterwards for Afghanistan and told Robin and Mike not to wait up. The record didn't fit any obvious category but got good reviews and was a surprise success in both Britain and the USA. By the time I left Elektra and was trying to figure out how to avoid going back to New York, they were almost ready to make a second. Mike and Robin's agreement that I should manage them – along with the launch of UFO – enabled me to stay in London.

In the studio that winter, two musicians sounded sparse after the varied textures produced by the trio. We were still using four-track tape machines in 1966, but the concept of multiple over-dubs was being explored and expanded by Denny Cordell, Mickie Most, George Martin and other British producers. *Revolver* had shown what was possible, so we set out to make the sound of two musicians comparable to the original three. The explosion in dope smoking and acid in 1966 also helped to alter recording practices: the stoned ear loves complexity and Robin and Mike were nothing if not drug culture pioneers.

Edinburgh now has one of the highest heroin addiction rates in Europe, but the grim estates that provided the setting for *Trainspotting* in the 1990s were mostly on the booze in the sixties. Students and middle-class kids living in unheated flats in the beautiful Georgian buildings of the undeveloped city centre were leading the way in Britain's exploration of altered consciousness. Mike and Robin were part of a milieu in which hashish and LSD were constant factors of sociable life. They had both read Koestler's *The Lotus and the Robot* and Huxley's *Doors of Perception* and Robin was an expert on Blake, the hippies' favourite poet and painter. I found their approach to drugs comfortably familiar: it reminded me of the Cambridge folkniks. And in 1966, drugs could still be viewed as a benign phenomenon: thanks to the purity of the chemicals, bad trips were rare and acid casualties virtually unknown.

I had to wait for a visit to Havana in 1995 to have as much fun in a studio as I had making *The 5,000 Spirits Or The Layers Of The Onion*. Their new songs had strange lyrics and rich melodies and they kept coming up with off-the-wall ideas for harmonies and over-dubs; cramming all the ingenuity on to four tracks was our biggest problem. When we finished recording, I had my first experience of a sensation I came to relish in the coming years: I couldn't wait to get the musicians out of the way so that the engineer and I could start mixing the multi-track tapes into a stereo master.

Each track – which in those early days might include a combination of instruments or voices – could be positioned anywhere from right to left on the stereo spectrum by the proportion assigned to the two channels. The lead voice (and bass, if there was one) was always divided equally, meaning it went in the middle. Volume in relation to the other tracks was controllable by the fader on the mixing desk. Above each fader were the dials that added reverb (of which many varieties of length and texture were available) or subtly calibrated the high, low and middle frequencies. You were, in a sense, creating the ideal physical location for each instrument or voice: the violin in the Sistine Chapel, the singer in your mum's shower stall and the bass drum in Alfred Jarry's cork-lined bedroom. If a track sounded too quiet, one option was to simply turn it up. But if you changed the stereo positioning, that track might be more audible at the same volume. Or, by adding one decibel at a certain frequency, you could heighten its clarity or weight, making it appear louder, without making the others sound quieter. A glass can never be more than full: if you increase the level of one instrument, you reduce all the others.

My grandmother's studies with Leschititsky taught her the 'singing right hand': the melody line is made to ring out without being louder than the other notes. All the composer's intentions are heard, the melody line is clear but without distorting the balance between the notes. Those early years sitting under her piano influenced me: the ideal for which I strove was to hear everything in balance with the melody singing out clearly.

Mixing was an endlessly fascinating jigsaw puzzle with the reward of hearing a wonderful piece of music slowly emerging before you, like watching a print in the developing bath. But with sounds you could control the colour, the contrast and even the positioning. I found the prospect that my life would involve countless repetitions of this process very pleasing. Adding to the excitement was the conviction that a significant number of people would want to buy the music as soon as they heard what you had made of it. These feelings would often be delusional, of course, but in the case of *The 5,000 Spirits*, they were to be amply fulfilled.

chapter 16

WHEN I RETURNED TO NEW YORK on holiday in the summer of 1966, George asked me to help him with an outdoor concert at Lewisohn Stadium in Washington Heights. It was a double bill: the Miles Davis Quintet and the Duke Ellington Orchestra. On a balmy night, 3,000 people were seated across the infield of the stadium.

Ellington was viewed then as a little passé, but since it was a big band, dynamics dictated that Miles's Quintet would open the show. Their level of fame in the mid-'60s was as great as any ever reached by modern jazz artists. (Black ones, anyway; Dave Brubeck made the cover of *Time* magazine.) Dressed in Ivy League clothes – snug Brooks Brothers blazers or tweed jackets, button-down shirts and ties, horn-rimmed glasses, slim grey flannel trousers and brown loafers – they embodied a confident new ethos in the black community. Their hair was short and 'natural'. The girls who swirled around them backstage had either a 'Seven Sisters' (female Ivy League) look with gabardine skirts and hairbands or huge Afros, giant gold looped earrings and dashikis. Miles's set was muted and perfect. Afterwards there were handshakes all around and possibly a few early sightings of a high-five, but no exuberance. Everyone was extremely cool.

Backstage during their set, I would occasionally pass an older man in a rumpled suit and a head-rag whittling down a sax reed, or sorting through piles of sheet music. I would do a double-take and say to myself, 'Isn't that Harry Carney?' or 'Wow, that's Johnny Hodges!' The backstage hangers-on paid these men no attention whatsoever. When someone asked 'Anybody seen Duke?' the answer was that he was in the bus getting his hair fixed.

When I started setting up the famous Ellington music stands, Carney or Hodges or Paul Gonzalvez would come out to make sure their stand was just so, and to organize their sheet music. George, Father Norman O'Connor (the 'Jazz Priest') and Whitney Balliett from the *New Yorker* were just offstage talking to Miles when there was a murmur in the wings and someone hissed, 'Here comes Duke.' Parting the sea of flannel and tweed like a surreal Moses came Ellington in a suit of thick blue cloth. The jacket was 'zoot' length, almost to his knees, and his trousers broke fully on the tops of blue suede shoes. His shirt was a shade lighter than the suit while the third note in this triad cluster of blue, the broad tie, was darker than either. In his breast pocket was an impeccably folded bright orange handkerchief. From head to foot, Duke was clothed in Ivy League anti-matter.

'Good evening, Miles. Good evening, George. Good evening, Father.' As he made his way to the stage the beautiful hip girls, the tightly Brooks Brother'd men and even Miles seemed to evaporate. Duke just kept walking, took his seat at the piano, leaned into the microphone, and told the audience: 'Good evening ladies and gentlemen. I just want you to know that we *do*... love you madly.' At a nod of his head, the orchestra tore into the opening bars of 'Take The A-Train'.

A few months later, I was on the phone to George, having lost my Elektra job: the conflicts between my desire to be a producer and Jac's need for a marketing genius proved impossible to reconcile. A shortage of experienced tour managers and the impending start of Newport in Europe '66 meant our need was mutual. I headed for Barcelona where one branch of the tour kicked off. My first trip to the Catalan capital two years earlier had been a stressful visit with Hawkins and Edison. This time I arrived a few days ahead of the musicians and explored the city. The concerts were being held in the Palacio, a beautiful art deco hall: Sonny Rollins and Max Roach on opening night, followed by Illinois Jacquet, then a sold-out show with Stan Getz and Astrud Gilberto.

The pairing of these two had a tortured history. I heard a version of it late one night in the hotel bar from Stan's Swedish wife, Monica. The partnership was supposed to be between Stan and João Gilberto: Astrud was just the wife who could carry a tune on the demos they recorded. Monica claimed credit for persuading MGM to release Astrud's version of 'Girl From Ipanema' as a single. The record shot up the charts, but Monica suffered blow-back when Astrud and Stan began an affair on the resulting tour. João and Astrud divorced and Monica soon put an end to the collaboration. But going back to being simply Stan Getz or Astrud Gilberto was something of a financial let-down and George's offer had enticed them to work together again. Both arrived flanked by sexual bodyguards in the form of Astrud's muscle-bound *shtarker* (as another tour manager referred to him) and Monica. You could cut the air with a knife. When Astrud passed by in the hotel restaurant on the first day, Monica said, 'What a beautiful dress that is, Astrud.' (Pause.) 'Too bad it's not your colour.'

The pressure quickly got to the Getzes. Underwear and Swedish curses flew at Barcelona airport as bags were unpacked, divided and repacked in front of the check-in desk. If Stan expected Astrud to get rid of the boyfriend after Monica decamped to Copenhagen, he was mistaken. He took his revenge onstage: after agreeing 'Shadow Of Your Smile', he would whisper 'Ipanema' to the band and she would have a few beats to figure out which song they were playing. I was back to shuttle diplomacy in hotel corridors. In Rotterdam one evening, Stan told me that he never spent a night alone if he could possibly help it. I watched as he hit on girl after girl in a bar, eventually settling for a very plain waitress, the last to remain after everyone else had gone home.

I imagined that a switch to 'The Max Roach Quintet with special guest Sonny Rollins' would make a refreshing change. But I met them on a November morning in fog-bound Copenhagen airport awaiting a delayed flight to Vienna and it went downhill from there. Everyone else was on their way to Paris for a concert or a day off. The young guys in Max's group – Freddie Hubbard (trumpet), James Spaulding (sax) and Ronnie Saunders (piano) – were disgruntled: everyone had a girl in Paris or knew where to find one. Their day off that week had been in Oslo.

I had hung out with them a week earlier in Barcelona and Hubbard had inadvertently advanced my gastronomic evolution. George's schooling had not addressed my shellfish aversion, but when I accidentally spooned up a mussel from a bowl of Catalan *bullabesa* in a Ramblas restaurant, Freddie looked at me and said, 'Well, go on, man, *suck* the motherfucker!' What choice did I have but to cut the final cord to the peanut-butter-and-jelly land of my boyhood?

There were no such high spirits in Copenhagen, just gloom about the delay and the destination with duty-free Scotch for solace. The three of them were drunk by noon in the airport and snoring on the plane to Vienna. On the bus to

Graz in southern Austria the promoter had thoughtfully provided a case of beer that they eagerly attacked. Non-drinkers Sonny and Max sat up front ignoring the storm brewing in the rear. First it was the Beatles, who had 'ripped off black culture and made a fortune', then George Wein, 'the Jew who was sending us off to play for a bunch of Nazis' (Freddie had read that Hitler came from Graz). When we arrived at the beautiful opera house, the crowd was calmly seated, dressed very formally and glancing at their watches: the three musicians were raving and out of control.

I managed to get them onstage only a few minutes late, but it just got worse. The audience initially regarded bugle-calls from Freddie, birdsong from James and dissonant chords from Ronnie as interesting and avant-garde. But as Freddie staggered around the stage, they could be fooled no more and began to hiss. He responded by going to the microphone and suggesting that 'All you white mother-fuckers can kiss my black ass'.

I had to talk fast to convince the promoter not to stop the concert, refund the tickets and have the three of them arrested by the fierce-looking police who had suddenly appeared backstage. Having negotiated a five-minute reprieve, I signalled Max to play a stage-clearing drum solo. I succeeded in getting the three of them off and Sonny on, joining Max and the equally sober bass player in the scheduled second-half trio. We got half the fee and Sonny played well but towards the end one of the inebriated trio started throwing furniture out of the window of the locked dressing room. More police arrived and took them away in handcuffs.

Max, Sonny and I cruised Graz in a taxi until 2 a.m. trying to find out where they were being held. I would go into police stations and say '*Schwarzers?*' and get a shake of the head until we finally found them in the medieval castle that overlooks the city. Early the next morning I sprang them with a $300 fine for violating an Austrian statute against 'insulting the public' and we headed for the airport and Paris. They were exhausted and Freddie's wrist was swollen from the cuffs. Someone asked him whether it had been worth it. 'No, man,' he said. 'But almost.'

It is risky to treat the incident as emblematic, but it seemed in synch with other developments that year. The Civil Rights movement was not over, but the energy of the early sixties had dissipated. Young white activists had moved on to other things: the war in Vietnam, drugs, free speech. With the turning away of white liberals from the black cause came a rejection of the music. The biggest-selling jazz artist of the late sixties ended up being Charles Lloyd, a moderately gifted sax player who tapped into a melodic, oriental vibe that struck a chord with kids at the Fillmore. Coltrane died, and listening to Monk and Rollins began to seem like hard work. Theirs was heroin and alcohol music and kids were now into acid and grass.

In Paris the night after Graz I heard the rawest edge of black anger translated into music: the Ayler Brothers. Their recordings on the ESP label had startled a jazz world that thought it was ready for anything. Don Ayler played trumpet with a clear, vibrato-free tone, like a street musician from New Orleans, while Albert's sax playing was rich and fruity, like an R&B player's. They would start with a familiar melody, but the cohesion would erode with each repeat of the theme. Strict time from the drummer would judder into syncopations, returning to the four-four beat only to veer off again even more obliquely. Albert and Don would play the melody in unison at first, then start to edge away from each other, finding quarter tones either side of the tune. Eventually, the theme would disappear into a cacophony in which the original source was barely recognizable. For their theme that evening, they chose 'La Marseillaise'.

The fury that greeted Serge Gainsbourg's reggae version twelve years later gives some idea of what happened that night. People shouted and threw things at the stage; fist fights broke out as listeners tried to silence the objectors. Don Ayler looked like a bomb-making anarchist in his rimless glasses: strict, ascetic and aloof. No matter what happened around him, he continued to play the melody a demented quarter-tone sharp and always with that beautiful pure tone. It was great that people fought about music in those days.

The Aylers came to bad ends: addictions, mental institutions and suicide. It was more and more difficult for them to get work as the sixties wore on. They represented the musical branch of the shift in black consciousness as the gratitude towards white Civil Rights workers of the early sixties evolved into the fury of the Black Panthers in the later years of the decade.

I read about most of these developments from the calm distance of London. There was a measure of political engagement for us there – the Grosvenor Square anti-Vietnam demonstration, for example – but it seemed tame beside the struggles that were going on in the States.

In the spring of 1968, I flew from London to San Francisco for a meeting with Bill Graham about the Incredible String Band and found myself with some time to kill. A cinema near the Fillmore was showing *The Battle of Algiers*. The opening credits were rolling as I entered; the kasbah scenes were dark and my eyes hadn't adjusted from the California haze. I groped for a seat and kept finding bodies. That seemed odd; I had expected a weekday matinée at an art house to be pretty empty. A hand grabbed my sleeve and a hissed whisper guided me into an empty chair. The vivid scenes of urban guerrilla warfare quickly made me forget where I was.

When the film ended, the lights came up to reveal a packed house. Mine was the only white face in the audience. The men were wearing black berets, the women dashikis and they were all carrying notebooks.

chapter 17

A SUB-PLOT RUNNING THROUGH the Elektra year was my growing involvement with the so-called Underground. In 1966, it was worthy of the name: few outsiders were even aware of its existence. When it flourished in the spring of 1967, it was seen as a sub-culture of drugs, radical politics and music built around the *International Times*, Indica bookshop, *Oz* magazine, UFO, the London Free School, Release, Granny Takes a Trip, the 14-Hour Technicolour Dream and the Arts Lab. To me, the expression referred primarily to the fruits of the energy of one man: John Hopkins.

I first met Hoppy in 1964 when, in his photographer guise, he shot the musicians from the Caravan tour for *Melody Maker*. He looked like the mad ex-scientist he was: wire-thin build, intense brown eyes, unruly dark hair, well-worn jeans and an all-encompassing grin. I got him some tickets for one of our London shows and sealed the friendship by introducing him to a folk club promoter selling a block of very good hashish. Waiting to get back on George Wein's payroll that summer, I took up residence on Hoppy's sofa. There I learned about his Cambridge physics degree, his past as a security-cleared technician at the Harwell Atomic Energy lab, his commitment to nuclear disarmament (and the resulting forfeiture of his security clearance), his discovery of Sandoz LSD, and his recent break-up with Gala, London's most beautiful and wayward model. Hoppy always seemed in a process of discovery, treating the city as his research laboratory and uttering a delighted 'Wow!' whenever he came across something that pleased or interested him. He taught me how to develop film in his darkroom, directed me to the best artery-clogging breakfasts and the cheapest curries in West London, showed me the back doubles to avoid traffic lights and introduced me to a rogue's gallery of visionaries. In his purple Mini he dashed from one end of the city to the other, dropping off film, convening conspiratorial meetings, joining girls for afternoon assignations, scoring dope and bestowing favours.

In November 1965, shortly after I arrived to take up my Elektra post, Hoppy invited me to the first meeting of the London Free School. In retrospect, the founding principles sound heartbreakingly naïve: we planned to offer free classes to the poor and under-educated of Notting Hill Gate, mostly West Indian, Irish and Polish immigrants. The area was still recovering from years of Peter Rachman's slumlordship and the race riots of 1958. The side streets off Westbourne Park Road, later home to 'trustafarians', media types, artists, musicians and the odd record producer (and more recently colonized by stockbrokers), were full of after-hour shebeens and ganja dens, the kind of places Stephen Ward had taken Christine Keeler to meet Lucky Gordon a few years earlier.

Hoppy and his friends proposed courses in photography, French and politics. We leafleted the area and got a modest turn-out of suspicious locals for the introductory meeting in a now-demolished church near the Harrow Road. John Michell, the world's leading expert on the relationship between flying saucers and ley lines, offered us his basement in Powis Square. Peter Jenner and Andrew King, soon to become Pink Floyd's managers, were pioneering LFSers, as were Ron Atkins, for many years the *Guardian*'s jazz critic, and Barry 'Miles' Miles, founder of Indica Books, author of biographies on Ginsberg and Burroughs and numerous other books on the sixties.

The feathers of some local authorities were successfully ruffled: LFS advice helped people challenge the criminal justice system and claim unpaid benefits. But the Free School's enduring legacy is the Notting Hill Carnival. A Trinidadian activist friend of Hoppy's named Michael de Freitas (later Michael X) suggested moving an indoor celebration of Trinidadian culture on to the streets around Portobello Road during the August bank holiday. It was colourful and subversive, bringing together West Indians and freaks – the police's worst nightmare. Thirty-nine years later, over a million and a half people danced through the streets of Notting Hill on that same summer weekend.

The 1966 carnival was an auspicious beginning but it didn't raise any money, so we scheduled a series of concerts in All Saints Hall, Powis Square. Jenner and King booked a group they knew from Cambridge who were looking for some London exposure. Pink Floyd had started out as a blues band, but after being asked for an experimental score by a film-making artist – and after Syd Barrett began his explorations of psychedelics – their music had veered off in more original directions. From the first LFS benefit in September 1966 until their departure for an American tour in November 1967, the Floyd's music was the soundtrack for the Underground. The film score influenced more than just their music: they liked playing in front of moving lights so much they made it a central feature of their shows. The most enduring images of the Free School events, the

International Times launch party, UFO and the 14-Hour Technicolour Dream at Alexandra Palace are of the four Floyds bent over their instruments in concentration while purple and turquoise bubbles of light play over them.

In the murky glow, it was hard to pick out personalities, but if there was a centre of attention, it was Syd Barrett, with his impish girl-magnet looks, the screams of his slide guitar and the offhand way he sang his oddly melodic songs. Roger Waters also stood out for me. He is extremely tall and played a very large electric bass, often with his mouth wide open. His prominent nose and big oval head were sometimes the only human features perceptible in the gloom of the light show. Roger anchored the operatic chords, giving the group a foundation like no other. When Syd and his songs were long gone, the sound that would sweep the world was their classical harmonies underpinned by Roger's bass, decorated by Rick Wright's artfully cheesy organ and Nick Mason's elaborate drumming and crowned by Dave Gilmour's spacey blues guitar. Syd may be the most famous individual Floyd, but his songs have been heard by only a fraction of the millions who have bought Pink Floyd records.

Peter and Andrew didn't know anyone in the music business but me. I played a Floyd demo tape to Holzman a month or so before my departure but it didn't do anything for him. Once I was a free agent, I set out to find a deal for them – and for myself as producer. Through the jazz tours I knew a man named Alan Bates who worked at Polydor Records, so I invited him to Powis Square.

Polydor was the joker in the British deck in 1966. EMI and Decca had dominated the business for decades with only desultory competition. Warner Brothers had not yet ventured out of California, Dutch Philips was beginning a challenge and CBS had just opened a London office (the

Beatles and the Stones having demonstrated that any self-respecting major company needed a British A&R presence). Polydor, the pop subsidiary of Deutsche Grammophon, sent a man with the unlikely name of Horst Schmolzi to open up the British market for them. Initially, the biggest weapon in his arsenal was James Last, a kind of teutonic Lawrence Welk popular with middle-aged British listeners anxious to insulate themselves from the unsettling new sounds now dominating *Top of the Pops*.

Horst was a garrulous blond man in his early thirties who quickly became a fixture at the late-night hang-outs of London's pop fraternity. Within a year he had prised The Who away from Decca by giving Lambert and Stamp their own Track Records label. His deal with Robert Stigwood secured not only Clapton's Cream but the Bee Gees as well. When I met him, he had just signed an unknown American named Jimi Hendrix. It was a remarkable start for someone who came at the English with all the subtlety of a Porsche overtaking a Morris Minor in the inside lane. (Polydor executives were not known for diplomacy: the man sent to open their American office startled the crowd at the New York press launch by telling them he had wanted to live in the city ever since he had seen its skyline from Long Island Sound through the periscope of his U-boat in 1943.)

EMI and Decca executives would have had cardiac arrests at the royalty rates and independence of Horst's deals, which is why the wiliest managers went to him. The majors' policy then was always to use their own studios and their own producers. The fact that staff man George Martin was so monumentally successful with the Beatles in EMI's Abbey Road blinded them to the limitations of the formula.

Horst was a cartoon German – vulgar, loud and monumentally pleased with himself – but I liked him: he was genuinely enthusiastic about the music and fearless in his tastes. When he heard the Floyd, he got it immediately and we proceeded to draw up a contract signing them to Polydor through my new company, Witchseason Productions.

I had been stumped for a name when Donovan released a song called 'Season Of The Witch':

Beatniks out to make it rich
Must be the season of the witch.

I liked the image, and by the time I thought to wince at having a company named after a Donovan song, it was too late.

While lawyers haggled over the fine print we went into a Polydor studio to rehearse the first single. Everyone liked the choice of 'Arnold Layne', Syd's catchy number about a back-yard knicker-sniffer (based on a true case from Cambridge). On our second night there, Jenner rang me to say they had signed with an agency and the bookers wanted to come down to the studio and meet the band. I retain a vivid memory of the moment Polydor's night porter buzzed up to announce the visitors: Bryan Morrison, Steve O'Rourke and Tony Howard. Bryan now plays polo with Prince Charles, having made his fortune as a music publisher. Steve managed Pink Floyd from the 1968 coup that ousted Jenner and King until his death in 2003. In the 1970s, Tony Howard was a successful agent and managed Marc Bolan; he also became one of my dearest friends and died long before his time in 2001.

All I saw when we first met, however, was three thugs. Steve was tallest: with large horn-rimmed spectacles, he looked like the evil twin of Yves St Laurent. Tony was short, with the squashed features of a boxing trainer. Bryan had dark hair, narrow eyes and an arrogant expression. They were dressed in velvet jackets, scarves knotted around their throats, King's Road black boots, tight trousers and possibly one ruffled shirt. The dandyism only made them more sinister: they looked like monkeys dressed up for a PG Tips commercial and talked like Tony Secunda minus the charm. I felt in over my head again, a preppy Yank in the wilds of the London music business dealing with barrow boys far cannier and tougher than I could ever be.

Jenner rang the next day to say that Morrison had looked over the Polydor/Witchseason contract, found it wanting and proposed a Plan B. His agency would put up the money to record the single, then shop it to EMI or Decca as a finished master. Based on what he had heard in the studio, he was certain they could get a £5,000 advance for it. They wanted me to produce it, but as the Floyd's employee, rather than the other way around. After kicking the wall a few times and cursing, I rang back and said I would agree so long as I was guaranteed the right to produce the first album. Bryan said he understood my feelings but was concerned that EMI wouldn't like having their hands tied and we'd just have to play it by ear. For a couple of days I held out, then buckled, naïvely assuming that if the record was a hit, it would be in everyone's interest to keep a winning team together.

In early February we went into Sound Techniques, where we recorded and mixed 'Arnold Layne' and the B-side, 'Candy And A Currant Bun', over two nights. I liked the Floyd and the atmosphere was good. Even with a four-track machine, the mix was tricky. These days computers remember every movement of the faders so you can get the balance on one section just right, then go on to the next part. In '67, mixes were like recording takes; you had to get it in one pass or go back to the top and start again. While engineer John Wood and I controlled most of the balances, Roger leaned over my shoulder extending his big index finger on one of the faders to ensure that the surge of volume at the start of Rick's organ solo was just right. It was a nice team effort and we all felt good about the results.

As Bryan predicted, EMI loved the single and offered £5,000 to sign the group. The royalty rate was far lower than Polydor's, but the group needed the cash to buy a van. On the subject of producer, EMI stood firm. They wanted the group to use Abbey Road Studios and their staff man, Norman Smith, who had just had a novelty hit as a recording artist with 'I Was Kaiser Bill's Batman'. We had one final session together when Peter Whitehead filmed the band recording 'Interstellar Overdrive' at Sound Techniques as part of the *Tonite Let's All Make Love in London* documentary. The result is probably the closest you can get to hearing what the original Pink Floyd sounded like live.

I went to the launch party for the single and wistfully wished them well. Witchseason Productions would have to get along without the Floyd. 'Arnold Layne' got into the Top Twenty despite a BBC ban for 'indecent lyrics'. Norman Smith produced *The Piper At The Gates Of Dawn*, but John Wood and I were gratified that they had to come back to Sound Techniques to get the '"Arnold Layne" sound' for the second single.

One evening in May I ran into Syd and his girlfriend in Cambridge Circus. It is strange to recall that early on a weekday evening there was almost no traffic in the heart of London. Syd was sprawled on the kerb, his velvet trousers torn and dirty, his eyes crazed. Lindsey told me he'd been taking acid for a week. A few weeks later Floyd fans were lined up three deep along Tottenham Court Road for their return to UFO. There was no artists' entrance, so one by one they squeezed between me and the crowd, heading for the tiny dressing room in the back. I had exchanged pleasantries with the first three when Syd emerged from the crush. His sparkling eyes had always been his most attractive feature but that night they were vacant, as if someone had reached inside his head and turned off a switch. During their set he hardly sang, standing motionless for long passages, arms by his sides, staring into space. Dave Gilmour was added to the group soon afterwards to cover for him and by the end of the year Syd was gone.

I remember the UFO crowd sitting on the wooden dance floor in front of the stage, completely engrossed as the Floyd played those early gigs. Pete Townshend came down one evening and spent the whole night at the right-hand corner of the stage by Roger's amp, tripping on something. When I came by, he pointed at Roger's open mouth and told me it was going to swallow him. There were many pilgrimages to those shows: Hendrix, Christine Keeler and Paul McCartney on the same night (but not together), German TV shooting UFO's only surviving film clip. Hearing the descending opening chords of 'Interstellar Overdrive' takes me immediately back to those nights, when the lights would pulse and bubble against the stage, the crowd would cheer the familiar melody, the four of them would stare intently at their instruments and we would be off. The jaunty choruses of Syd's songs were like fertile planets in a void of spaced-out improvisation: returning to the theme after a ten-minute excursion was both exhilarating and reassuring. Even today, with Syd's era a dim memory and Roger off sulking on his own, there is something about a Pink Floyd song no one has ever been able to emulate.

Jenner and King were – like me – out of their depth once the Morrison Agency came on board and it was only a matter of time before they, too, would walk the plank. None of us imagined that decades later you could go to the remotest parts of the globe and find cassettes of *Dark Side Of The Moon* rattling around in the glove compartments of third-world taxis along with Madonna and Michael Jackson.

Pink Floyd's success is difficult to analyse or explain. What they brought with them from Cambridge was all their own; London in 1967 just happened to fall in love with it first.

chapter 18

HOPPY AND I STARTED UFO because we were both broke. I had decided to stay in London and start my production company while Hoppy had given up his career as a photographer to launch the *International Times*. Neither venture was likely to yield much cash in a hurry.

We spent an early afternoon in December 1966 speeding around London in the purple Mini, looking at derelict cinemas and nightclubs fallen on hard times. (In those days, you *could* speed around London on a weekday afternoon.) Our last stop was a Tottenham Court Road basement next to the Berkeley and the Continentale cinemas (all now buried under concrete) with a small sign outside reading THE BLARNEY CLUB. A wide stairway with faded red carpet bolted to cement steps led down to a gloomy, low-ceilinged ballroom with a tiny stage and a smooth wooden dance floor. To the left was a fluorescent-lit hallway opening on to a seedy bar area. The owner, Mr Gannon, was slinging around soft-drink crates, counting under his breath between puffs on a Woodbine. We enquired whether the club might be for rent on a weekend evening. 'I suppose I could let you have a Friday night for fifteen pounds,' he said, 'but I'd have to sell the soft drinks.' Since most of our customers were likely to suffer from dry-mouth syndrome or tight-throat syndrome and we knew nothing about the soft drinks business, we shook on the deal and booked the last two Fridays in December. Pink Floyd was engaged as the house band. We couldn't decide between Night Tripper and UFO, so we put both on the flyers handed out in Portobello Road market the previous Saturday. We had no idea who would turn up that first night, 23 December 1966, but freaks came out of the woodwork from all over the city and we made a profit. There was a general feeling of surprise and recognition; few had any idea there were so many kindred spirits.

Over the coming months, UFO introduced London to Pink Floyd, the Soft Machine, the Crazy World of Arthur Brown, light shows, tripping en masse and silk-screened psychedelic fly-posters. We opened every Friday at 10.30 and closed around 6 a.m. when the Tube started running. Indica Books sold posters from the Fillmore and Family Dog ballrooms in San Francisco so we decided to create some of our own. My friend Nigel Waymouth was a partner in Granny Takes a Trip, King's Road's most extreme boutique, where they sold floral jackets and mattress-ticking suits and shirts with collars that drooped to the nipples. Nigel had painted their shop window in a post-Beardsley acid-dream style with the front end of a car protruding on to the pavement. I nominated him for the task of creating our first poster.

Hoppy had his own artist, Michael English, who had worked for *IT* and the Free School. In a typical 1967 solution, we introduced them, shut them in a room and told them not to come out until they had designed London's first psychedelic poster. It worked a treat: they adopted the nom de plume 'Hapshash and the Coloured Coat', turned out over thirty posters in eighteen months, made an LP and eventually went their separate ways to successful careers as painters.

Hapshash's first, a huge gold field with a giant peppermint-swirled UFO across the middle, might be my favourite, but their collected works constitute a particular English style of psychedelia – celebrated with an exhibition at the Victoria and Albert Museum in 2000. The silk-screen process was uneconomical – no cost reduction as the quantity increased – but it altered the face of London. Thieves were spotted with steam kettles, peeling them off fences. The protection racket that controlled the sites began selling instead of fly-posting them, so we set up a short-lived poster marketing business to capitalize on their popularity.

When you consider that ceilidh bands and green-skirted Irish teenagers had been the Blarney Club's standard fare, Mr Gannon handled the influx of freaks (we preferred the term to 'hippies') remarkably well. On one of our first evenings, he took me aside for 'a little word'. He had a lovely brogue and there was a lilt in his voice when he said that he wasn't sure, and didn't want to jump to conclusions, but he had a feeling 'there's a few people smokin' dope in here'. The downward melody of the 'o' in 'dope' I recall being particularly charming.

'Well, Mr Gannon, I can't say this with absolute assurance, but I certainly hope you are mistaken.'

'Well, that's as may be, and that's as may not be, Joe. But all the same, I think it might be a good idea to turn on the fan.'

On another occasion, a stranger asked whether we would like to present the British premiere of the New York underground film *Flaming Creatures* by Jack Smith. I remembered reading about it in Jonas Mekas's film column in the *Village Voice* and knew it was considered a classic. About 2 a.m., I made the announcement and watched as the images unfolded on the screen. Women dressed like flamenco dancers posed languorously on a bed as strange music played. Eventually a skirt was lifted to reveal a most unfeminine organ. I was horrified to see that Mr Gannon had left his post by the soft-drink stand and was staring at the screen. I assured him that I had had no idea about the content of the film when I agreed to show it. (These were the days of the Lord Chamberlain's office, when licences for public entertainment could be withdrawn for four-letter words or nudity.) 'Oh, I wouldn't worry about it, Joe,' he said, 'I've seen far worse than that in the navy.'

Besides the Floyd, we booked the Exploding Galaxy dance troupe, avant-garde jazz outfits such as Sun Trolley, and ten-minute comedies by the People Show. Yoko Ono cast her *Bottoms* movie mostly from UFO audiences, who signed up for it in a book by the door. One night she asked for a contact microphone on a long lead, an amp and a stepladder. When the place was packed we cleared some space in front of the stage for the ladder, taped the mic to a pair of scissors, plugged it in and cranked up the volume. Yoko emerged from the dressing room leading a beautiful girl in a paper dress who smiled serenely atop the ladder as Yoko cut the garment off her, the amplified scritch-scritch of the scissors booming across the club.

A week after his agency took the Pink Floyd record deal away from me, Tony Howard came down to see the club and have a chat. We grabbed a couple of bottles of Mr Gannon's synthetic orange soda and repaired to a tiny alcove off the main ballroom. The Floyd were becoming more and more famous, getting bookings all over the country; Tony said they couldn't continue to work for £50 on a Friday night in central London. 'But they're only getting higher fees because of the publicity generated by UFO!' I spluttered. If we paid more, we would have to raise the ten-shilling admission price. Tony suggested that this was my problem, not the Floyd's. We finally agreed a compromise:

they would play two more gigs for £75 each, then, regardless of how big they were in June, they would come back and do a final show for the same fee. I envisioned it as I sat there: they would be the hottest group in England by June and UFO would have them; we'd get huge publicity and a packed house. It turned out as predicted, but it was a hollow triumph: by June, Hoppy would be in jail and Syd present in body but absent in spirit.

Now I needed both to replace the Floyd at UFO and to find a band for Witchseason Productions. The Soft Machine were perfect for UFO, but as recording artists, they didn't convince me. The name, taken from a William Burroughs novel, epitomized their problem: it was trying just that little bit too hard. The Floyd's mysterious plundering of the Carolina backwoods for theirs was more opaque and offhand.

I loved drummer Robert Wyatt's hoarse vocals and Kevin Ayers was an alluring songwriter whom girls adored, but I had trouble with Daevid Allen's hectoring presence as lead vocalist. Later that year I was hired to bring some 'Arnold Layne' production magic to their first single but it sank without trace. Thirty years later, after Robert's back-breaking fall transformed him into a sedentary but profound *chansonnier*, I had the honour of releasing his catalogue of recordings on my Hannibal label.

In March, a jazz buff named Victor Schonfield tipped me off about a group playing in a bar in the Shepherd Market red-light district. In a tiny room a dozen customers nursed cocktails while an organ-based trio pounded out a jazzy fusion. After a few choruses, out popped Arthur Brown in a Merlin cape and make-up with his head on fire. He began and ended his set with a raucous but catchy hymn to the 'God of Hellfire'. He quickly became a UFO favourite. I pondered trying to sign Arthur, but decided he was a one-song wonder. I was right about the limited repertoire, but that one song got to the top of the British charts a few months later.

I billed Arthur with comedy surrealists the Alberts. We had already established the connection between psychedelia and Dada humour with visits by the Bonzo Dog Doodah Band. I liked to think this demonstrated that UFO was more than just an outpost of the revolution, and the diverse entertainments never seemed to put anyone off. From LPs of Pakistani classical singing by the Ali Brothers between live sets, to the W. C. Fields shorts we showed in the middle of the night, the audience lapped it all up.

About 2 a.m. one night I was accosted at the entrance by a little guy in a flared mod suit. His hair was blond and short and his gigantic speed-dilated pupils were further magnified by large thick spectacles. He talked so fast I could barely follow what he had to say, but it was clear he wanted a free pass into the club. His name was Jeff Dexter, resident DJ at Tiles, an all-night mod club in Oxford Street, and his visit was portentous. When Jeff entered UFO, he began a metamorphosis that would eventually transform him into an elder statesman of flower power. He was like the first swallow of spring, a harbinger of a general migration. In the coming months, the curious from other tribes would come to find out what all the fuss was about. When 'Arnold Layne' hit the charts, the floodgates opened.

A new vein of talent was opened up for me by the once feared Tony Howard. He offered a peace treaty: I would tell him the groups I wanted and he would do the negotiating, splitting commission with the group's agency. He had a clear sense of the cachet adhering to a UFO booking and introduced me to established bands keen to jump on the psychedelic bandwagon. This wasn't as cynical as it sounds: many of them had been transformed by their experience of drugs and their music had changed as a result. Gigs by

Tomorrow and the Pretty Things were the first fruits of this new relationship.

As the club's popularity grew, Hoppy and I tried hard to maintain the original atmosphere. We still showed Kurosawa movies before dawn; Jack the Nudist from Watford (clothed for the evening) continued to project his light show in the corner while people tripped and danced around him; our security staff still sold some of the best acid in London; the corridor between Mr Gannon's soda stand and the dance floor remained crowded with tables offering leaflets on political prisoners, the legalization of drugs and the upcoming porno festival in Amsterdam, while celebrities, journalists, 'straights' and converts appeared in ever greater numbers. UFO became a crucial spot in the London music scene and Hoppy and I were able to survive off the proceeds.

UFO's success became the object of envy. There was a feeling in the Underground that it should belong to the community, rather than to any individuals. UFO money certainly flowed into the scene as the staff – all freaks – were well paid and *IT*'s stall raked in plenty of cash each week. Any cause, no matter how radical, was welcome to proselytize on the premises. But when *IT* had a financial crisis following a raid by the Obscene Publications Squad and it was felt that UFO ought to provide rescue funding, I resisted and Hoppy didn't disagree. We passed a bucket, made pleas over the PA system and pre-paid our advertising bill a few weeks in advance.

Hoppy and some *IT* staff organized the 14-Hour Technicolour Dream at Alexandra Palace in April. I thought them a bit ambitious, but publicized it at UFO and hoped they didn't lose their shirts. I don't think much money was made, but none was lost and the event got huge publicity plus royal visits from Lennon and Hendrix. The gigantic hilltop building looked fantastic all lit up that night. Next morning I lay outside on the grass surrounded by crowds streaming away in the bright sunshine. There was no stopping this juggernaut; the Underground was becoming the mainstream.

An early visitor from the Soho music business world was Denny Cordell: he loved the crowd and invited me to his office to hear his latest production. It was by an unknown group with incomprehensible lyrics and was based on a sedate piece of eighteenth-century chamber music. I immediately booked Procol Harum to play UFO the evening 'A Whiter Shade Of Pale' was released. There was something familiar about the strange words. When Denny introduced me to Keith Reid, the lyricist, it all came back. He had sauntered into the Elektra offices a year before looking for a deal based solely on some typewritten verses. I found him amiable but crazy. Who ever signed someone on the basis of a few stanzas of doggerel? (Let's see now, that's Steve Winwood, Lovin' Spoonful, Cream, Pink Floyd, the Move, 'Fire' and 'Whiter Shade Of Pale' that slipped through my fingers…)

I also loved Cordell's next single, 'Say You Don't Mind' by Denny Laine and the Electric String Quartet. UFO provided them with some of the very few gigs they ever played. Laine was one of the era's great singers, immortalized by his vocal on the Moody Blues' 'Go Now', and eventually successful singing harmony with McCartney in Wings, but he never got the recognition he deserved. His amplified strings may have started stable-mate Bev Bevan thinking about ELO.

Tony Howard had the idea for a 'milkman's matinée' audition slot at 5 a.m. One of the first to be given this opportunity was a Dublin blues band called The People. Their manager – an Irish photographer doing it for a lark – appeared around eleven, all anxious and speedy. He thought the starting time on the contract must be a misprint: they were outside in the van and ready to go on straight away. I explained the deal to him and his face fell. He asked for the £5 fee in advance and I said they had to play first. I did agree to his last request: that someone bang on the side of their van at 4.30 as an alarm call. They had no money to do anything in the intervening period but sleep.

A short while later, a man in a tweed jacket, white shirt and tie came down the stairs. I had met him before: Mike Jeffreys, manager of Jimi Hendrix and the Animals. He complimented me on the size of the crowd; as a former club owner in Newcastle, he knew about crowds. (As a former Newcastle club owner he also knew about a great many other things, best explained by renting a DVD of *Get Carter*.) When I told him Soft Machine and Arthur Brown were on the bill that night, he said, 'I just signed the Soft Machine for management and Arthur Brown is signed to Lambert and Stamp.'

He was turning to leave when I added: 'And there's an Irish blues band at five a.m.'

He spun round and looked at me intently. 'Irish? Do they have Irish passports?' I assumed they must, since they came from Dublin. Jeffreys found a spot against a wall and stood there, with only an occasional trip to the toilet or the soda stand, for six hours. In our audience, a guy in serious glasses, coat and tie seemed the most outlandish of all.

The People were good and got the sleepy crowd up on its feet. The leader, Henry McCullough (also later with Wings), harangued and charmed them, the approach was original, the band was tight. They got two encores before we started shooing people out into the street. Because we'd had such a good night, I gave their manager two crisp £5 notes. A few minutes later, he sought me out again. 'Look, Joe, can you give me a hand? There's some nutter in the dressing room upsetting the lads. He says he manages Jimi Hendrix and he wants them to open for him on a tour to America starting next month. Will you help me get rid of the guy?'

When I told him that Jeffreys actually did manage Hendrix, he looked at me wide-eyed for a second, then dashed back to the tiny dressing room. Jeffreys had lined up a US tour starting after the Monterey Pop Festival and needed an opening act but hated the idea of giving a break to someone else's band. He had the further problem of 'exchanges': you couldn't get a work permit in either country without a balancing number of dates being played at comparable salaries by musicians travelling in the opposite direction. Alternatively, you could find Irish musicians who fell outside the agreement and you could change their name from The People to Eire Apparent.

A decade later I was running a film distribution company and wanted to release a documentary about Stiff Records and their post-punk line-up of stars such as Elvis Costello, Ian Dury and Madness. I went to see Dave Robinson, the infamous boss of the label, and discovered that he was that same Dublin photographer. The American tour with Jeffreys had provided him with a music business education. As for the film, despite other offers, he had decided to let me have it 'seeing as how you gave us that extra *foiver*'.

As UFO's popularity grew, so did the conflict between me and the revolutionary vanguard who staffed it. Hoppy was the beloved leader whose heart was clearly on their side; I was the breadhead who cared only about his music business career. The majority of the UFO crowd just wanted to get high and laid and listen to great music. They believed in the social and political goals of the movement, but weren't prepared to dig a trench on the front line to achieve them. For those who were ready to live in squats, fight policemen and radically alter their lives, music was important more for its message than its artistic qualities. Their spiritual (and perhaps literal) progeny reappeared in England in the late ’70s during the punk movement and again in the late ’80s with the New Age travellers and crusties.

Leading the radical faction was Mick Farren. Hoppy had dragged me to Shoreditch one snowy night in January to hear Mick’s group, the Social Deviants. I hadn’t much liked Hoppy’s description of them and when we entered the damp, chilly basement and got a glimpse of Mick’s gigantic white-boy Afro and his glum band-mates, I viewed the audition as even less promising, if that were possible. There is no twist in this tale; they were as bad as they looked. Mick’s singing was devoid of melody and his group could barely play their instruments. Hoppy conceded the point, but his unerring nose had spotted a willing and able trooper in Farren. I said the Deviants would play UFO over my dead body.

As predicted, Mick made himself indispensable. He saw that the girls handling UFO’s door money were in over their heads and took over the box office while fellow Deviants helped out as guards at the back door. Every week, he would ask me when they could have a booking. In unguarded moments he acknowledged that musically they were crap, but in his mind that detail was outweighed by their *commitment*. I think he also imagined that once he strutted his tight jeans and mega-hair on the UFO stage, female adulation would be his. Despite my continued refusal to sully our stage with them, Mick and his boys became a key part of my support team. Eventually, after some sterling work coping with bigger and bigger crowds, I gave in. You can see them in the list of billings on 14 April 1967. At least I held out for three months.

Despite differing notions of what the revolution was about, an atmosphere of *agape* was pervasive in 1967:

people were fundamentally quite nice to each other. Most hippies pitied, rather than hated, the 'straights'. I suppose it helped that we were stoned much of the time. Another factor was Hoppy. Most movements are unified behind an inspiring leader at the outset and ours was no exception. It is difficult to over-emphasize the effect Hoppy had on the Underground community from the launch of the London Free School in October 1965 until his jailing in June 1967. At the LFS, then *IT* and UFO, his enthusiasm for music *and* revolution smoothed over most disagreements. He would propose an elegant compromise or point out the solution with such good-natured clarity that the corrected party never felt humiliated.

Gathered behind each of us were the massed ranks of our respective constituencies: his radicals who did so much of the hard work at both *IT* and UFO; my music fans ready for any new challenge to their eyes and ears. Hoppy and I saw this dichotomy as a source of strength rather than a problem and always had complete confidence in one another.

Tensions mounted as the regulars got crowded out of the increasingly popular club and Hoppy's June trial date approached. Nothing so symbolized my apostasy in radical eyes as booking The Move. Ever since the club had become successful, I was determined to introduce our audience to my favourite *faux* psychedelics. When the staff heard about it, they were horrified. We were already swamped by 'weekend hippies' who were more likely to have downed a beer than a tab of Sandoz's best before setting out. When the night arrived, the club was packed and the band played well enough, but the small stage inhibited them and perhaps the crowd did as well. It was a good, but not a great, night.

Hoppy's role as Pied Piper of the Underground meant that policemen, journalists and outraged parents became aware of him. It has been suggested that the search warrant

EMI photo archive

Tomorrow: Junior, Steve Howe, Twink, Keith West

Lonnie Johnson in the late 1940s

Joe Boyd collection

John Byrne Cooke

Maria d'Amato (later Muldaur), New York, 1963, with Bob Neuwirth and Tex Isley

Val Wilmer

Sister Rosetta Tharpe, England, 1964

Reverend Gary Davis, on tour, England, 1964

Val Wilmer

John Hopkins

Dressing room harmony, England, 1964: Otis Spann, Muddy Waters, Brownie McGhee, Sonny Terry

Ransom Knowling, Willie Smith, Muddy Waters on stage, England, 1964

Val Wilmer

John Hopkins

Berlin Jazz Festival, 1964: Roland Kirk, Tété Montoliu, Tommy Potter, Kenny Clarke

Coleman Hawkins and Harry 'Sweets' Edison, on tour in Europe, 1964

John Hopkins

Brian Shuel

Ian Campbell Folk Group: Lorna Campbell, Ian Campbell, Brian Clark, John Dunkerly, Dave Swarbrick

John Lee Hooker playing a blues all-nighter at Alexandra Palace, London, 1964

John Hopkins

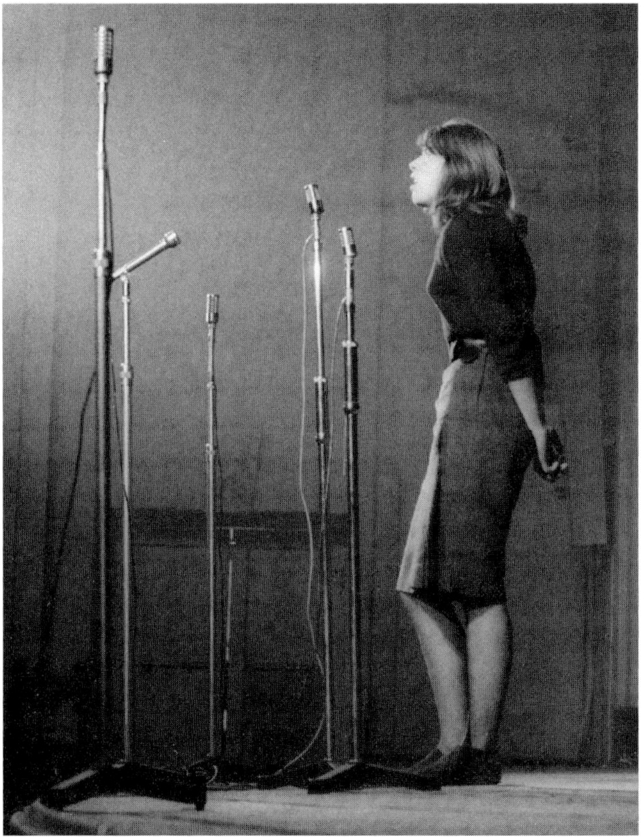

Brian Shuel

Anne Briggs, Cecil Sharp House, 1965

Paul Butterfield, Elvin Bishop, Mike Bloomfield, 1965

John Byrne Cooke

Brian Shuel

Padstow Hobby Horse in the streets, May Day 1964

Brian Shuel

The Watersons: Lal, John Harrison, Mike and Norma

We Shall Overcome, Newport 1963: Peter, Mary and Paul, Joan Baez, Bob Dylan, the Freedom Singers, Pete Seeger, Theodore Bikel

John Byrne Cooke

John Byrne Cooke

Paul Rothchild and Bob Dylan, near Woodstock NY, 1965

Newport 1965: Eric Von Schmidt (beard), Joe Boyd (hat), Tom Rush, Geoff Muldaur, Maria d'Amato (Muldaur)

Jim Floyd

Redferns Music Picture Library

The Move in caftans: Ace Kefford, Trevor Burton, Carl Wayne, Bev Bevan, Roy Wood

John Hopkins in Portobello Road, 1965

Adam Ritchie

Robin Williamson and Mike Heron, 1966

London Free School Notting Hill Carnival, 1966

Adam Ritchie

courtesy Vashti Bunyan

Vashti Bunyan, 1966

Richard Thompson takes aim

Nick Drake at the piano, 1968

Victoria Waymouth

Joe Boyd

Bob Squire, Beverly and John Martyn, Hastings, 1970

Marian Bain and Nick Drake, Witchseason office, 1970

Joe Boyd

Val Wilmer

Blue Notes, ICA, 1965: Dudu Pukwana, Mongezi Feza, Johnny Dyani, Chris McGregor

Incredible String Band on tour, 1969: Joe Boyd, Rose Simpson, Mike Heron, Christina McKechnie and Walter Gundy

Joe Boyd collection

Joe Boyd

Linda Peters (later Thompson), 1971

Fred McDarrah

Jimi Hendrix and Devon Wilson, New York, 1970

Fairport Convention, rehearsals for Liege and Lief: Ashley Hutchins, Dave Swarbrick, Sandy Denny, Richard Thompson, Simon Nicol, Dave Mattacks

for his flat was triggered by a phone call from the worried and titled parent of a teenager who was dancing in the UFO lights, but it could have come from any one of a number of sources. We all assumed he would get off with a fine, but as the trial date approached the prosecution appeared to be playing for keeps. At a South London magistrates' court in early June, we heard the eight-month sentence handed down. Everyone was devastated. Hoppy handed full control to me and I decided to try to make the club as commercially successful as I could. Half the profit would still go to Hoppy and he would need it when he came out.

The Billings for the UFO club as printed on posters and in ads, December 1966 to September 1967:

Dec 23/30:	*Freakout under Berkeley Cinema; Warhol movies; Pink Floyd sounds; Anger movies; Heating warm; IT god*
Jan 13:	*Pink Floyd; Marilyn Monroe movie; The Sun Trolley; Technicolor strobe; Fiveacre slides; Karate*
Jan 20:	*Pink Floyd; Anger movie*
Jan 27:	*AMM Music; Pink Floyd; Five Acre Light; Flight of the Aerogenius Chpt 1; International Times; IT Girl Beauty Contest*
Feb 3:	*Soft Machine; Brown's Poetry; Flight of the Aerogenius Chpt 2; Bruce Connor Movies*
Feb 10:	*Bonzo Dog Doo Dah Band; Ginger Johnson; Bank Dick WC Fields*
Feb 17:	*Soft Machine; Indian Music; Disney Cartoons; Mark Boyle Feature Movie*
Feb 24:	*Pink Floyd; Brothers Grimm*
Mar 3:	*Soft Machine*
Mar 10:	*Pink Floyd*
Mar 17:	*St Patrick's Day off*

Mar 24:	*Soft Machine*
Mar 31:	*Crazy World of Arthur Brown; Pink Alberts; 'spot the fuzz contest'*
April 7:	*Soft Machine*
April 14:	*Arthur Brown; Social Deviants; Special: the fuzz*
April 21:	*Pink Floyd*
April 28:	*The Smoke (29/30 14-hour technicolour dream)*
May 5:	*Soft Machine; Arthur Brown*
May 12:	*Graham Bond Org; Procol Harum*
May 19:	*Tomorrow; Arthur Brown; The People Show*
May 26:	*The Move*
June 2:	*Pink Floyd*
June 9:	*Procol Harum; The Smoke*
June 16:	*Crazy World of Arthur Brown; Soft Machine; The People Blues Band 4.30 a.m.*
June 23:	*Liverpool Love Festival*
June 30:	*Tomorrow; The Knack*
July 7:	*Denny Laine; Pretty Things*
July 14:	*Arthur Brown; Alexis Korner; Victor Brox*
July 21:	*Tomorrow; Bonzo Dog Doo Dah Band*
July 28:	*CIA v UFO; Pink Floyd; Fairport Convention*
Aug 4:	*Eric Burdon; Family*
Aug 11:	*Tomorrow*
Aug 18:	*Arthur Brown; Incredible String Band*
Sept 1/2	*UFO Festival: Pink Floyd; Soft Machine; Move; Arthur Brown; Tomorrow; Denny Laine*
Sept 8:	*Eric Burdon & The New Animals; Aynsley Dunbar*
Sept 15:	*Soft Machine; Family*
Sept 22:	*Dantalians Chariot w Zoot Money & His Light Show; The Social Deviants; The Exploding Galaxy*
Sept 29:	*Jeff Beck; Ten Years After; Mark Boyles New Sensual Laboratory; Contessa Veronica*

chapter 19

THE SURGE IN ATTENDANCE and publicity UFO experienced during its first six months may have been in keeping with the *annus mirabilis* 1967, but it was also part of a historic pattern. No matter how pure and impassioned the intention, the inevitable effect of most artistic or cultural revolutions is to feed the public's appetite for titillation. London's first commercial 'hit', *The Beggar's Opera* (which ran almost continuously from 1721 to 1790), was based on the gallows confessions of highwaymen and cutpurses and the broadsheets that memorialized them. Clergy and Tory politicians were furious at its success; they felt it undermined all that was good and proper in English society. Which, of course, explains its popularity.

In the nineteenth century, the French refined the process by which the newly enlarged bourgeoisie avoided boring itself to death. Adventurous sons left the safety of the middle-class hearth, lived in sin with seamstresses in garrets, took to drugs or drink and espoused radical philosophies. They would then create a daring novel/play/painting/poem/opera to provide vicarious thrills for those still working at their respectable jobs, earning enough as a result to reassume the trappings of bourgeois life in their old age. These rituals, speeded up and modernized (and extending now to daughters), can currently be followed in the popular press.

The twentieth century's new twists to the old formulae involved drawing the audience farther into the subversive worlds celebrated by the artists. Few in the crowds attending *The Beggar's Opera* dreamt of hanging out with thieves and murderers. Nineteenth-century audiences loved reading *Scènes de la Vie Bohème* and going to the opera, but would never trade their comfortable homes for garrets. And most wouldn't tolerate their children getting up to any such behaviour.

White New Yorkers taking the A-train to Harlem in the '20s to catch Duke Ellington at the Cotton Club demonstrated that audiences were becoming as interested in experiencing the dangerous ambience as they were in listening to the dangerous music or reading the dangerous book. When preachers fulminated against rock'n'roll for luring innocent white teenagers into sexually subversive black lifestyles or – heaven forfend! – dancing with black folk, they knew what they were talking about. Fifties teenagers were pushing the boat out that much farther than slumming jazz fans thirty years before.

What London witnessed in the spring of '67 was more than an endorsement of a new musical style, it was a mass immersion in the sub-culture that gave rise to it. We saw them pour down the stairs week after week in search of a transcendent experience. Thanks to the chemistry in the back pockets of my security staff (freelance, of course, nothing to do with the club), they often found it. Drugs meant there was less of the toe-in-the-water tentativeness of the A-train passengers in 1928: at UFO, the grinning crocodile of psychedelics wrapped its lips around your ankle, dragged you in and licked you all over. Such experiences began to transform society, but not as we had hoped.

By the summer, kaftans and beads were everywhere and UFO was swamped by tourists and weekend hippies. But were we anything more than the latest in a line of English style tribes, following Teddy boys, Rockers and Mods? We had aspired to greater things: to be as threatening to the good order of society as the authorities had feared.

The march to Fleet Street and Tomorrow's dawn call to revolution ushered in July, but the month passed relatively calmly as our crowds continued to grow. When the *News of the World* spiced the nation's Sunday breakfast at the end of the month with shocking tales from the 'Hippie Vice Den', Mr Gannon got a call from a local policeman: if UFO opened that weekend, a warrant would be sought for a raid and his licence could be lost. Our Blarney Club days were over.

I persuaded Centre 42, playwright Arnold Wesker's foundation for the encouragement of 'workers' theatre', to rent us the Roundhouse, a magnificently decaying brick hulk at the edge of the railway yards in Camden Town. That Friday we handed out leaflets in front of the Blarney Club telling punters they could find UFO – starring the newly mind-blown Eric Burdon – a few stops away on the Northern Line. In some respects, the Roundhouse UFO was glorious. Its extraordinary space and huge stage were liberating after the cramped confines of the Blarney Club. I looked forward to a future of big crowds and soaring profits. One problem, however, was barely noticed that first night: after eleven, the local pubs filled the streets with their inebriated Irish and skinhead patrons. A few of our customers got hassled, but we thought little of it.

By the following week, word had spread. Skinheads hadn't had too much contact with hippies up to then, but they could smell a natural enemy. The minute our audience arrived in the neighbourhood, they were under attack. Bells were snatched from around necks, handbags stolen, eyes blacked. A group of skins charged through a fire door and started hitting anyone they found, myself included. A few police came but they seemed to enjoy seeing the hippies getting a kicking.

Our door staff were useless against the thugs, so I turned to Michael X and his Black Nationalists to provide a security patrol. He showed up the following week with seven big, mean-looking guys in black turtlenecks, tight black trousers and shaved heads. I got to know a few of them later: an actor, a film director and a writer, and they could not have been gentler souls. But when they scowled and struck karate poses, the skinheads weren't to know that, were they? Their services, however, didn't come cheap.

Everywhere I turned, costs soared. The rent was far more than we had been paying Mr Gannon and I could no longer use the tiny capacity of my venue as an excuse for keeping musicians' fees down. More lighting was needed and more staff. Commercial promoters, now regularly booking the Floyd, Soft Machine or Arthur Brown, had become competitors. The eager idealists who had worked long and hard began to fade away without Hoppy to inspire them. Week after week I paid out the door cash to musicians, staff and to cover expenses with little or nothing left for my rent or Hoppy's nest egg. For the first time, UFO began to lose money.

There were some high points amid the gloom. The balcony platform that circled the Roundhouse halfway up the high brick walls inspired me to track down the company that had 'flown' Peter Pan during a recent production in the West End. Arthur Brown made his first Roundhouse entrance high over the audience, his head in the trademark halo of flame, with another novel device – a radio microphone – amplifying his vocal. For a moment, I thought the Roundhouse might be worth it after all.

A side benefit of our larger size was the increased tithe paid to Release from our door takings. The bust-fund buckets passed in the spring had evolved into an organization. Michael X, always urging us to think about practicalities, called a meeting of interested parties, including an exotic-looking, dark-haired young woman who volunteered for the difficult jobs and accomplished them all impeccably. She had become active in protesting against arbitrary policing after plainclothes men stopped her Jamaican lover on the street and offered him a choice of felonies: a sack of ganja or burglars' tools. Despite her efforts, he went down for three years. When I gave her a lift home after the second meeting, she showed me a painting she was working on: a phalanx of naked Amazons charging towards the viewer.

I recalled a visit to a friend a few months earlier. Over his fireplace, he proudly displayed his new acquisition: a pink-hued oil painting depicting pubic hair and moistly parted labia, viewed from below. He told me he had bought it from an artist who supported herself by nude modelling – including a *Mayfair* cover clad in nothing but gold paint. He had an option on her next work: his description of it matched what I saw on the easel. This was my introduction to Caroline Coon: artist, feminist, journalist and campaigner.

Caroline set up Release and ran it with an effectiveness that was out of step with most underground organizations. Of all the idealistic enterprises begun during year zero of our cultural revolution in West London, only Release and the Notting Hill Carnival still carry out their original functions. Many in the Underground were uncomfortable with her businesslike attitude, but sex and class played their parts as well. Caroline is the well-spoken rebel daughter of an upper-middle-class family. Her intelligence and determination unsettled many men in the theoretically progressive scene and her accent and manners bothered many of the radicals.

By the autumn, Release had a twenty-four-hour answering service for legal help and was supplying lawyers for busted dopers all over London. Caroline met with Home Office officials and demanded that young people be permitted their statutory phone call and be given legal aid forms. These approaches were far too straightforward and effective not to annoy our self-styled anarchists. A group led by Mick Farren stormed the Release offices and threw out Caroline and her staff, but the complexity of Release's tasks so daunted the rabble that they abandoned their mission after a few days. Caroline calmly reclaimed the office and she and her staff carried on as before.

For UFO, September was a downward spiral of bad bookings, smaller and smaller crowds, higher and higher costs. At the end of the month I decided to quit while we were ahead. My only consolation was that enough money had been put aside so that Hoppy could escape to Morocco with his loyal girlfriend when he got out.

Weekends at the Roundhouse were quickly picked up by two rival promoters: Blackhill Enterprises (Floyd managers Jenner and King) and Middle Earth, run by the pleasant if slightly vague Dave Howson. They alternated while Centre 42 weighed up the virtues of granting one or the other a permanent franchise. Initially, both contributed to Release's upkeep. Blackhill, however, was allied with Farren, and withdrew their support after the humiliation of the abortive coup. Release's earnings from the Roundhouse door were halved and finances were precarious.

The following summer, the well-connected Blackhill were chosen to present the UK debut of The Doors and Jefferson Airplane on a Roundhouse double-bill. Whoever promoted this show was likely to generate enough cash and momentum to control the future of the Roundhouse. I pleaded with Jenner and King for an end to the feud that was starving Release of funds but they were unyielding.

What happened next gave me, I confess, immense pleasure. I called Paul Rothchild, who put me in touch with the Doors' management, then rang Bill Graham's office, who put in a word with the Airplane. If these groups wanted the cachet of an 'underground' appearance in London, they needed to learn about the local struggles in which they were pawns. Within days, the British agent summoned Granada TV (who were filming the Doors), Blackhill and the Institute of Contemporary Arts (friends of Blackhill's who were providing 'cultural' cover for the work permits). As all watched in horror, the agent crossed Blackhill's name off the contract and wrote Middle Earth's in its place. Caroline and I took it over to the late-sleeping Howson and shook him gently awake with the news that he was promoting the Doors and the Airplane; we got him to up his Release donations from 5 to 10 per cent of the door as well. In the years to come, Middle Earth would be a cornerstone of support for Release. It was, I felt, my finest *éminence grise* moment.

During these years, Release quietly gave George Harrison and Mick Jagger legal assistance on drug busts. In gratitude, Harrison summoned Caroline to the Apple offices in 1969, shook her hand and gave her an envelope which, when she ripped it open after leaving the office, was found to contain a cheque for £5,000. Thirty years later, Jonathan Green's book about the sixties, *All Dressed Up*, asserted that both stars' donations had been inspired by blow-jobs provided by employees of Release. The memory of the years of hard work by the mostly female staff and the tears of joy shed on the pavement outside Apple that day fuelled Caroline's resolve. She sued Green and Random House, fired a solicitor who suggested an inadequate settlement, fought off foreclosure on her flat over legal bills, argued the case herself in the High Court and won a stunning victory that involved retraction, apology and substantial damages.

Beneath the surface, the progressive sixties hid all manner of unpleasantness: sexism, reaction, racism and factionalism. It wasn't surprising, really. The idea that drugs, sex and music could transform the world was always a pretty naïve dream. As the counter-culture's effect on the mainstream grew, its own values and aesthetics decayed. The political setbacks of the coming years grabbed the headlines while the dilution of ideals happened more quietly, but nonetheless vividly for those who noticed.

For me, the closure of UFO was sad but liberating. Pink Floyd were now a successful touring rock attraction, Arthur Brown was in the charts, the Soft Machine and The People Blues Band were touring America with Hendrix and 'A Whiter Shade Of Pale' had become one of the biggest singles of all time. It was time to get down to business. Almost unnoticed among the support acts that summer, I had found Witchseason's next group. While they wouldn't make my fortune, they did provide the foundation for a great deal of my work over the next fifteen years. I thought I had seen the last of folk-rock but it came back to get me in the end.

chapter 20

ONE EVENING IN THE EVENTFUL month of June '67, I went to hear Sandy Denny at Les Cousins in Soho. I still wasn't convinced: she insisted on performing songs by her American ex-boyfriend Jackson C. Frank and other undistinguished singer-songwriters. Her voice often seemed more big than expressive. She was entertaining company, though; her laugh was the loudest thing in a room. She had a way of jerking her cigarette to her mouth so that the ash scattered everywhere and she was very adept at knocking over drinks. I once saw her upend three mugs on one trip to the kitchen to freshen up the teapot. When playing the guitar, she would stare at her left hand, keeping a wary eye out for the inevitable slip. It was only when she sat at the piano, her first instrument, that she became serene and graceful, the dignified lady she longed to be. She was clever and quick and a brutal punisher of fools, but she wore her neediness and her heart very much on her sleeve. The only redeeming feature of the *Bridget Jones' Diary* film for me was Renée Zellweger's uncanny replication of many of Sandy's insecure gestures.

We talked music all that first night; dawn found us listening to a tape of Radio Luxembourg's sneak preview of *Sgt Pepper* at her parents' home in Wimbledon. The ferocious impact of the Beatles' masterpiece was magnified by the hushed and surreptitious circumstances as we huddled by the speakers so as not to disturb the sleeping household. Sandy was tired of slogging around the folk clubs with her guitar: she wanted to sing in front of a band. 'A Day In The Life' and 'Lucy In The Sky' made solo folk singing seem a very limited palette. She had made an LP with the Strawbs, but wasn't convinced they were the right band for her. When she gave me an advance copy, I was startled by how great her voice sounded on record. The best track was her own first stab at songwriting, 'Who Knows Where The Time Goes', which Judy Collins was about to make the title song of her new LP. (Composer royalties from this song would, over the years, prove to be the most reliable source of income she ever had.) I was impressed and fascinated, but when I found the perfect band for her, I failed to make the connection.

Fairport Convention made their UFO debut a month later. They were well-behaved middle-class kids from Muswell Hill whose taste in American singer-songwriters was better than Sandy's, but not enough to keep them from performing hack-work like Eric Andersen's 'Thirsty Boots'. Towards the end of their set I winced as they took up the challenge of Butterfield's 'East-West'. But when Richard Thompson embarked on his version of the Bloomfield guitar solo, I was stunned. This seventeen-year-old was extraordinary! After their set, I stormed into the dressing room, Mike Jeffreys-like, and offered them a deal.

There was a curious inevitability about it. Here was a group of well-educated kids approaching rock'n'roll as if they were doing a doctoral thesis. They idolized the Kweskin Jug Band, listened to Django Reinhardt and Duke Ellington and played the kind of American folk-rock I had dreamed of creating three years earlier with Sebastian and

Yanovsky. I had reached for the glamour of The Move and Pink Floyd and ended up with an English version of myself.

Richard was the key. He can imitate almost any style, and often does, but is instantly identifiable. In his playing you can hear his evocation of the Scottish piper's drone and the melody of the chanter as well as echoes of Barney Kessell's and James Burton's guitars and Jerry Lee Lewis's piano. But no blues clichés: like Bix Beiderbecke or Django Reinhardt, he is unapologetic about his whiteness.

Fairport already had a girl singer. Her name was Judy Dyble and her voice was tentative, but she was Thompson's girlfriend and bullying them into sacking her didn't seem like the right way to start off a relationship. Moreover, although Fairport came from the same kind of suburban grammar-school background as Sandy, their temperaments could not have been more different. It wasn't that Fairport never drank, for example; they just never seemed to get drunk. Hard as it was to keep Sandy quiet, it was sometimes difficult to get them to say anything at all. You heard more four-letter words in a five-minute conversation with her than in a month of Fairport rehearsals. Sandy and Richard, two of the greatest talents I ever worked with, made their way slowly towards each other without any help from me.

We addressed Fairport's vocal weaknesses by adding Ian Matthews, a former professional footballer from Scunthorpe with a pop tenor voice. He and Judy shared vocal duties on the eponymous first LP, which included a couple of unreleased Joni Mitchell songs. When Richard and Judy Dyble split up, I thought of proposing a change, but was afraid Sandy would eat them for breakfast and spit them out for lunch.

In the end, they approached her while I was in New York. I rushed round to a rehearsal the minute I got back to find Sandy as docile as could be. She was in awe of Richard and overjoyed to have a great band behind her. Inspired by her, Richard started writing songs. The second LP, *What We Did On Our Holidays*, was streets ahead of the first. Sandy's voice used to overwhelm her guitar but it fitted perfectly with what was becoming a powerful band. Simon Nicol evolved into the most solid, sympathetic rhythm guitarist I ever worked with. Ashley Hutchings, always an elegant bass player, developed a style that would influence legions of taste-free heavy-metal musicians. Martin Lamble was a fluid, jazzy drummer who gave Fairport a distinctive swing. He was also the fashion plate of the group, turning out in velvet jackets and a knotted scarf when the rest seemed sewn into their jeans.

By the time we began work on *Unhalfbricking*, they bore little resemblance to the group I had heard at UFO. The songs Sandy and Richard were writing no longer suited Ian's vocal style, so the tradition was established: no two consecutive Fairport Convention records have ever featured the same line-up. Ian had always been somewhat of an outsider, bemused by the enthusiasms of the others for jazz, blues and folk music. I imagined many post-Fairport futures for him but never the one he created for himself: making consistently high-quality recordings for more than thirty years in a folk-rock style, and having a bigger hit with Joni Mitchell's 'Woodstock' than anything Fairport ever managed.

As the album took shape, I got more and more excited. Sandy's 'Autopsy' and Richard's 'Genesis Hall' were mature compositions that showed they could fulfil all the ambitions I had for them. During a break in recording, they summoned me to a gig in Bristol to hear two new songs. First a French version of Dylan's 'If You Gotta Go, Go Now' performed Cajun-style, then a traditional ballad Sandy had taught them called 'A Sailor's Life'. The first became their only hit single, the second turned English folk music on its head. The implications of their version of this old ballad have reverberated far and wide. A member of Los Lobos told a friend of mine that they had been just another rock band from East LA until 'A Sailor's Life' challenged them to find in their own Mexican traditions something as rich as Fairport had found in their English ones. Many bands around the world have begun to look to their own culture when they come up against the limitations of the Anglo-American 'rock' model. The map for such journeys leads back to that night in Bristol. And when Fairport were themselves in need of inspiration at a time of trauma and tragedy, they would find it in the same place.

Martin created the Cajun washboard sound for 'Si Tu Dois Partir' by stacking some plastic Eames chairs and running his drumsticks along them. The percussion break was supposed to feature an empty milk bottle lying on the topmost chair, but when the time came it fell and smashed on the floor. I signalled frantically to keep playing: the crash of broken glass was absolutely in time and worked perfectly, a good omen for the session. Guest violinist Dave Swarbrick was still getting used to playing through an amplifier when we recorded 'A Sailor's Life', but on the first take he followed Richard's solo with one of his own, pointing the way to Fairport's future. The album cover photograph was taken in the Dennys' garden with Sandy's parents in the foreground and the group spread out on the grass, dressed with scant regard for the styles of the time. With no type on the front cover, it conjures up a confident future that wouldn't necessarily be fashionable, but it would be successful. It would also never happen.

I took a copy of the finished disc to New York, where I played it to some of the Newport Folk Festival board, who assured me an invitation awaited us. I had a meeting scheduled the next day with Frank Barsalona, the most important rock agent in America, but I was awoken at dawn that morning by a call from my office. Fairport's road manager had fallen asleep on the M1 and the van had plunged off the motorway. Martin Lamble and Richard's American girlfriend, Jeannie Franklin, were dead and Richard and Simon were in hospital. When *Unhalfbricking* came out it was hailed as a great record. But by then the group was determined never again to play the repertoire they had worked on so carefully and for so long with Martin.

chapter 21

SIX YEARS AFTER *SGT PEPPER* swept across the globe, pervading the consciousness, it seemed, of everyone on the planet, LPs by Carole King and Neil Young far outsold the Beatle masterpiece. Ten years later, sales of Michael Jackson's *Thriller* would dwarf those of all Beatles records combined and he would buy up the publishing rights to Lennon & McCartney's song catalogue with his pocket change. I set up my production company in an innocent age of comparatively modest expectations.

One night in the summer of '67, I went to hear a singer named Tod Lloyd, who was opening for Paul Simon at the Troubadour in Earl's Court. After the gig, Simon told me he had made a record in New York with his friend Artie from Forest Hills and to his alarm, their producer had over-dubbed a cheesy drum track on one of the songs. Now he was being summoned back to promote its release as a single. Paul loved his flat in London and his folk club circuit and was reluctant to leave. The song was 'The Sound of Silence' and the folk clubs of England never saw him again.

Tod gave me a demo he had made with his sitar teacher. It was an interesting fusion of folk and Indian, but didn't tempt me to risk money I didn't have. Tod, however, turned out to have a small inheritance he was itching to invest in a musical enterprise. He became a partner in Witchseason and moved into my capacious flat in Bayswater (rent £15 a month). We set up office in the front room.

My trip to the USA with the Incredible String Band for the '67 Newport Folk Festival in early August led to a visit from Joni Mitchell. I promised to introduce her to music publishers who could collect her songwriting royalties on George Hamilton IV's recording of 'The Circle Game'. Her first night at the flat was brought to a spectacular end by the Flying Squad breaking down the door at 6 a.m. They had a search warrant for 'seditious literature, guns and ammunition'. Tod had come to the attention of the police by providing bail for Michael X when the Black Power leader was arrested for incitement to riot. His photograph leaving court with Michael appeared in the *Daily Telegraph* and his name must have gone into a few notebooks. We had to stand in the hallway in dressing gowns while they took the flat apart. They opted not to plant any drugs or bombs, but it was certainly an exciting welcome to London for Joni.

Among the useful things I learned during my year at Elektra was where to find the best espresso in Soho. This was not a matter of trial and error: I was led to a now defunct café off Old Compton Street by a dapper gentleman named Danny Halperin, who knew similar spots in cities all over Europe and North America. Danny, the next piece in the Witchseason jigsaw, had been designing Elektra's ads and catalogues before I arrived and continued to do so during my time there.

Halperin was from Toronto, where his father had been an official of the Canadian Communist Party and done time in jail for sedition. After the war, he organized a conference of anti-colonialist leaders from around the British Empire: Albert Luthuli from South Africa; Mohammed Ali Jinnah from what would soon be Pakistan; Kwame Nkrumah from the Gold Coast (now Ghana); and Nnamdi Azikiwe from Nigeria. Danny got to meet them all. He was working for the *Toronto Globe and Mail* a few years later when Azikiwe got in touch. Would he come to Lagos to run a pro-independence newspaper? Of course he would. He gave up his Toronto flat, broke up with his girlfriend, stopped in New York to say goodbye to his mother and boarded a Pan Am Clipper bound for the Azores, Dakar, Conakry, Monrovia, Accra and Lagos (no long-haul jets in those days). The plane taxied, but did not take off. A couple of brown-suited men got on and asked to have a word in private with Danny.

'You don't really want to go to Lagos, do you, Mr Halperin?'

'Of course I do.'

'No, Mr Halperin, I don't think you do, really. It would be a big mistake.'

'It would be an even bigger mistake if I didn't. I've signed a contract, given up my flat, broken up with my girlfriend and said goodbye to my mother.'

'But if you go, you'll end up in jail like your father.'

'That's OK, my contract says I get paid double for any time spent in prison.'

Despite what Danny might or might not wish to do, they insisted, he was not going to Lagos to run a newspaper. They had promised their pals in the British Colonial Office and must keep their word. When he threatened to go to friends on the *New York Times* and raise an almighty fuss, they tried another tack.

'Mr Halperin, if you could work on any newspaper in any city in the world, which one would you choose?'

'I suppose, in an ideal world, I would live on the Left Bank and write about jazz for the Paris edition of the *New York Herald Tribune*.'

One of the brown-suits left the windowless office at Idlewild airport and made some calls. They waited. Someone called back. A brown-suit went away and returned with a first-class ticket on Pan Am's next flight to Paris. The following week Danny started work at the *Herald Tribune*. That was his story, anyway, and he told it well.

Over the years, I met various members of Danny's *karass*. I could always identify them by their old-fashioned hipster jargon: 'Listen, baby, you dig?' I had only to hear that nasal urban drawl and the quaintly out-of-date beatnik vocabulary and I would ask, 'Do you know Danny Halperin, by any chance?' And Alan Douglas, for example, the man who produced Jimi Hendrix's last recording sessions, or Marvin Worth, who used to manage Lenny Bruce, would say, 'Danny? Of course I know Danny, man! We used to snort coke together in Paris in the fifties with Charlie Parker/Django Reinhardt/Bud Powell.'

Danny was of medium height, with olive skin and a nearly hairless battering ram of a head. His sensitive artist's eyes were situated uneasily in a face dominated by a jutting jaw and defiant lower lip. He strode briskly around Soho, cashmere coat over his shoulders, his impeccable footwear skipping carefully over puddles, trash and dog-dirt. He had a way of shooting his cuffs and rotating his neck at the same time that you only see in '50s *film noir* (like George C. Scott in *The Hustler*). He smoked Gitanes incessantly and his drugs were of the highest quality. When he took his leave, he would pat you on the cheek, saying, 'Be good now, baby, see you tomorrow.'

Danny fulfilled his graphic design contract for a pharmaceutical company with a minimum of effort, leaving him free to design jazz LP covers and organize advertising for Blue Note and Elektra. He worked out of the Track Records office in Old Compton Street where a member of his *kerass* was a silent partner (with far deeper pockets than Tod's). Pete Kamron managed the Modern Jazz Quartet and had done very well when there was money to be made in jazz. He also looked after Terence Stamp, the dream boy of British cinema, dabbled in film finance and had an elegant Knightsbridge flat. He was an impressive *éminence grise*.

Danny introduced me to Terence's brother Chris and the other Track partner, Kit Lambert. Chris Stamp was cockney and sardonic and cut quickly to the chase, as we say in the future. Kit was the tortured gay son of '30s composer Constant Lambert: brilliant, alcoholic, mercurial, original, tragic, and there have been entire books written about him so I won't go on. With Kamron's backing they created a brilliant machine for making The Who international superstars. They masterminded *Tommy* – the LP, the tour and the film – but could not survive success. Chris now lives quietly on Long Island while Kit died, raving and addicted, in 1981.

They loved the UFO posters and thought there was money in them. They were confident that their distribution deal with Polydor could be expanded to include selling them in record stores the world over. They also liked Fairport Convention and they seemed to like me. They were expanding and needed to reclaim Danny's office space, so in an adroit shuffle they advanced me some of Polydor's money for posters and folk-rock. Witchseason spent it on an office in Charlotte Street and Danny took over the back room to run a graphics business.

It seemed like an elegant parlay of mutual interests, but in the wake of The Who's triumph at Monterey, the release of a Fairport Convention single was an obscure footnote. Polydor, moreover, was perplexed by the notion of distributing something that didn't come in a 12″ x 12″ cardboard sleeve. Kit and Chris disappeared off to the

Mexican jungles to take peyote and mushrooms in celebration of their American triumph and could not be reached for a month. I folded the poster enterprise and moved Fairport over to Schmolzi's Polydor label for the album release. Horst wouldn't give me my own label, as he had with Kit and Chris and Robert Stigwood, but he did grant me our witch-on-a-broomstick logo beside Polydor's, control over marketing and promotion, generous budgets and plenty of leeway in signing artists. All seemed well with the world: UFO had hardly bitten the dust and I had a West End office and a production deal with a major label.

But one day there was a tug on the line and Horst was reeled in back to Polydor HQ in Hamburg. He had seized 12 per cent of the UK domestic market from a standing start and signed hugely profitable artists in his two London years, but perhaps he was enjoying the late nights too much. Even more un-German, he was spending the profits on lavish promotions and new deals like mine. It was time for more sober hands to hold the sterling cheque book and attempt the age-old (and now ubiquitous) corporate fantasy of cutting costs while holding on to the income. When Horst left they were paying my studio bills and giving me overhead money every month, but the contract had yet to be signed.

I was halfway into the second Fairport LP when they presented me with the final draft. Gone were the freedoms Horst had promised: in a traditionally structured document, rights adhered to the larger company, obligations to the smaller. I decided to go to Hamburg and plead my case with Horst as I was getting nowhere with the bureaucrats who had replaced him. I knew it was probably hopeless, but I had an ulterior motive. The previous summer, I had met a German couple at a Legalize Marijuana rally in Hyde Park. Uwe Nettelbeck was a journalist writing a piece about the London Underground scene for *Die Zeit*. His wife Petra, in the wheelchair she had occupied since breaking her back in a fall seven years earlier, was a stunning beauty. I invited them out for an evening and we went to the Speakeasy, the after-hours basement club where *le tout pop London* hung out. At the top of the stairs Uwe scooped up his wife and handed her to me saying, 'You take Petra, I'll take the chair.'

Between top and bottom steps, I became completely entranced. It seems I was not alone. After her injury, she became a presenter on German television, guiding viewers through the evening, reading news bulletins and introducing shows. The whole country fell in love with her during her two years in that role. Then she met and married Uwe, quit television, became a photographer and had two daughters. I found the couple fascinating and decided to take them up on an offhand invitation to visit.

I brought some rough mixes to play Horst, hoping it would inspire him to intercede with his masters. There were a few tracks showing what a different proposition Fairport were with Sandy Denny and some songs by an unknown songwriter I had just started to record. Fairport had taken part in an anti-Vietnam War marathon held at the Roundhouse that winter. Ashley Hutchings's decision to stick around after the others left reverberates to this day: at three in the morning he heard a young singer named Nick Drake. Ashley handed me his phone number a few days later, saying, 'You ought to call this guy, he's pretty interesting.'

Horst took me to lunch by the lake and afterwards we listened to the tape. He loved the Fairport tracks and was impressed by Nick, but he was powerless to help me. I looked at my watch and told him I had to be downstairs in ten minutes to meet my ride.

'Don't be stupid. Sit down, have a drink, they can call up.' I got up and shook his hand. I had to be downstairs. He demanded to know why.

'Because the person picking me up can't get out of the car to come to reception to ask for me.'

'What are you talking about? Who do you know in Hamburg that can't get out of an automobile?'

For Horst, fate was beckoning. When I told him who was picking me up in her hand-controlled VW, he was astounded. *'You know Petra Nettelbeck!?'* When I introduced them in the front driveway, Horst was like a shy teenager. He invited her and Uwe to be his guests in a box at a Frank Zappa concert the following week. I spent a great weekend, smoking powerful dope on the grass-turfed roof of their self-designed house in Lüneburg Heath, enjoying the first of a four-decades-long parade of remarkable meals at their table and meeting their clever and beautiful daughters.

For Horst, the Nettelbecks provided him with an entrée to the kind of Bohemian world he had been missing since his exile from London. Uwe and Petra were at the centre of radical life in Germany, politically and culturally. He showered them with invitations and visited them in the country. Soon Uwe had a production deal with Polydor. Uwe made wonderful records and played the game with the savoir-faire of an old hand, recording the groups that would forever change the image of German music: Faust and Slapp Happy. Both are written about endlessly in collectors' and specialist magazines, their recordings (particularly the transparent vinyl of Faust's first) treated like gold dust. But neither group sold. Horst continued to throw money at them until Polydor management did their sums. Less than three years after I introduced him to Petra, he was out of a job.

It is a story of *kismet*, perhaps, but not a sad one. Horst set up an independent label and acquired the rights to a singer named Roger Whittaker, who proceeded to sell millions of LPs during the 1970s. Jimi Hendrix it wasn't –

more like Burl Ives – but it made Horst his fortune.

When I got back to London, *my* moment of *kismet* awaited me. Mixing *What We Did On Our Holidays*, I tried to keep my mind on the music and not worry about the deal, but it wasn't easy. I hated the new Polydor and the contract they were forcing on me. The unrecouped advances totalled over £10,000, a huge sum in 1968, particularly if you weren't having hits. As I arrived for a session at Morgan Studios one day, I brushed past someone leaving as I was coming in. We both stopped: 'Aren't you Joe Boyd?' 'Aren't you Chris Blackwell?'

Blackwell is the only child of Blanche Pereira, heiress to a palm oil fortune and an estate on the north coast of Jamaica, just down the hill from Noël Coward's Firefly and along from Ian Fleming's Goldeneye. Local lore has it that she was a staunch friend of the former and a lover of the latter. When I stayed at Goldeneye in the early '80s, my girlfriend and I were invited round for tea. As we arrived, we could see servants manicuring the lawn and watering the garden. Inside, every conch shell on every marble table-top held a fresh orchid.

Blanche received us in her bedroom as she was feeling under the weather. Tea was brought on a silver tray while she perched on the four-poster bed, observing us as we surveyed the room. It was full of paintings and photos, many of Chris. She saw me looking at a large photo of a dashing young man in uniform with a Sam Browne belt and the visor cap of a junior officer.

'Chris's father. Terribly handsome man, don't you think?'

Their marriage did not last long but it produced a son of universal appeal. According to tribal custom, Blanche's Portuguese-Jewish heritage makes Blackwell a Jew. Blond and handsome, he moves effortlessly through a world dominated by Middle-Eastern-descended merchants like a golden WASP, seemingly above such vulgar concepts as 'trade'. Ahmet Ertegun, Turkish boss of Atlantic Records, dubbed him 'the baby-faced killer'.

After an idyllic childhood in colonial Jamaica, he was sent to Harrow. Passing up university, he settled in London and began to dabble: a bit of real estate and a wholesale appliance business whose clients along the Harrow Road had many West Indian customers. Hearing that he was headed home for a visit, one suggested he bring back some local records as the scarcity of Jamaican music in London made it hard to sell phonographs. Chris returned with a trunk full of bluebeat 45s that sold out in days. On his next trip he decided to learn more about the Jamaican music business. Soon he was shuttling back and forth carrying licensed master tapes instead of vinyl. The Island label sold tens of thousands of records up and down the Harrow Road, not to mention Brixton, Handsworth, Moss Side and Toxteth.

When he started producing his own music, he came up with a track too hot for Island to handle. It was by Millie Small, a fourteen-year-old girl from Tivoli Gardens, one of the poorest slums of Kingston, and it was called 'My Boy Lollipop'. Licensed to Philips, it became an international hit and Pepsi-Cola invited Millie on a promotional tour of Africa and Latin America. Chris went along as chaperone and loved every minute. At the end of the tour, a heroine's welcome awaited Millie in Kingston. The motorcade wound its way through cheering, flag-waving crowds: this was Jamaica's first international success following independence. Finally, it reached Millie's shack in Tivoli. She jumped out of the limo and ran towards her mother with open arms. The older woman backed away fearfully from the most famous person in Jamaica and bowed low. 'Welcome home,

Miss Millie,' she said, holding out her hand.

In that instant, Chris's high opinion of himself plummeted: he felt his ambition had estranged a mother and daughter. In years to come, he would be an exceptionally protective manager, giving first Steve Winwood and then Bob Marley all the leeway they needed to live their personal lives, to follow their hearts and never be ruled by The Deal.

He signed the Spencer Davis Group and licensed them to the Philips marketing machine. When Winwood left to start Traffic, Blackwell decided the time was right for Island Records to cross the street. He had just released Traffic's 'Paper Sun', the label's first 'white' record, when our paths crossed at Morgan. He told me how much he liked Fairport Convention and chided me for not bringing them to him before going to Polydor. When I said it might not be too late, we made a date for dinner the following evening.

On the proverbial paper napkin in an Italian restaurant, we sketched out a deal. He would take over the funding of Witchseason from Polydor and I would have the freedoms Horst had promised me. We drew up the contract in full and signed it, with a clause suspending its execution until the £10,000 cashier's cheque made out to Polydor Chris had given me cleared his bank.

Polydor thought I was coming in to sign *their* contract and had a photographer on hand to record the moment for the trade press. When I told them I wasn't signing, they shooed the photographer away, tutted and cajoled, and finally got angry: 'What about the ten thousand pounds you owe us? You can't just walk away from that, you know.' That was my cue to place the anonymous bank draft on the table. Afterwards, Chris made me describe the expressions on their faces. They held out for a few days, trying to change my mind, but in the end they cashed the cheque and let me go. Fairport Convention and Nick Drake became Island artists.

The early years of Island are legendary. Successes poured out of that small office in the late sixties: Traffic, Jethro Tull, Cat Stevens, Spooky Tooth, Free, King Crimson. My roster of Fairport, Nick, Sandy Denny, and John and Beverley Martyn made only a modest contribution to their bottom line, but our critical acclaim added to their reputation as the hottest label in Britain.

Chris had purchased an old church near Portobello Road and built a couple of studios in it. One end held the label's offices while tucked up in the opposite corner was Chris's flat. The Island office was a room dominated by a large circular table with all the employees sat round it. Typewriters and a conference area were a few paces away. The energy was intense, the communication unparalleled: e-mails can't begin to match overhearing every conversation and discussing events as they happen. Chris's chair was the same size as everyone else's. Island became the first British label to have its own hip image. Pink-label pressings from the late sixties are among the most sought-after vinyl treasures today on eBay.

Chris's style hasn't changed over the years. He always wears tennis shoes and jeans, never a tie, rarely a jacket. He has the air of a hip plantation owner who never raises his voice and always thinks laterally. We loved haggling, either with each other or teaming up against a third party. Whenever our deal was renegotiated, we came up with more and more complicated financial structures. At the end of one particularly arduous session, having got his way, Chris turned to me and said: 'Now how much do you really need?' and wrote me out a cheque for far more than called for in the contract.

One day John Gaydon and David Enthoven (managers of King Crimson) and I spent a Sunday with Chris at a house in the country. We held a mini-Olympics of back-yard sports and indoor games: croquet, ping-pong, pool, badminton and backgammon. Proceeding from game to game and always playing hard, close-fought contests, there was never any variety in the result. Chris's will to win is the fiercest I have ever encountered.

Witchseason started a booking agency and a publishing company and slowly took on more staff to deal with the growing business. It was a reasonably efficient, bustling office staffed by people who loved the music and worked hard. Marian Bain, my assistant, held it all together. But we never sold enough records. As long as Island continued to advance money, we were OK, but one of two possibilities was always around the corner: a hit, or a day of reckoning. No prizes for guessing which arrived first.

chapter 22

FOREBODINGS WERE VERY much in the background with the Incredible String Band. Everything unfolded as I imagined it: no long years of building up a following through club tours; no puzzled critics or indifferent audiences. I bypassed the folk scene and booked them into UFO and venues like the Speakeasy and the Sunday concerts at the Savile Theatre with Pink Floyd. I hired 'The Fool' – Simon and Marijke Posthuma – to design the cover of *The 5000 Spirits Or The Layers Of The Onion*. (Their lurid psychedelic style provided the huge mural for the Beatles' Apple shop in Baker Street as well as the paint-job on John Lennon's Bentley.) Personally, I found their style auto-parodic, but I knew it would send the right signal. When John Peel started playing a track every night on his *Perfumed Garden* pirate radio show, we were off and running.

I sent a copy to the Newport Folk Festival committee, who immediately invited them to the 1967 New Folks concert along with Joni Mitchell and Leonard Cohen. The Americans regarded them with amazement. Joni was particularly impressed: the four of us sat under a tree one evening while they swapped songs. She had yet to make her first record, but I felt I was in the presence of three timeless talents.

When the third LP, *The Hangman's Beautiful Daughter*, was finished in early 1968, I thought it was the best thing I had produced. I persuaded Roy Guest to book the Royal Festival Hall, Birmingham Town Hall, Manchester Free Trade Hall and the Liverpool Philharmonic. He thought I was mad, but the tour began a few weeks after the release of the LP and most of the halls sold out. Watching the audiences enter those staid bastions of classical music reminded me of the early UFO audiences coming down the stairs at the Blarney Club a year before. They were delighted with themselves: freaks in the provinces didn't realize they were so numerous.

I flew to San Francisco that spring to see Bill Graham and secure an opening spot with Jefferson Airplane at Fillmore West. Within six months, we were selling out our own concerts there as well as at Graham's Fillmore East in New York. *5,000 Spirits* sold ten times what the first LP had and *The Hangman's Beautiful Daughter* did even better, making the Top Five in the UK and the US Top Thirty. In London they played the Albert Hall, creating a dreamy, unworldly atmosphere in the stately old rotunda. Girls placed home-baked cakes and other offerings on the stage before the concert. I remember looking smugly down on the packed hall and marvelling that I had been the only one to imagine this unlikely triumph: even Mike and Robin thought I was crazy when I told them how successful they would be.

When the Rolling Stones started their own label, they sent a limousine round to try to woo them away from me and Elektra. Two of the world's greatest songwriters, the Brazilian Caetano Veloso and Silvio Rodriguez from Cuba, have told me how inspirational the ISB were to them. Rodriguez decided to become a songwriter while recovering from a bullet wound in a Cuban military hospital in the Angolan jungle and listening to a bootleg cassette of *5,000*

Spirits. Paul McCartney selected *Hangman* as 'the best album of 1968'.

Younger readers may find all this hard to believe. History has deemed the ISB terminally unhip, forever identified with an incense-drenched, tripped-out folkiness. The Beatles may have worn flowers for a brief interlude, but they are usually recalled either in early mop-top guise or the sober-suited *Let It Be* period. Stones fans give *Satanic Majesties* a wide berth. Mike and Robin represent aspects of the sixties its survivors find most embarrassing. Seeing this in my crystal ball in 1968 would have shocked me, but in truth, the seeds of their decline were planted early.

Mike and Robin were Clive's friends rather than each other's. Without him as a buffer, they developed a robust dislike for one another. Fortunately, the quality and quantity of their songwriting were roughly equal. Neither would agree to the inclusion of a new song by the other unless he could impose himself on it by arranging the instruments and working out all the harmonies. They also tended to avoid confrontation, making it hard to reach decisions. I would have to ring them both, cajoling them into a consensus – once they got telephones, that is. In the early days, they would phone the office and I would hear the clunk of pennies dropping to the bottom of ancient Scottish callboxes.

Like many rivalries at close quarters, theirs was further complicated by a girl. In this case it was Robin's girlfriend, Christina 'Licorice' McKechnie. Initially, I sized her up as a temporary passenger – how wrong could I be? She had a sweet small face marred by a chipped front tooth she never sought to repair. Her dark hair hung down lank and uncombed. She wore wool or corduroy skirts so carelessly that her aversion to underwear became obvious. At first I had only the vaguest notion of her personality as she rarely spoke and when she did it was in a squeaky voice with the thickest of Scots accents. When she began attending recording sessions and coming along on tours, however, it became apparent that Robin was under her thumb more than vice versa. She could alter the direction of a discussion with a steely glance or a murmur.

We used the new eight-track tape machines during the recording of *Hangman*, so the possibilities for over-dubs were doubled. Robin liked to inject Licorice's tiny dog-whistle voice at certain points; she also proved useful keeping time on hand drums and finger cymbals. Robin began to mutter about the possibility of including these embellishments in live shows.

On a rare excursion to London without Licorice, Robin turned up at my flat with a girl they had encountered after a concert at York University. In the middle of the night she left Robin's sleeping bag – 'I realized I was in the wrong bed' – crawled in with Mike and stayed with him for the next three years. Rose Simpson was – and still is – as bright, cheerful and outgoing as Licorice was dour and secretive. Her laughter is as hearty as Mike's and the pair were a delight to be around. She was further unlike the other three in that she *wasnae Sco'ish*! We hit it off immediately and I began to rely on her to inject clarity into discussions that took place out of my presence. She and Licorice were like a dog and a cat living in the same house: they ignored each other bar the occasional low growl or hiss. The day Robin proposed that Licorice join the group, Mike went out and bought Rose an electric bass. 'Learn this,' he said, 'you're in the group now, too.'

One of the most remarkable acts of pure will I have ever witnessed was Rose's evolution into the ISB's bass player. She has no natural rhythm or aptitude for music; her voice is tuneless, with no sense of pitch. Licorice was far more musical but could no more have learned to play the bass than fly to the moon. Mike would work out the parts and Rose, her lower lip firmly clasped between her teeth, would practise them. She memorized not just notes, but phrasing and feel. Later, when Mike was making a solo LP and Steve Winwood came to play organ on a track, he watched in amazement as she played an unusual and tricky part perfectly, take after take, as the guest musicians rehearsed the song in the studio. Steve rang me the next day about having her play on a track of his; knowing she could never manage it, she asked me to tell him she was unavailable.

On stage, Licorice had her virtues as an enigmatic figure, switching from one percussion instrument to another and singing weird but effective harmonies. Rose just grinned and glowed and audiences adored her. Shows now had the air of a family gathering. Musically, however, it was the beginning of the decline. Liccy and Rose were little more than extensions of the wills of two extraordinarily talented people. The first recording with the girls' full participation, *Wee Tam & The Big Huge*, lacked the wall-to-wall richness of earlier LPs. It's a shame the girls were on board for the first extended American tour: outside Newport, US audiences never got a chance to see the duo at its undiluted best.

Shortly after the girls joined, I accompanied the group on a Swedish tour. The final concert was in Lund, a university town near the southern tip of the country. The following morning we took the tram from Malmö down the coast to the end of the line. We got off in front of a huge old wooden hotel on the point looking south towards East Germany. It had once been a fashionable tourist destination but was now eerily empty except for two rooms on the fourth floor where the new owner, the Maharishi Mahesh Yogi, was staying with one of his aides. Now that the whole world was getting high, Robin and Mike were plotting their next spiritual move. The five of us grouped ourselves around a bed where the tiny guru was perched dressed in a white dhoti that seemed an extension of the bed sheets. Mike and Robin had been to Krishnamurti's lectures, studied Hinduism and Buddhism and were eager to discuss meditation. But the Yogi had no interest in oriental philosophy: meditation, he said, was only of value when the mantra had been given personally by him or one of his cohorts, and that meant joining the organization and paying the fees.

It puzzled me that they left the hotel that day so disillusioned yet a few months later were ready to sign on for something far more businesslike and formularized. The Maharishi wasted no tears on his failure to convert the String Band. Within a few months of our meeting, he was welcoming the Beatles to his ashram in India.

As their popularity continued to grow, the rituals of an ISB concert were celebrated at every stop: the long-haired girls in flowered dresses, the men in velvet or oriental finery, the aroma of incense, the home-made gifts lining the apron of the stage. The crowds knew the songs and joined in on familiar choruses such as that on 'You Get Brighter Every Day' (although to their credit, Mike and Robin never encouraged sing-alongs). The pair had lost some of their amateur spontaneity and could now orchestrate the sweeping waves of affection that passed back and forth between stage and auditorium with professional ease.

In November '68, they played to a sold-out Fillmore East for the third time in less than a year. I had an early morning flight to LA and a late date and the tour manager had other tasks so I was anxious to see the group sorted out as quickly as possible after the show. I knew a nice vegetarian place called the Paradox a few blocks from the hall. While they chatted to fans and signed autographs, I ran down the street to hold a table.

When I entered the restaurant, I was surprised to see David Simons greeting guests and snapping his fingers at waitresses. I knew him from Cambridge, where he had been Jim Kweskin's court jester. For a year or so he became a member of the Jug Band, adding some wacky vocals on old ragtime tunes and a bit of earnest harmonica. He did a nice line in pseudonyms, appearing on one Jug Band LP as 'Rex Rakish' and on another as 'Hugh Bialy'. I ran into him in Greenwich Village in 1965 during the folk-rock supergroup period and he told me he was forming a band called Wolfgang and the Wolf Gang. I had heard nothing of him in four years.

When the group arrived, David ushered us to a large corner table. After they ordered, I told them the saga of David Simons: the deals, the names (Mike found 'Wolfgang and the Wolf Gang' hilarious), the shrugs from old Cambridge friends if I enquired about his whereabouts. The kid I knew in Harvard Square was never on time for anything, dressed like a bum, and never looked anyone in the eye. What a contrast to the bright-eyed, super-efficient, highly energetic maître d' who had just seated us! They listened, gripped by this tale of transformation in ways I failed to comprehend.

In years to come I often pondered this moment when, despite the girl waiting at the bar of Max's Kansas City, I couldn't resist the sound of my own voice. Fate feeds off such egotistic impulses. I told them to have a good time and I would see them when I returned from California. By the time I met up with them next, Simons had enrolled them all as Scientologists.

chapter 23

'UH, HELLO?' THE VOICE ON the other end of the line was low and soft, almost embarrassed. In the years to come, I would get used to Nick Drake's way of answering the telephone as if it had never rung before. When I told him why I was calling, he was surprised. 'Oh, OK, uh, I'll bring it in tomorrow.' He appeared at my office the next morning in a black wool overcoat stained with cigarette ash. He was tall and handsome with an apologetic stoop: either he had no idea how good looking he was or was embarrassed by the fact. He handed me the tape and shuffled out the door.

When I had some peace and quiet later that winter afternoon in 1968, I put the reel-to-reel tape on the little machine in the corner of my office. The first song was not one of his best: 'I Was Made To Love Magic'. The sentimental chord at the beginning of the chorus became one of the few moments in a Nick Drake song to annoy me. But that first time, it drew me in: it was, after all, the first Nick Drake song I ever heard. Next came 'The Thoughts Of Mary Jane', then 'Time Has Told Me'. I played the tape again, then again. The clarity and strength of the talent were striking. It was like the moment I heard Robin Williamson's 'October Song' or Richard Thompson's solo at UFO, but there was something uniquely arresting in Nick's composure. The music stayed within itself, not trying to attract the listener's attention, just making itself available. His guitar technique was so clean it took a while to realize how complex it was. Influences were detectable here and there, but the heart of the music was mysteriously original.

Nick came in the next day and listened as I explained what I wanted to do. He nodded and stammered, staring down at his hands, then asked whether I minded if he smoked. I couldn't take my eyes off his hands: they were huge and stained with nicotine, the fingers strong and articulate, with long, evenly trimmed nails caked with grime. He moved them constantly as he listened to my plans for him.

My productions had until then been mostly with working groups, which meant simply recording what was already there. But Nick's compositions cried out for arrangements, an ideal setting for each song. One source of inspiration was John Simon's production of the first Leonard Cohen album. Simon had adorned the tracks with choruses, strings and other additions that set off Cohen's voice without overwhelming it or sounding cheesy. Cohen's voice was recorded close and intimate, with no shiny pop reverb. Nick hadn't heard it, but he liked the idea of strings. He described performing with a string quartet at a Cambridge May Ball, the first moment of our meeting when he became animated.

His accent was at the aristocratic end of 'received pronunciation'. Born in Burma, where his father was a doctor in the Colonial Service, he attended Marlborough and was now at Cambridge, reading English. I had met many public schoolboys (Chris Blackwell, for example) who seemed to have not an iota of doubt in their entire beings. Nick had the accent and the offhand mannerisms, but had somehow missed out on the confidence.

One evening, Nick played me all his songs. Up close, the power of his fingers was astonishing, with each note ringing out loud – almost painfully so – and clear in the small room. I had listened closely to Robin Williamson, John Martyn, Bert Jansch and John Renbourn. Half-struck strings and blurred hammerings-on were an accepted part of their sound; none could match Nick's mastery of the instrument. After finishing one song, he would retune the guitar and proceed to play something equally complex in a totally different chord shape.

Sixties London was not brimming with good arrangers. George Martin did his own. Denny Cordell and Mickie Most used John Cameron, but I felt he would have been too jazzy. I rang Peter Asher at Apple and asked him about Richard Hewson, who worked on the first James Taylor record. Peter spoke well of him and gave me his phone number. I sent him a tape of three songs and we paid him a visit. Nick looked at his shoes a great deal and muttered agreements to things I said. It must have been painful for him to go through this process, knowing Robert Kirby was back in Cambridge. But I never thought to ask who had written the arrangements for the May Ball and Nick didn't volunteer.

In those pre-computer days, there was no way to hear an arrangement before recording it. On the day of the session, Nick, engineer John Wood and I sat in the control room as the musicians rehearsed their parts, trying to imagine how they would sound with the songs. When Nick joined them in the studio, I listened as carefully to his performance as to the instruments. I needn't have bothered: Nick was perfect every time. The arrangements, on the other hand, were competent, mediocre and slightly fey, distracting from the songs rather than adding to them. After we listened back to our morning's work and I admitted it hadn't worked, Nick breathed a sigh of relief: you could see how wary he was of complaining. After a silence, he said, 'I know someone at Cambridge who might be able to do the job.' John and I looked at him. 'He's already done some arrangements for my songs. They, uh, well, they're not too bad.'

I wasn't sure what to make of Nick's suggestion. I wanted a world-class production, so the idea of using a fellow student struck me as a step backwards. Yet for the supremely cautious Nick to recommend his friend was impressive. I agreed to drive up to Cambridge the following week to meet Robert Kirby.

What can you tell about a musician from meeting him? Kirby was hearty and jolly like a young music tutor, but beneath the banter there was no hiding the deep affection he had for Nick and his music. I liked their ease together. When Robert talked about the songs, he was down to earth and practical. Encouraged, I set a date for the recording.

They started the session with a song I hadn't heard because Nick didn't play it on the guitar. As John isolated the sound of each instrument, adjusting the mic position or the equalization, I could barely contain my impatience to hear the full sextet. The individual lines were tantalizing, unusual and strong. When at last John opened all the channels and we heard Robert's full arrangement of 'Way To Blue', I almost wept with joy and relief.

We moved quickly on to 'The Thoughts Of Mary Jane' and 'Fruit Tree'. Each arrangement was devoid of clichés and affectionate towards the song, setting off Nick's voice and lyrics perfectly. The consistency of Nick's performances gave us the luxury of recording everyone together in the same room, Nick and the strings moving together under Robert's direction. John experimented with different microphones for Nick's voice, eventually settling on a Neumann U67 that brought out the depth and also captured its breathy, delicate quality.

The words to 'Fruit Tree' didn't particularly strike me that day. I took them as a gloomy romantic ode to the lives he may have read about in English class at Marlborough: poet Thomas Chatterton, for example, dead at nineteen and acclaimed decades later; Shelley, drowned in Italy at twenty-four; or maybe Buddy Holly and James Dean. How were we then to grasp the implications of his words?

Fame is but a fruit tree
So very unsound
It can never flourish
'Til its stalk is in the ground.

And then:

Safe in your place deep in the earth
That's when they'll know what you were truly worth.

These lyrics didn't seem at all prophetic that first year. Nick was shy and unsure of himself, but seemed to have plenty of friends. He travelled frequently between London and Cambridge and was pleased to be working on his record. Sometimes I ran into girls at parties who would say, 'Nick? Oh I simply adore Nick, isn't he wonderful?' One, Alice Gore, always made a point of telling me what great friends they were. Lord Harlech's daughter, later Eric Clapton's girlfriend and fellow addict in the early '70s, Alice would die of an overdose a few years after Nick's death.

We took our time finishing *Five Leaves Left*, taking stock after each session before planning the next. I had worked with Danny Thompson a few times by then. He is a large man with a formidable technique on the double bass who brings an inimitable energy to a session. His drive propels 'Three Hours' and 'Cello Song' and his no-nonsense attitude worked wonders with Nick. Most people, myself included, were too careful, wary of disturbing his silences. Danny would slap him on the back, tease him in rhyming slang, make fun of his self-effacement and generally give him a hard time. Nick would crack a hesitant smile and be relaxed and laughing by the end of the session.

Blackwell made me a present of John Martyn. He had released a couple of LPs on Island but Chris didn't really know what to do with him and thought I ought to. I admired his playing but had never been a huge fan. When John started living and performing with Beverley Kutner, an ex-Denny Cordell artist Tod Lloyd wanted to sign to Witchseason, I was stuck with him. I recorded an album with the couple in America using a New York pianist named Paul Harris as musical director. I thought Paul's style would work for 'Time Has Told Me', so when he came to London to finish John & Beverley's *Stormbringer*, I introduced him to Nick.

Paul spent hours talking to Nick, visiting him and working on 'Time Has Told Me' and 'Man In A Shed'. He kept scratching his head, as if trying to figure out what planet this kid was from. This was typical of the responses musicians had to Nick: they couldn't figure out how to categorize him. Some, like Harris, recognized the fragility of his genius and became extremely protective of him.

Richard Thompson would listen to a song of Nick's, ask to hear it again, then again, frowning in concentration, then come up with a great part. He would stand in the door of the control room listening to a playback, concentrating quizzically. Richard likes to figure out every kind of music he hears, but Nick puzzled him. Where did that *come* from?

Five Leaves Left's final piece fell into place when Kirby announced that he was not up to 'River Man'. He had tried, but just couldn't manage what he knew Nick wanted and what the song deserved. John Wood immediately suggested

Harry Robinson, aka Lord Rockingham. When rock'n'roll first invaded British television with *6.5 Special* the resident band was Lord Rockingham's Eleven. Harry had also been on the board of Island Records in the early years but had sold his shares years before. As a composer he had scored all those Hammer horror movies starring vampires-in-chief Christopher Lee and Barbara Steele. After telling us these colourful but irrelevant facts, John came to the point: as an orchestrator, Harry was a master mimic. You want Sibelius? He could give you Sibelius. Since Nick wanted 'River Man' to sound like Delius, Harry, said John, was our man.

Nick and I went to visit Robinson at his house hidden in the middle of Barnes Common, just below the tree that was to kill Marc Bolan ten years later. Having heard a tape, Harry was already intrigued when we arrived. Nick played the song through, then strummed chords as the tape played, showing Harry the textures he wanted for the string parts. I had never heard him so articulate or so demanding. Harry made notes and nodded. The result was a track which – next to the Volkswagen ad's 'Pink Moon' – is the most often played and discussed of all Nick's songs. Whenever I saw Harry in later years, he would talk about the day we recorded it, with Nick surrounded by the orchestra, playing and singing while Harry conducted – just like Nelson Riddle and Frank Sinatra.

Five Leaves Left was released in the summer of 1969. My expectations, like my production approach, had been influenced by Leonard Cohen. His first album sold over 100,000 copies in America while Cohen refused all offers to perform. But when Nick's album was released in Britain, we had no radio outlets like the American free-form FM stations that played 'Suzanne' so often. John Peel played Nick's album, but he was one of the few; Radio One was all about 'pop' in its myriad British guises, none of which bore much resemblance to Nick. And many critics were dismissive: 'an awkward mixture of folk and cocktail jazz', said *Melody Maker*.

Island had no US office in those days, so Chris and I had made deals with A&M for Fairport Convention and Warner Brothers for John & Beverley Martyn. Some American A&R men liked Nick, but none actually made an offer; they said they needed to see him perform. David Geffen loved Nick, but somehow a deal with Asylum never materialized.

That autumn saw the re-emergence of Fairport Convention and the release of *Liege and Lief*. To honour the occasion, Roy Guest booked the Royal Festival Hall and we made it a Witchseason night: John & Beverley would open, then Nick would finish the first half. Never having seen him perform in front of an audience, I was nervous; Nick remained his usual monosyllabic self. I introduced him to scattered applause. The emotion surrounding Fairport's fatal accident meant that the audience was very respectful. They listened in silence while he sang 'Three Hours', then erupted in applause. Nick looked at them suspiciously, not sure how much to smile. The silence resumed during Nick's wordless retuning. Finally, he played the opening chords of 'The Thoughts Of Mary Jane'. As each song was rewarded with huge applause, I could feel the affection surging towards the stage. When he finished, the cheering soared and I pushed him back on stage for an encore. As I stood watching from the wings, my mind was racing: *Nick can tour. He can play concerts after all. It doesn't matter that he can't talk to an audience. He'll learn how. He can have a real career. I'm not whistling in the dark, after all.*

Everyone in the Witchseason office adored Nick and was thrilled by his performance. The next morning we started booking his first British tour. Two months later he set off for a series of club and university dates around the country. I was busy in the studio but planned to see one of the shows later in the tour. When he called me from the road after the third date, his voice had the crushed quality of defeat: 'I, uh, I don't think I can do any more shows, uh, I'm sorry.' He just wanted to come home.

I spoke to the promoter of one of the shows. He said people talked a lot and when Nick started tuning between songs they talked more and bought more beer. The noise of glasses clinking and conversation became louder than Nick's music. He never said anything on stage, just tuned and sang, and when the noise became too much, looked at his shoes for a minute then got up and walked off the stage.

I felt briefly angry with Nick. *Why can't he just say something? Why can't he be more professional?* By this time he had left Cambridge and had no supporting group of friends near at hand. After the abandoned tour he retreated to his room in Hampstead. He had always smoked hashish, but that now became the pattern of his days: play guitar and smoke joints, go out for a curry when he got hungry. He came to life when we started recording the second album but between sessions he went back to his isolated existence.

I was aware of only three regular social outings. One was to Bob Squire's to play liar dice, another was home to visit his parents and the third was up the road in Hampstead to John and Beverley's. Beverley took on the role of Jewish mother, making him chicken soup, chiding him about his hair and sometimes even washing his clothes. She loved him and was tremendously kind to him. John is a complicated character who certainly admired Nick and even said that he loved him. But I doubt any guitar player could watch Nick play without envy. I joined Nick at John and Bev's for dinner sometimes and we would all get high and listen to records.

Even in these relaxed surroundings, Nick remained guarded and quiet.

Françoise Hardy, the long-haired chanteuse ruling the French charts, sent word that she was a fan. Letters and messages were exchanged about a collaboration. Nick and I travelled to Paris and climbed the ancient stairs to take tea in her top-floor flat in the Ile St-Louis. The entire time, he barely uttered a word. I think she found him too strange and nothing came of it.

Despite the lack of sales, the absence of an American deal and the failure of the tour, I couldn't wait to make another record. I looked forward to being in the studio with Nick more than with any other artist. We started creating more rhythm tracks with Nick's vocal and guitar plus electric bass and drum kit, adding an instrumentalist or an arrangement afterwards. Robert was stretching out, writing for brass as well as strings. When I heard 'Poor Boy', I thought of 'So Long, Marianne' on the Leonard Cohen album and its mocking chorus of girls' voices. When I suggested it to Nick, he looked at me for a minute, unsure how to respond, but didn't seem entirely convinced.

I was virtually living at Sound Techniques by then, with more artists joining the Witchseason roster and none being dropped. The day we recorded the track for 'Poor Boy', I had spent the morning mixing a record by the South African jazz pianist Chris McGregor. When Nick and the other musicians arrived, Chris asked whether he could stick around to listen. Chris had grown up in the Transkei bush, smoking dagga with the Xhosa boys from the village. That day he sat at the back of the control room in his dashiki and pillbox cap, stuffed his pipe full of grass and listened. After the morning mix, my ears were full of Chris's piano. When Nick, Dave Pegg and Mike Kowalski started running through the song, I turned and saw Chris grinning. I asked whether he was thinking what I was thinking. While John went to get the microphones, I buzzed down to the musicians in the studio, 'You're getting a pianist in a minute,' then introduced Nick to Chris. He had a look at the chord sheet Nick wrote out and we turned on the tape. That first-take piano solo on 'Poor Boy' is one of my favourite moments in the studio.

I had been stunned by John Cale's arrangements on Nico's *The Marble Index* and shocked that Elektra failed to pick up its option for a second LP. I convinced Warner Brothers to finance a sequel and after a week of recording in New York, Cale flew to London to help me finish off *Desertshore*. After a session one day, he put his feet up on the mixing desk, waved his arm imperially at John Wood, and said, 'Let's hear what else you guys are working on.' We played him a few things, and eventually got to Nick. Cale was amazed. 'Who the fuck *is* this guy? I have to meet him, where is he? I mean, where is he *right now*!' I rang Nick and told him that John Cale would be over in half an hour. Nick said, 'Oh, uh, OK.' I wrote out Nick's address, John grabbed it and ran down the stairs.

The next morning I had a call from Cale. 'We're going to need a pick-up for the viola, an amp, a Fender bass and bass amp, a celeste and a Hammond B-3 organ. This afternoon.' I had scheduled a mix on another project that day but Cale had decided it was time to record 'Northern Sky' and 'Fly'. They arrived together, John with a wild look in his eyes and Nick trailing behind. Despite his domineering manner, Cale was very solicitous towards Nick, who seemed to be guardedly enjoying himself: his only choice was to relax and be carried along.

Bryter Layter is one of my favourite albums, a record I can sit back and listen to without wishing to redo this or that. The playing of the rhythm sections, Robert's arrangements and the contributions of McGregor, Cale, Richard

Thompson, sax and flute man Ray Warleigh and Doris Troy and P.P. Arnold are a constant source of pleasure. John Wood never got a better sound and we mixed it over and over until we were absolutely satisfied. But when the album was finished, Nick told me he wanted to make his next record alone – no arrangements, no sidemen, nothing.

Looking back, I can see that we were all so enamoured of Nick's music we moved happily into the vacuum created by his diffidence. Nick, I think, felt left out of his own album. His refusal to include my favourite – 'Things Behind The Sun' – and his insistence on including those three instrumentals were his way of stamping his foot. His ghost is having the last laugh: the stark *Pink Moon* is his biggest selling album, while *Bryter Layter* trails in third place after *Five Leaves Left*.

Since then I have listened to more than one man's fair share of anglophone singer-songwriters. When I ran the Hannibal label, I had a box for demos marked 'WPSEs' – White People Singing in English. Many claimed Nick as their primary influence: gentle breathy vocals, sad introspective lyrics and arpeggio guitar figures. *Next!* Few bear comparison to Nick's form, much less his essence. The only ones who even slightly reminded me of Nick turned out to be unaware of him.

chapter 24

NICK SEEMED HAPPIER AT Sound Techniques than anywhere else (with the possible exception of Bob Squire's kitchen). I was pretty happy there myself. It was a former dairy – a plaster cow's head marked the doorway – on a side street off the King's Road near the World's End. Across from the studio, where Manolo Blahnik now has his flagship shoe store, was a 'provisioner', a throw-back grocery that sold potatoes, onions, carrots and canned or packaged goods. I stopped in during a recording session in 1966 and saw a blackboard listing 'fresh-cut' ham sandwiches and cheese sandwiches. Being American, I asked for a ham and cheese sandwich. The two ageing white-smocked proprietors looked at me blankly: they made ham sandwiches or cheese sandwiches, but the combination was not on the menu. I stared back in disbelief. After a brief stand-off, I ordered one of each, threw two slices of bread on the counter, stuffed the ham in alongside the cheese and walked out the door.

In talking about how we used to make records I sometimes feel like one of those ruddy, besmocked shopkeepers who refused to countenance the concept of ham *and* cheese. I have never used a drum machine, never sequenced anything, never sampled. Whenever I pass the old dairy and see the flats that have replaced the studio, I feel a wrench. It is hard to find places like Sound Techniques today. There is a small anti-digital movement, but even studios with this approach rarely have a room that sounds anywhere near as good.

When I took up my London post, Elektra was already using Sound Techniques for an instrumental series of Holzman's devising called *Signs of the Zodiac* (string players in London were better and cheaper than in New York). I had to bring a wad of cash down there one day in February 1966 to pay the musicians and started chatting with John Wood, the heavy-set engineer. We got along pretty well and I liked the feel of the place. The control room looked down on the studio from a box above one side while the offices were built over the opposite side. It looked awkward, but the differing ceiling levels meant that you had three different acoustics in the same studio; you could move things around until you found the sweet spot for an instrument or a singer.

These days most engineers confronted with a displeasing sound reach for the knobs on the console and tweak the high, mid or low frequencies. When that process is inflicted on more and more tracks of a multi-channel recording the sound passes through dozens of transistors, resulting in a narrower, more confined sound. With the added limitations of digital sound, you end up with a bright and shiny, thin and two-dimensional recording. To my ears, anyway.

When John heard a sound he didn't like, he would lift his bulky frame off the chair and lumber down the stairs, muttering all the way. I began to be able to predict whether he was going to try a different microphone, reposition the existing one or shift the offending musician to another part of the studio. When I listen to records we made together in the sixties, I can still hear the air in the studio and the full dimension of the sounds the musicians created for us. I can hear the depth of Nick Drake's breath as well as his voice, the grit in the crude strings of Robin Williamson's *gimbri* and Dave Mattacks's drum technique spread out warmly in aural Technicolor across the stereo spectrum.

John started out as an editor at Decca, taking a razor blade to recordings of operas and symphonies. When I brought the Incredible String Band into Sound Techniques, he had never heard anything like them. He took care of the sound, I looked after the musical side of things and we learned from each other. When I wanted to do something he thought unwise, he would give me a withering sneer. 'You want to *what*?!?' If I were sure of my ground, I would tell him to just do it and not give me any shit. If my resolve melted in the face of his contempt, it probably wasn't such a good idea in the first place. Professional session musicians regarded the pair of us with curiosity: the normal deference of engineer towards producer didn't seem to apply. Later, in California, when I worked with yes-men engineers, it was hard to adapt.

Most studios now have large control rooms so outboard gear can be plugged directly into the console: drum machines, electronic keyboards, sequencers, etc. Most music recorded today is created by performers – or operators – sitting beside the engineer; it passes directly on to a hard disk rather than reverberating in the air to be captured by microphones. As a result, the 'studio' room itself is often shrunk to a modest space for vocalists or single instruments. The ideal acoustic is now a dead one: digital reverb can supposedly synthesize any atmosphere from Madison Square Garden to your bathroom. In the quest for the perfect track, each part is added separately so that any mistakes can be easily corrected; inflexible rhythms are generated by a machine. Musicians in the sixties were still recording a large part of each track playing together in the same room at the same time, maintaining at least some of the excitement of a live performance, with vocals and solos usually added later. Rhythm sections breathed with the other musicians, accenting and retarding the beat as mood dictated. The acoustics of different studios varied widely, as did the styles of engineering and production. Computers theoretically let musicians and producers choose from an endless palate of varied sounds, but modern digital recordings are far more monochromatically similar to each other than were older analogue tracks.

When Fairport Convention visited Los Angeles for the first time, their ambition was to record at Gold Star, where Phil Spector built his famous 'wall of sound'. A&M, their American label, booked a day for us there and we recorded a couple of tracks. The control room still had 'rotary pots' (Bakelite dials) to calibrate the levels instead of faders. The acoustic was amazing; sounds jumped out of the speakers and off the tape. When we got back to London with our rough mixes, we listened in awe: the punch of the recording was astounding. But our Gold Star tracks were never completed and the studio was torn down soon afterwards to make room for a strip mall.

Musicians were obsessed with 'sounds' in those days. Drummers often asked John whether he had heard the latest by so-and-so and what he thought of the drum sound. When we recorded *Liege and Lief*, Dave Mattacks wanted to match Levon Helm's snare sound on The Band's *Big Pink*. Drummers usually want their snare to have a lot of 'edge' so the backbeat jumps out of the mix, but Levon had gone the other way, producing a sound that resembled an expensive cardboard box being struck with a pair of velvet slippers. John would impatiently explain that you can't just *create* sounds, you had to actually *play* like that. 'Records get the sound they deserve' was his motto. John could be infuriating, but no Witchseason musician wanted to work with anyone else. With John you knew no nasty surprises were awaiting when it came time to mix. I am a great believer in 'bad news first', and with John you got all the bad news, all the time.

When Warner Brothers asked me to produce an album with Geoff and Maria Muldaur after the Kweskin Jug Band broke up, John and I settled in at a Boston studio where aspiring comedian Martin Mull was the assistant engineer. *Pottery Pie* got some nice reviews, sold a few copies, and is immortalized as the source of the version of 'Brazil' that is repeated throughout Terry Gilliam's film. That track was recorded as guitarist Amos Garrett's departure for his flight home loomed ever closer. The more Amos pressed, the worse it got. Finally, he gave up and hailed a taxi. John pieced together one composite verse from various takes, mixed it down to stereo and copied it back to the multi-track four times for four verses. Then we added the vocals and the rest of the over-dubs. A primitive form of sampling, I suppose, but without today's computers it was certainly more of a challenge.

As we were mixing another track we found flakes of Ampex tape on the floor in front of the eight-track recorder. The tape was falling apart! There was a huge chunk missing from the vocal track and we couldn't ask Geoff to re-sing it as all the other tracks were full. John recorded a new vocal verse on a mono tape, getting it in synch with the master by listening through a set of headphones, speeding it up with his finger or slowing it down with the heel of his hand so I could insert the missing word into the mix at exactly the right spot. He ended up with blood on his shirt and the tape console but the mix sounds perfect.

As the pace of my recordings picked up during 1969 and 1970, I would block out weeks at a time in Sound Techniques, go to the office in the mornings for a couple of hours, then head to the studio, where John and I would stay until midnight. It seemed natural that when I left London for California in the early 1970s, he would take over as producer for many of the Witchseason artists. But without our 'good cop/bad cop' routine, they were left with just the latter. When other producers hired him as an engineer, they were appalled at the way he sassed them back. He produced some great records in the 1970s, including the early Squeeze albums, but eventually moved to Scotland and opened a hotel. Strong-minded artists and I periodically drag him out of retirement.

One artist relationship of John's that was never in question was with Nick. He adored John and John's wife doted on him. They would invite him out to Greenwich for a home-cooked meal when he began to look pale. John could sense when Nick was uncomfortable with something I suggested and would give me a hard time on Nick's behalf, which Nick appreciated enormously. In early 1971, after I had moved to California, he produced *Pink Moon* as starkly and simply as Nick intended.

The five years I spent making records in London saw huge leaps in technology. From the four tracks I began with, we went to eight, then sixteen, each increase doubling the tape's width. Just before I left for California came the beginning of the decline: some bright spark figured out how to squeeze twenty-four tracks on to the two-inch tape that previously held sixteen. The reduction in track width significantly degraded the sound quality. A few young engineers today realize how great two-inch sixteen-track recording sounds. The best sound of all, of course, is straight to stereo, no mixing, no over-dubbing – and no digits.

Listeners may not know *why* they like something, but it is a good bet the response to an album of 'performed' music recorded properly will be much better than to the same thing recorded in modern hi-tech over-dubbed fashion. An engineer who used to work at Sound Techniques is now the torch-bearer for traditional values. Jerry Boys runs Livingston Studios in North London and started travelling with me for world music projects in the late 1980s. When we got back from Havana in 1995 with the first Cubanismo CD, Nick Gold at World Circuit hired Jerry to go back to Cuba for a project with Ry Cooder.

I have seen people enter pubs and bars where the *Buena Vista Social Club* CD is playing and look around for the source of the music; they seem startled to be entering a three-dimensional acoustic space. There were many recordings already on the market with similar Cuban singers and material when *Buena Vista* was released. Its success is usually ascribed to Cooder, the film or the brilliant marketing, all of which were certainly relevant. But I am convinced that the sound of the record was equally if not more important. Not only is it music from another era, magically preserved in the time capsule of Castro's communism, but it was recorded using equally outdated techniques and painstakingly transferred to a digital master so that it retained as much of its analogue warmth as possible. The old Egrem studio in Havana is huge, an excellent but unforgiving room. Jerry, Cooder and Gold experimented a great deal with microphone placement. The recording captures the full sound of the three-dimensional space in which the musicians performed – live. If it had been made at one of the new digital studios in Havana, trying so hard to be 'modern' with their tiny dead recording spaces and big control rooms, I doubt very much whether anyone beyond a few thousand Latin music enthusiasts would even know it existed.

On second thoughts, make that a straight cheese sandwich, please.

chapter 25

LIAR DICE INVOLVES FIVE poker dice and any number of people around a smooth-topped table. It resembles poker but with more treachery and no betting. It helps if the players are fuelled by cups of strong English tea and good Afghan hashish. This was the regular *après-studio* entertainment for a number of Witchseason artists and its proprietors. The venue was Bob Squire's kitchen.

Hapshash & The Coloured Coat – Nigel Waymouth and Michael English – designed their posters in a small studio near Holland Park. Arriving to collect artwork for the printers one day, I noticed a green Morris Minor convertible outside the house next door with a FOR SALE, ENQUIRE WITHIN sign. As my 'sit-up-and-beg' Rover was on its last legs, I rang the doorbell. It was answered by a seedy-looking man in a string vest and braces, a roll-up dangling from his mouth, two days' growth of grey-flecked stubble and dark, thinning hair. We haggled a bit, he asked me in for a cup of tea, and the deal was done. Bob Squire had entered our lives.

Bob was East End Jewish. He had been a tout for strip clubs in the West End and vaguely knew the Kray twins. In the early sixties, he had suffered a nervous breakdown and was given a 'grace and favour' flat in Princedale Road by a villain who owed Bob an obligation – I never dared ask why. He had a wife and two kids and made ends meet buying and selling used cars, stolen goods and hashish (which he learned to love while stationed in Palestine after the war). Besides his addiction to PG Tips (loose in a strainer, boiling water poured slowly through into the cup, milk in first, three sugars), he had a prescription for three Nembutals a day.

He started looking after the transportation needs of my various groups: driving the Incredible String Band to gigs in his Ford Sedan; finding a van for Fairport Convention; having John Martyn's motor repaired. We found his company so agreeable that we would stop by late at night to smoke dope, drink tea, chew the fat, listen to music and play liar dice or *kaluki*.

The cramped space with its linoleum floor, a few wobbly chairs and a Formica-topped table became a haven for us. The pressures of coming up with new songs, finishing mixes in time for release dates or juggling cash flows seemed to evaporate in its benign confines. His musical tastes were impeccable: Jimmy Smith and Stanley Turrentine were favourites and he was always playing Dr John's *Night Tripper*. The cockney clichés flew thick and fast: 'If you drink the water you die. And if you don't drink the water you die'; 'He didn't know whether to shit or go blind'; 'Needs must when the Devil drives'. Money was counted in 'ponies', 'monkeys' and 'scores'. No one ever chickened out, he 'dropped his bottle'. Your face was your 'boat' (race); you got high on 'sausage' (and mash); and drank cups of 'Rosie' (Lee). No one was ever 'an arsehole', they were the double rhyme of 'a right Charley' (Smirk, the jockey; then Berkshire Hunt). The police didn't warrant a rhyme, they were simply 'the Old Bill' or 'the Filth'.

I came across an anthology called *The Elizabethan Underworld* with a piece by Robert Greene, a contemporary of Shakespeare's. In it he describes a con man who is forever saying, 'Needs must when the Devil drives.' Bob would dismiss an annoying person by calling them a 'shmurry abbott'. The only clue to this mysterious insult was the ancient church of St Mary Abbott's a short distance away. I felt Bob was part of a long and deep river flowing underneath all the kings, prime ministers, playwrights and poets of England.

Bob could sense what was going on in the internal politics of Witchseason before I did. With Nick, he added to Danny Thompson's aggressive cockney affection a gentle wisdom about human nature. Many people loved Nick, but Bob was able to express it in concrete terms that demanded nothing in return: hot tea, a welcoming chair, friendly and stimulating surroundings. I never saw Nick more relaxed than in Bob's kitchen and few things seemed to give him more pleasure than winning a round of liar dice. When Tod Lloyd chafed at his lack of involvement in Witchseason, Bob took him under his wing. He introduced Tod to *spielers* – illegal card games – and he was soon going to croupier school. Tod later worked in Lake Tahoe as a blackjack dealer.

I took Bob and his wife June on holiday with me to Morocco in 1969. We had a great time, apart from June's alarm at her first experience of a shower. Bob loved the markets there and was determined to return with a sword cane. He spotted an exquisite one in the souk in Marrakesh and started haggling. Bob made an offer far below that proposed by the dealer, who then came down a bit, made tea, wandered off to talk to another customer, returned with a slightly lower offer, made some more tea, changed the subject, suggested a cheaper cane, made a lower offer, etc. Bob never budged from his original price. Twice we left the shop; each time the trader tracked us down with yet a lower price. I asked Bob why he didn't play the game and make a slightly higher bid. Bob was adamant: he knew the object's worth and would get it at his price. Twenty minutes later, halfway across the market, the defeated trader, out of breath from running up and down alleyways looking for us, capitulated. Bob grinned but professed not to be surprised. I could never have matched his self-control.

Friends from Bob's other worlds would drop by and play whatever game was going that evening. One regular was a neatly dressed man involved in 'debt collection'. At the end of a particularly long and stoned evening, everyone started putting on their coats and finishing their tea. A hashish high often involves a fascination with the details of something without being clear about the big picture. I found myself intrigued with the movements of this man's hands. He was doing something very specific, but I couldn't quite grasp what it was. He was as stoned as I was, so it had the feeling of an obsessive, habitual action being repeated hypnotically. Finally, I got it: he was wiping his fingerprints off everything he had touched since he had entered the kitchen.

Jaded urbanites that we were, we would have scorned the idea that we were in need of family. Bob provided just that. When he and June moved to Worthing, I would go and visit, but something was lost for all of us; most of all, I think, for Nick.

chapter 26

CHRIS MCGREGOR WAS BORN IN rural Transkei, where his Scottish father was a missionary. Obsessed with Duke Ellington in his youth, he grew up to become South Africa's most adventurous jazz pianist. In the early sixties, he formed the multi-racial Blue Notes and they defied the apartheid regime by performing from Cape Town to Pretoria. Their tours were often nightmares of police harassment, pass law restrictions, padlocked venues and township violence. Out of that forge of hatred, repression and indifference, McGregor and his group – Dudu Pukwana, Mongezi Feza, Louis Moholo and Johnny Dyani – created music of extraordinary power and beauty.

When they were invited to the 1964 Antibes Jazz Festival, the South African authorities happily gave them passports in the hope they would never return. They stood out in Antibes both for the originality of their music and for their unrefined personalities. Unlike American jazzmen, they had no frame of reference for the sophistication of the European jazz milieu. They drew huge crowds playing every evening at the TamTam bar in Antibes, but despite numerous approaches there were no concrete offers. Promoters couldn't categorize them and their drinking and shouting at each other in Xhosa made people nervous.

They finally secured a two-week stint at Ronnie Scott's in London and got a great reception. But the British Musicians Union wouldn't allow them membership until they had lived in Britain for a year and they couldn't work until they were members. How were they to survive? Towards the end of their year of waiting, I came across them at the Old Place in Gerrard Street, where musicians earned only what was tossed into a bucket by the door. From the moment I heard their blend of Ellington, South African choral music and free jazz, I was a convert.

I got them a deal with Polydor (jacket design by Danny Halperin) and my agency took on the task of booking them. It seemed clear to me that they were playing music more vital than anything else in the British jazz scene, but that turned out to be part of the problem. In South Africa they had dreamed of an England where protests against apartheid were regular occurrences and racial equality reigned. They imagined meeting, jamming and exchanging ideas with American and British musicians. But the British, once they realized this was no two-week splash of colour that would soon return to Africa, felt threatened. Like British jazzmen, the Blue Notes had studied the classic American canon but that didn't stop them throwing their South African culture uninhibitedly into their music and in so doing making most British jazz of the period sound derivative. (Danny Thompson was the only British musician imagining a Morris dance/jazz fusion and he was keeping very quiet about it.) Visiting Americans weren't much better; most refused requests to jam – except of course the Ayler Brothers, who hung out with them for weeks.

The desperate sorrow of being such a long way from home manifested itself in behaviour that made things harder: they drank, they were late, they shouted at promoters. In the polite British scene, impatience and intemperance were not rewarded. There was no going back to South Africa: the apartheid laws had been tightened, making the touring they had done in the early sixties impossible. Chris started working as a soloist and with his multinational big band, the Brotherhood of Breath. Johnny moved to Copenhagen and took up heroin. Then Mongezi came down with tuberculosis: modern medicine is supposed to be able to treat it but couldn't cure the scrawny Monks and he died.

In the early years of the Blue Notes, Dudu Pukwana's sax playing was the show-stopper. As Chris combined the spirit of Ellington with gospel piano, Bartok, Monk and the anarchy of Cecil Taylor, so Dudu mixed township jive with Johnny Hodges and Albert Ayler. Both made music steeped in their Transkei roots. I spent evenings at Dudu's flat near King's Cross listening to his *mbqlanga* and *kwela* records; he had all of Spokes Mashyane's hits. We plotted a fusion of township jive and rock that would have pre-empted *Graceland* by fifteen years. He taught Richard Thompson and Simon Nicol to play the Zulu guitar rhythms and we recruited exiled South African stars the Manhattan Brothers for the vocals. It didn't always work, but we were getting somewhere. We decided to take the record as it was to Johannesburg. I could hear some of the music up close, he could catch up on new developments and maybe I could sell the South African rights.

South Africa in 1970 lived up to its billing. I saw white truck drivers at red lights spit on black pedestrians crossing in front of them. When I went to a movie, black passengers waiting for a bus to Soweto were still there when I came out while empty 'white' buses passed constantly. The movie was *Hurry Sundown*, about poor whites and blacks joining forces in the American South. The liberal audience hooted at the clumsy excision of an embrace between Jane Fonda and Diahann Caroll and cheered the feel-good racial-harmony ending – then sailed past the beggars outside with hardly a glance.

I couldn't get a permit to visit Soweto, but Dudu and I met every day at Dorkay House, the Black Musicians' Union headquarters, and I played snooker and ping-pong at the Bantu Men's Club next door. The suppression of the theatre and music scenes meant the club was full of unemployed actors and musicians. I will never forget being approached by men dressed in rags who would ask me whether I had seen the new Harold Pinter play at the Royal Court or heard the new Miles Davis LP.

I licensed Dudu's record to a man at Trutone Records who lectured me about Miriam Makeba, the 'traitor' who had libelled her homeland and who, one day, would 'crawl back on her knees'. The minute I had the cheque, I rented a car, picked up some friends from Dorkay House and headed for Swaziland. I couldn't take any more of Johannesburg.

Dudu and I never completed the project. In the countdown to my departure for California, I had a lot of records to finish and time was tight. He was drinking a lot and spent an evening in the studio playing the worst solos I had ever heard from him. The unfinished tapes are still lying in a vault.

Chris and his wife Maxine moved to a mill in Gascony where they raised their kids and Chris found a more welcoming atmosphere in the French jazz world. Dudu persevered in London with a *kwela*–jazz fusion group, achieving small triumphs, growing fatter and drinking more. Johnny Dyani overdosed in 1986 in Denmark. In 1988, I helped Chris make *Country Cooking*, a wonderful recording of the re-formed Brotherhood of Breath for Virgin. He fell sick soon after and the doctors found cancer throughout his body. He flew home to the Valley of the Lot and lay in his bed, surrounded by family, friends and candlelight, and died within days. Two years later, Dudu succumbed to a heart attack.

Chris was a remarkable man, with his rural Transkei accent, his sophisticated musical skills, his wry sense of humour and his mix of African and European clothes and mannerisms. He never got to America, but at least the French loved his music, and a generation of European and African jazz musicians revere him.

Of the original quintet, only Louis Moholo survives: he now runs drum clinics in the new South Africa. None of the others lived to see Mandela walk out of prison and into the President's Palace. Whatever the cause of death on the certificate, homesickness and exile were their true afflictions, and the potential cure of being welcomed by their adopted British homeland was never really on offer.

chapter 27

THE FIRST INKLING I HAD of what took place after I left the Paradox Restaurant came when the Incredible String Band's US agent telephoned me in LA. Rather than send the tour proceeds to our London bank as agreed, they wanted it all paid in cash. I got through to Licorice, who told me they needed it to pay for Scientology courses. I knew little about the cult, but what I had heard wasn't good. When I arrived back in New York I was confronted with a strangely unified foursome: they wanted the money and they wanted to give it to the Church of Scientology.

Before vacating my seat at the Paradox, I couldn't have set Simons's sales pitch up any better. The group had all been intrigued by my account of his transformation – due entirely, he said, to Scientology. He invited them to the 'Celebrity Center' the next day and they quickly signed up. Back in London, they spent weeks being 'audited'. They told me about 'going clear' as the auditing process reaches its first plateau of accomplishment. I hated the jargon, but began to notice interesting changes in their personalities. They had always avoided discussions about money; now they eagerly convened meetings about group finances. Touring schedules and recording plans were sorted out quickly and efficiently and they even took time to thank me for the job I was doing (previously unheard of). Internal jealousies seemed to evaporate overnight. They stopped taking drugs or alcohol. Everything I'd read or heard about Scientology seemed horribly obscure, self-important and dubious. But the results appeared to be a happier, saner group of people who had become a pleasure to deal with. They were coming up with good new songs and the recordings were proceeding smoothly. To my surprise, they never attempted to convert me.

I was also intrigued by their sexual evolution. Mike and Rose remained close and shared a cottage in the Row (a group of eight cottages on the Tennant estate in Scotland where they all now lived) but they seemed to sail effortlessly through other liaisons: Rose with David Crosby during a visit to San Francisco; Mike with various girls that Rose just laughed about; a brief affair between Rose and myself; and a more serious one between Mike and Suzie Watson-Taylor, the woman I had hired to deal with their day-to-day management.

But soon the new compositions began to lose their wild melodic beauty. In the studio, there were fewer moments of surprise and inspiration. Was this a natural decline after years of original output, or was it Scientology? I resisted the thought that creativity might be linked to unhappiness or neurosis.

Mysterious practices surfaced one evening in Amsterdam. A midnight show at the Concertgebouw paired them with Fairport Convention. The crowd was full of flower-bedecked girls and gaudily dressed men, led by the poet Simon Vinkenoog in a lemon-yellow linen suit: the counter-culture seemed to be in charge in Holland. Onstage, clunky chromium microphones for the Dutch radio broadcast stood alongside the modern ones from the PA system. As Mike set down his electric guitar after the first song, he brushed his leg against an ungrounded radio mic. There was a crackling sound and he levitated, hovering a few feet above the stage for what seemed an age, then landing with a thud, his guitar and the mic stand glued to his chest, humming. I ran onto the stage and flung the stand into the orchestra pit. Mike had turned a pale green.

They carried him to the dressing room and locked the door, barring the house doctor; they would take care of him using Scientology methods. After a hurriedly summoned Fairport finished their set, the ISB made a triumphant return. The crowd roared as Mike, still looking pale, played and sang as well as I ever heard him. Licorice told me they had treated him with 'touch assists'.

Album sales and tour income, meanwhile, continued to grow. Next up was the Woodstock Festival where they – along with Joan Baez and John Sebastian – were topping the bill on Friday night. That morning in New York, reports started coming in about the crowds thronging to the site. By the time we landed at Monticello airport, the access roads had turned into parking lots. They used an old army helicopter with a permanently open door to take us to the site, the six of us (including Walter Gundy, the tour manager) strapped in, staring down hundreds of feet at a Catskill countryside filled with traffic jams, tents and small colourful armies marching across the fields. When we reached the site, it was almost too much to take in: a city had formed around the stage. As we banked and turned over the sea of people, the small landing strip behind the stage appeared to be the only unpopulated area for miles around.

At sunset, candles and small fires appeared in the crowd and torches were lit along the top of the hill. It seemed a sight from a distant century (a past one, let's hope). The first raindrops started to fall while Baez was onstage. As at Newport four years before, there was a small tarpaulin strung between poles keeping no more than a fraction of the stage dry. The band's days as an acoustic duo were long past. Rose's bass needed an amp, Mike played electric guitar on several important songs, and oriental instruments were amplified through pick-up microphones. We huddled with our friend John Morris, one of the festival producers, and talked about what to do if it didn't clear up.

I am generally immune to regret, but I find it painful to write about what happened next. As the rain came down more heavily, Morris offered us a spot the following afternoon. Faced with the prospect of radically altering their set and trying to play through the rain, and with reports of clearing weather to the west, the group opted to stay over then race to New York, where we had a gig the next night. To my eternal chagrin, and against my instincts, I went along with the plan. We were vaguely aware of the cameras and the recording truck parked beside the stage, but we couldn't know that Melanie would step into our spot, revelling in the downpour and transforming herself into a star. Nor could we know what Saturday would be like.

There was no way off the site that night (the helicopters stopped flying at dusk), so the six of us slept in a cramped tent with John Sebastian, Melanie and her boyfriend. At dawn, we were 'coptered out to a motel in Monticello to wash and get a few hours' sleep in a real bed. When we returned and looked out at the crowd, our hearts sank. It was sunny all right; the hillsides were baking in the heat. The sylvan beauty of the hippy crowd the day before had changed beyond recognition; now it looked like a battle zone. Everyone was caked in mud, many dancing crazily in the dust, out of their heads. Following the thunderous boogie of Canned Heat, the ISB were the last thing anyone wanted to hear. The group were exhausted and the set fell flat.

Having given up trying to collect ticket money, the

organizers had run out of cash, so dozens scrambled for a few seats on the last 'copter flight before the charter company took their unpaid bills back to Albany. Licorice was pushed off, Robin got off to stay with her and Walter got off to look after them. Somehow, they made it out with a driver who knew a dirt track through the woods and we got to New York just in time to go onstage. We knew we had blown it: the extent of the error became clear in the months to come as the Woodstock film reached every small town in America and the double album soared to the top of the charts. Had they played in the rain that night, would they have made the cut in the film and on the record? I had nightmares about the might-have-beens: the ISB gloriously recapturing the acoustic spontaneity of their early years, their songs and voices perfect for that magical first night, their careers transformed by the exposure. It was a phenomenon and, like that last helicopter, we had failed to hold on to our seats on board.

Economists will tell you there is no such thing as stasis: if you aren't going up, you're going down. Their next two albums had some strong tracks, but overall they were no match for the earlier ones. They moved a group of dancers and Scientologist friends into the Row and created a pageant called *U*. I tried to discourage them: with a cast of ten plus sets and costumes, it was going to be very costly to tour. The lyrics were even more obscure than their opaque masterpieces of the past and the tunes weren't as good. Promoters who had been happy to book the ISB were dubious about *U*. Guarantees were reduced everywhere, putting the group financially at risk.

Scientology is not designed to engender timidity. Confidence flows from the belief that you are eliminating the weak points in your personality. The group refused to contemplate the notion of failure and *U* went ahead full-speed. The fact that it was a disaster artistically, critically and financially failed to dent their confidence, but it hastened my search for new challenges.

The Incredible String Band carried on into the '70s with ever declining audiences and less and less interesting records. Rose escaped back into a normal life, got married and had a daughter. For a while in the '90s, she was the girlfriend of the chairman of Aberystwyth town council and took on the role of Lady Mayoress. Dressed in the sensible tweeds befitting her status, she sat with me in the audience at an ISB reunion concert in London in 1997. Licorice disappeared somewhere in California and is presumed dead. Mike and Robin went their separate ways; both eventually left Scientology. Robin tours the world reciting bardic tales and playing the Irish harp and the fiddle. A recent reunion – including Clive – has served primarily to rekindle old feuds.

chapter 28

ON A RAINY FRIDAY afternoon in August 2002, I left London and headed for Fairport Convention's annual Cropredy Festival in Oxfordshire, an event I honour with my admiration more than my presence. There are real ale stands, a *Mojo*-sponsored CD stall and a cartoonist's dream of beards and anoraks. When I arrived, the hoods were up and the face furniture dripping wet, but over 15,000 stood in the soggy pasture to hear a reunion of Fairport's earliest line-ups. Barring occasional feuds, current and former members participate on a rotating basis, while Richard Thompson, star that he is, gets invited every year.

That evening they played songs that hadn't been performed since the M1 crash. Curiosity and nostalgia propelled me through the downpour to hear Ian Matthews and Judy Dyble singing with Richard Thompson, Simon Nicol and Ashley Hutchings again on 'Time Will Show The Wiser' and 'Jack O' Diamonds'. With ex-Fotheringay drummer Gerry Conway taking Martin Lamble's seat, the understanding between the three old friends from Muswell Hill was as instinctive as it had been thirty-five years before and the originality of their take on American 'folk-rock' as clear that night as it had been in the summer of 1967. Hearing them through a great PA system, with every detail sparkling in the chilly air, reminded me what a wonderful group they were and what a future was lost along with their friends in the crash. After an hour exploring the first three albums, Dave Swarbrick was assisted onstage with a tank of oxygen beside his wheelchair and they started in on the music created by the new line-up in a Hampshire farmhouse that mournful summer of 1969.

As they pondered the future that spring, the record on all their turntables was *Music From Big Pink* by The Band. It had thrown down a gauntlet: *You want to play American music? Well, try playing something as American as this!* It was a revolutionary record: their schooling in the Southern roadhouses with Ronnie Hawkins followed by their work as Dylan's backing group meant they were at once both source and emulators. Fairport couldn't face going back to the pre-crash repertoire and they felt *Big Pink* meant that a return to their trademark style wasn't an option. They decided to pick up where 'A Sailor's Life' left off and create a repertoire as English as *Big Pink* was American – to turn a rebuke into an inspiration.

First they added Swarbrick, then found drummer Dave Mattacks in a ballroom dance orchestra. Mattacks's strict-tempo schooling was a perfect foundation for their reinvention of English traditional music. He has been endlessly – and depressingly – imitated, but no folk-rock drummer has ever trumped what he conjured up in his first months with the group. Ashley Hutchings spent weeks trawling through the Cecil Sharp House archives, consulting sages like A. L. Lloyd and assembling a set of ballads that would lend themselves to Fairport's approach. In August, after two months of rehearsal, we were in the studio, and by November *Liege and Lief* was out and selling better than any Fairport record before.

Making English folk music fashionable was an extraordinary accomplishment, pushing against the historic diktat that nothing could be less hip. But the team didn't stay together long enough to enjoy the acclaim. Sandy loved what they were doing but wanted to be in a band that would perform her new songs as well. She had also fallen in love with a man known for his roving eye and was reluctant to leave him unchaperoned while Fairport was on tour. When she refused to board a plane to Copenhagen for a TV appearance, the implications were clear.

Ashley, on the other hand, had the passion of the newly converted. Traditional songs may have been old news to Sandy, but he had a vision of transforming English folk music and bringing it to a wider audience. Even with Sandy gone, he knew Richard wouldn't want to be tied to a strict repertoire of traditional material. He persuaded Martin Carthy and Maddy Prior to join him in forming Steeleye Span. Two wings of Fairport had broken off.

The remaining members loved the road, couldn't wait to tour the new material and were dying to get to America. Richard and Swarb could handle the singing; all they needed was a bass player. They indulged the folkie Swarbrick when he insisted on an audition for his Birmingham mate who played stand-up bass with the Ian Campbell Group. Throwing him in at the deep end, they took 'Mattie Groves' and 'Tam Lin', with those impossible bass lines of Ashley's, at breakneck speed. Dave Pegg blinked and tore into what Swarb had warned him to learn by heart. I watched from the doorway as Fairport's future took shape in front of me. Pegg played everything they threw at him with a hooligan edge that Ashley could never have matched. The legendary rhythm section that would grace albums by so many different artists had just been formed.

In 1970, Fairport toured as widely and as often as we could find bookings. On the night of their American debut at the Troubadour in Los Angeles, Linda Ronstadt cheered them from the audience. When they ran out of encores, they invited her to join them. 'I don't know any English songs,' she shouted. 'That's OK, we know all of yours,' said Simon. Pushed onstage, she nervously sang the first a cappella notes of 'Silver Threads And Golden Needles', then heard Fairport enter on cue, re-creating her arrangement perfectly. When Richard took an expert James Burton-esque solo, she almost fainted in astonishment. The set lasted another forty minutes, covering songs she had forgotten she knew. On another occasion at the Troubadour, Led Zeppelin (old Birmingham buddies of Dave Pegg) turned up and Jimmy Page and Richard jammed on R&B numbers. John Wood and I were recording the show that night and the tape reveals Plant's vocal being louder than any of the amplifiers, Page trying to keep pace with Richard on jigs and reels and Zep manager Peter Grant at a front table cursing and abusing the waitresses.

From the moment Sandy left the group, she and I did nothing but argue. I could get a big advance from A&M for a solo LP, but she wanted to form a group with boyfriend Trevor Lucas. Successful women in show business often have trouble maintaining relationships. Or rather, men have problems dealing with a star performer. Many women solve the problem by ending up with their lead guitarist/producer/manager/musical director or by casting their (usually unqualified) man in one of those roles. Fotheringay, as she wanted to call the group, after Mary Queen of Scots' prison, would be a castle built on false foundations. The money keeping everyone on salary was Sandy's, but she made me write the contract for the egalitarian benefit of all. Blackwell, A&M and I were clear about what we wanted: a record of Sandy's songs, sung by Sandy with Sandy's name in big letters on the cover. (She was voted 'best female vocalist' in the 1971 and '72 *Melody Maker* polls.) But she was determined to make Trevor her equal. The record we made includes some of her best performances: 'The Sea', 'The Pond & The Stream', 'Winter Winds', 'The Banks Of The Nile'; but the rest of the album is filler.

Fotheringay hurtled through Sandy's advance, buying a huge PA system (nickname: 'Stonehenge') and a Bentley to get around in. The musicians earned higher salaries than Fairport could afford to pay themselves. Sandy was bankrolling the group without having the power to lead or the money to keep going much longer since she refused American tours because of her fear of flying. Her relationship with Trevor was turning her into a nervous wreck. I turned over the managerial role to Roy Guest.

Fairport's first all-male album, *Full House*, with hilarious liner notes by Richard, was far better than I could have hoped. The only cloud on the horizon was a variation of the problems appearing all over the Witchseason realm. Inexperienced musicians recording for the first time need a producer's guidance and are grateful for it. By the fourth or fifth album, the process has been demystified and many become less willing to be told what's good and what isn't. With only one track usually available on the old eight-track tapes, Richard had always let me decide whether to keep or retake a guitar solo; now when I wanted to keep one, he insisted on erasing it and vice versa. Discontent stalked the land. Many of them had been seemingly successful for a few years and didn't have much to show for it. If I was such a great manager and producer, why weren't they rich?

In 1970, I finished sixteen LPs: I was working myself to a frazzle. In Charlotte Street, the financial wolves were circling; we owed money in every direction and the more success we achieved, the more we seemed to spend. Break-even was a horizon that kept receding. I started thinking about radical solutions.

chapter 29

IN THE LATE SIXTIES, John Sebastian's ex-wife Lorey settled in a Hertfordshire cottage with her remarkable record collection. One evening, I brought some tapes and acetates of things I was working on plus some records I thought she wouldn't know and we reminisced and took turns playing DJ. When I played her an advance copy of *Five Leaves Left* she went crazy, telling me how wonderful it was and how big a success it was going to be.

Listening to Nick Drake led to a search for 'Sunny Girl', an English-language single by a Swedish outfit called the Hep-Stars. Lorey had gone to Stockholm with the Spoonful a few years earlier and someone took them to hear this local group perform their new hit, an obvious copy of Sebastian's 'Daydream'. She thought it was a clever tribute and she adored the lead singer, who had broken his ankle skiing and performed on crutches. Lorey gave me her extra copy of the record; she was right – the lead voice did remind me at times of both John Sebastian and Nick Drake.

In 1969, Witchseason's booking agency landed a deal to arrange Frank Zappa's European tour, and I joined the Mothers of Invention for their trip to Stockholm. I was thumbing through the racks in a local record store when my eye caught a familiar name: Lorey's Hep-Star Benny

Andersson in a duet album in Swedish with Björn Ulvaeus. The record was great, full of rich melodies and harmonies. When *Liege and Lief* started to sell in Scandinavia, I needed a local music publisher to collect the composers' income and help promote my artists. In other territories I relied on colleagues' recommendations about the best sub-publishers, but for Scandinavia I looked no further than the credits on the back of the Andersson/Ulvaeus LP.

I met Stig Anderson in the Polar Music offices in Stockholm in October 1970. He was bemused at being offered the publishing rights to artists he had barely heard of but brightened when I told him I didn't want an advance, just a swap. I would give him Fairport, Nick Drake, Sandy Denny and John Martyn for Scandinavia and he would give me the English-language territories on Benny and Björn's songs. He suggested I join them all for a drink at a downtown hotel that evening. After a friendly chat, Benny and Björn invited me to stick around: their girlfriends were starring in a turn-of-the-century revue in the hotel lounge, complete with top hats, high-kicking routines and old Swedish music hall songs.

After the show, the five of us (yes, the dancers were Agnetha and Frida) went back to Benny's flat. We spent half the night talking, drinking and playing records, mostly by obscure American soul singers. I told them they should go back to writing in English. We joked about whether or not they could ever write a song as successful as 'Daydream'.

Back in London, there were two pieces of paper on my desk. One was a letter from Stig Anderson confirming our reciprocal arrangement: he had checked on Fairport's and Sandy Denny's sales figures and was reasonably pleased with what he found. The other was a message to call Mo Ostin at the Dorchester Hotel.

Everyone in the music business knows Mo Ostin. Once

Frank Sinatra's accountant, the legendary boss of Warner/Reprise Records presided over the greatest company in the most wildly successful years of the recording industry. His gentle demeanour, his willingness to delegate to the 'good ears' that worked for him and his loyalty are legendary. He is a short man, whose wide black-framed spectacles, bald patch and benign smile make him look a little like Sergeant Bilko. I had met him on an early visit to Los Angeles and we hit it off well. He hired me for the Geoff & Maria Muldaur project and picked up John & Beverley Martyn for North America. Whenever I was in Los Angeles, I would stop by his Burbank office to say hello.

Things got more complex when he started asking me questions about Chris Blackwell and Island Records. Warner had no European outlet then and were considering buying their way into the market. I waxed lyrical about what a great company Island was. Mo sent accountants to go over their books and when Chris balked at the first proposal, Mo went out on a limb with the Warner Brothers board and made a huge offer matching what Chris said he wanted. Blackwell's response was 'Let me think about it'. *Think about it?* Mo was beside himself. Then an interview appeared in a British trade paper where Chris explained that Philips had first option on buying Island and anyway, he wasn't in the mood to sell. Mo seethed with quiet fury. He had learned the business from Mickey Rudin, Sinatra's fearsome attorney, and underneath the smiling exterior, Mo was not a man to take kindly to a slight.

It later occurred to me there was more to my Dorchester visit than his flattering offer to run the film music department in California. He gave me a schedule of upcoming projects that included *Clockwork Orange* and *Deliverance* and I asked for a few days to think it over. On the same trip he offered Chris Wright and Terry Ellis at

Chrysalis their own label deal in the USA, and eventually – when Warner set up in Europe – in the UK as well. In one short visit he had removed two of Island's sources of new artists and successful releases.

Blackwell was away looking after Steve Winwood on Traffic's first American tour. I found him on a snowy November morning in a hotel room in Northampton, Massachusetts, far from the headquarters of his growing empire, adding up petty cash receipts. Chris had never forgotten Millie Small and was determined to take good care of his prodigy. If he sensed what lay behind Mo's offer, he never let on. I had to do it, he said, it was the chance of a lifetime. Never mind that it left him with a stable of artists in turmoil, all poised at crucial points in their careers. Suffering studio burn-out and terrified by the mounting bills, I was in no state to judge the situation clearly. The Incredible String Band's devotion to Scientology and refusal to listen to my advice, coupled with my arguments with Sandy, the growing recalcitrance of Fairport and Nick's simple concept for his next album all combined to make me feel that everyone might be happier with me out of the way. And the only certain way to balance Witchseason's books was to sell it to Island: at least that way I could make sure everyone got paid.

I flew to Burbank to meet Ted Ashley and John Calley, the heads of the film company. I was dazzled by the studio and the rich possibilities that seemed to open up and I buzzed with ideas about using John Cale for film scores and getting Nick to write title songs. I had *done* records; it was time to move on to a bigger game on a larger playing field. The contract with Stig Anderson lay unsigned on my desk; Island Music would buy my publishing company and they had their own relationships in Scandinavia. What was a deal for a few songs by some Swedish songwriters that might never be written compared with the new world beckoning in California?

Back in London, I started arriving at Sound Techniques at ten every morning and leaving after midnight. The Fairport schism had left me another group to produce while Mike Heron's prodigious output of songs led to a solo album, and the chance to record him with John Cale, Pete Townshend, Jimmy Page, Steve Winwood and Dudu Pukwana. And there were now another two female artists: not only had I taken on Nico, but a singer I had pursued in 1966 suddenly re-appeared.

Early in my Elektra year I attended a poetry reading at the old Institute of Contemporary Arts in Dover Street. Singers were scattered through the declamatory line-up and one intrigued me. Her voice was small and delicate but the quieter she sang the more attentively the audience listened. She disappeared before I could speak to her and when I finally tracked Vashti Bunyan down, she had just signed with Andrew Oldham's *Immediate* label as 'the new Marianne Faithfull'.

Oldham's recordings were overproduced flops, so Vashti had headed north in a horse-drawn caravan with a man she and her previous boyfriend picked up hitch-hiking one night. She started writing songs again and remembered my interest from four years earlier. I visited their winter-quarters somewhere near Lancaster and was smitten once again with her and her music. Her new ultra-rural life and impending motherhood made her an even trickier commercial proposition than Nick Drake, but I couldn't imagine saying no. With new Chris McGregor configurations, John and Beverley Martyn and Dr Strangely Strange, Ireland's quirky answer to the ISB, my 1970 productions came to 16 LPs. All needed to be mixed and mastered before my January departure for LA.

One night in December working on the second Fotheringay LP, I lost my temper after the fortieth unsuccessful take of *John The Gun*. Sandy and I went out and got drunk. She asked if I would stay if she broke up the group and made a solo album. I said I would take time off to produce it and if there was anything that would have tempted me to turn Warner Brothers down, it was that. The next morning Sandy rang to say she had disbanded Fotheringay: when could we start work on her new record? I said I would have to discuss it with Warner Brothers once I got there.

'Get there? But you're not going now!' I told her if she had broken up the group thinking I would walk away from a signed contract, she had better re-form it pronto. She replied that it was too late, two of the band had signed on that morning for a long tour with Cat Stevens. She never forgave me for the confusion of verb tenses, but at least, I thought, she wouldn't go bankrupt financing Fotheringay.

There was a long list of issues that needed resolving about the integration of Witchseason into Island Records. A meeting was scheduled for my first day off from the studio in over a month. The night before, Suzie Watson-Taylor, Nigel Waymouth and I ended up around midnight at the Baghdad House, a Chelsea institution run by an enigmatic Iraqi and his red-haired Scottish girlfriend. The basement had alcoves perfectly designed for the discreet smoking of substances and long after-hours evenings of wine, song, flirtation and conspiracy. The music business and the criminal fraternities – often quite different people – adored it.

We watched a madly dressed fiddler playing and dancing in the middle of the room, who then passed around a cup of 'hot wassail'. Suzie wrinkled her nose and demurred. Nigel and I were suspicious of its contents, but each took a tiny sip, just to be polite. Soon we all went home to bed. Suddenly I was wide awake and the walls were dancing. *Shit!* I picked up the phone and rang Nigel. His wife told me yes, he had been tripping, but she had given him two Mandrax and now he was sleeping like a baby. I told her I would be right over for some of the same. I drove the half-mile to and from their flat at 10 mph, took the pills, got into bed and tried to read to take my mind off the hallucinations. The big meeting started the next morning at ten o'clock.

Suddenly the phone rang. I picked it up with a start. Who could be ringing me in the middle of the night? It was Marian, my assistant. As she talked, asking me where I had been all day, I realized the light in the room involved more than just my bedside lamp. It was mid-afternoon and the phone beside me had been ringing for hours. I had slept through it all, my head cradled in the palm of my hand, the book still open to the right page. All the undone business had been sorted out without me. It was time to pack for LA.

A week after my arrival, I was woken at dawn in the Chateau Marmont by a roar that shook the whole of creation. My immediate thought was that someone had dropped the Bomb. I was dead, but at least I had plenty of company. A few seconds of rational analysis altered the event to earthquake. In all my years in recording studios, I had never heard a sound so low. The vibrating object had to be unimaginably large to make such a noise. Like a wet dog, the earth was trying to shake us off.

That day at the Music Bungalow on the Warner Brothers lot, I got to know my new staff. Malcolm Beelby had been working there for almost forty years. He asked whether I remembered the scene from Busby Berkeley's *Gold Diggers of 1933*, with the circular staircase full of girls playing fluorescent violins. I did. That scene was shot during his first week at the studio, on the day of the 1933 Long Beach earthquake. He remembered helping screaming girls off the tottering tower, the wired violins crackling and sparking as they fell. The peroxide blonde in the accounts department with the Cupid's-bow lips had been one of the dancers.

A few weeks into my new California life, I got the news that Richard Thompson had left Fairport. I was stunned: it was the last thing I would have predicted. I was even more astonished when I picked up a two-week-old copy of *Melody Maker* and read an interview in which he said, 'It didn't seem the same after Joe left.' You could have knocked me over with a feather. Or flown me back to London with it.

Next came a distressing telephone call from Molly Drake. Nick had returned to Tanworth, no longer able to handle living in London. They wanted him to see a psychiatrist, but he felt people would judge him crazy if he did. (Such attitudes were not unusual in England in 1971.) She asked me to tell him I thought it was a good idea, which of course I did. Nick sounded terrible on the phone. His hesitant manner had always seemed to shield an inner core about which he was certain, even if he had little ability to communicate it other than through his music. Now it felt as if both core and shield had been shattered. He sounded frightened.

Settling into my new job, I discovered that the last thing film directors wanted was 'creative input' from a kid from the music business. They tended to score their films at the last minute and usually wanted John Williams or his ilk. When I persuaded the producers of *Omega Man* to let me and John Cale score a ten-minute sequence of the film on spec, they were horrified at the results. John and I thought it was perfect.

I cleared rights to Leonard Cohen songs for *McCabe and Mrs Miller* and organized regular screenings of new releases for the LA music business community. I went to

A&R meetings at the record company across the street and attempted to coordinate the activities of the two branches of the multinational now called Warner Communications. I tried to hire the great Cambridge banjo wizard Bill Keith to play the theme for John Boorman on *Deliverance*, but Bill was travelling in Europe and wanted to visit a girl in Ireland, so he suggested I get Eric Weissberg instead. I went to Atlanta with Eric and recorded 'Duelling Banjos' frontwards, backwards, fast, slow, upside down and sideways. Boorman was so delighted with the results he insisted it be released as a single. I took it to an A&R meeting and everyone laughed. We humoured him by pressing up 500 white-label promo copies to play on radio interviews he was doing around the country.

The morning after his first interview in Minneapolis I got a call from someone in the warehouse, asking whether I knew anything about a mysteriously numbered single. It was 'Duelling Banjos', of course, and the Minneapolis branch had just ordered 5,000 copies. I had been so contemptuous of its merits as a single, I hadn't even bothered to put my name on the label as producer. Within a few weeks, it became my only number one hit.

Working with Stanley Kubrick was fascinating, but consisted of little more than taking orders. When I compressed the copy on the back of the soundtrack LP for *Clockwork Orange* by crediting 'G. Rossini' instead of 'Gioacchino Rossini', I was woken at 6 a.m. in LA by Kubrick insisting I stop the presses and restore the full spelling of the composer's first name.

My ties to England remained close. My Scottish girlfriend, Linda Peters, followed me to Los Angeles, went back to London, came out again. We broke up and got back together several times. Finally, she stayed in England, married Richard Thompson and became his singing partner.

chapter 30

MY CONTACT IN THE Warner Brothers publicity department was Don Simpson, the man destined to become the symbol of '80s Hollywood excess, producer of *Top Gun*, *Beverly Hills Cop* and *Flashdance* and victim in 1996 of an overdose of prescription drugs. He was bright, well read (barring anything written before 1960 or in Europe) and very ambitious. The California self-improvement cults fascinated him, Scientology in particular. He had read of an experiment conducted at the Stanford University Research Laboratory cyclotron in which psychics were asked to bend the path of an accelerated electron. Ingo Swann, a Scientologist, was the most successful, and of the seven other 'benders', four were Scientologists. He was intrigued to hear about my experiences with the String Band.

Don liked quoting a William Burroughs story about a man who ventures into the rainforest in search of a tribal ritual with extraordinary powers of spiritual transformation. When he reaches the jungle clearing and meets the witch doctor, he discovers that the experience involves 'fucking the sacred crocodile'. Don and I made a pact: we would fuck the crocodile and find out what was so powerful about Scientology.

Through the ISB, I knew the head of the 'LA Org' and

got us special treatment at their optimistically entitled 'Celebrity Center': no proselytizing by mail or phone and we could skip the tedious introductory 'Communications Course'. We started 'auditing', paying $30 an hour for sessions in which you sat opposite an 'auditor' holding a pair of tin cans wired to an 'E-Meter', a primitive lie detector that measures galvanic skin resistance. Commands are designed to elicit memories that trigger 'engrams: cellular records of incidents involving pain, loss, unconsciousness and a real or imagined threat to survival'. When a memory triggers an engram, the meter reacts. You go over the incident in your mind, without judgement, recalling its sights, smells, sounds and emotions until the needle 'floats', showing that the 'charge' has been erased through acceptance of the experience. The same incident can be called up a day later and provoke no reaction from the meter. The next command is 'Recall an earlier similar incident'. You keep going in this vein until you can recall no 'earlier similars'. I was surprised by how much I could remember from childhood years.

The theory makes sense. If, at age two, you fell on your head in a room with pale blue walls, chicken soup on the stove and Haydn on the stereo, your mood might well decline for no apparent reason if thirty years later you should encounter those same sounds, smells and sights. A 'Clear' is someone who has completed the first course of auditing and is deemed ready to graduate to higher 'OT' ('Operating Thetan', Scientology-speak for free spirit) levels. Once 'clear', you become able – in theory, at least – to respond to the present unfettered by the charged unconscious memories that weighed you down. You should become lighter, happier, more effective. And following some auditing sessions both Don and I had moments when we felt elated and energized.

But there was more to Scientology than auditing. Founder L. Ron Hubbard (known to everyone as LRH) had rules for everything. If Clears followed them, their efforts must, by definition, produce 'up stats' – Scientology jargon for success. When I asked about cases where rules were followed, but 'stats' were not 'up', I discovered the notion of 'Suppressive Personalities' and the obsession with past lives. An 'SP' is a Thetan who has suffered such a painful death in a previous lifetime that nothing will deter them from an agenda of vengeful destruction in the current one. When an organization run according to the thoughts of Chairman Ron fails, the inevitable SP within it must be isolated and expelled – a textbook example of self-justifying paranoia, circular logic and scapegoating.

When Clears spoke about 'earlier similars' taking them into past lives, they seemed always to have defied enormous odds by being Egyptians or princes or something colourful and romantic. An unsettling air of certainty pervaded the Celebrity Center: everyone had big plans – usually for show-business careers – and there was no possibility of failure. It sounded like a chapter from one of Hubbard's bad sci-fi novels, but then it was easy to be sceptical in those pre-Tom Cruise and John Travolta days.

One weekend I hurt my neck body-surfing. Auditing cannot take place if you are suffering pain or discomfort so they sent me to a chiropractor. The waiting room was full of literature from the far-right John Birch Society; I decided the place was too unpleasant and left without treatment. I was summoned to the 'Guardian's Office' to explain myself. When I proposed letting time heal the injury, they asked whether I had been associating with 'persons hostile to Scientology'. I said that most people I knew were hostile to Scientology and I had no intention of cutting myself off from my friends. Robot-like, they repeated admonitory phrases from Hubbard's texts. I left the center and never went back. Don had a similar run-in soon afterwards.

For recruits without our Hollywood salaries, hours spent hustling passers-by earned auditing credits. We met devotees who had been volunteering for years and had not yet earned as many hours as Don and I had purchased out of curiosity. The more time and effort invested, the less receptive people were to questions or doubts. I read *Barefaced Messiah*, which exposes Hubbard's lies about his naval career and recounts his 1948 address to the Science Fiction Writers' Convention in which he advises the delegates that if they really want to make money they should forget about science fiction and 'start a religion'.

After this failed experiment, meetings with Mike Heron and Suzie Watson-Taylor were strained, but I stayed in touch with Suzie after they – and the group – broke up in the late '70s. Suzie is a delightfully positive upper-middle-class girl, who adored Mike and had done a great job in difficult circumstances as ISB's manager. She was sad she and Mike had not had children; she had a good job at Warner Brothers Records but was finding it hard to meet men who could understand her experiences or tolerate her devotion to LRH. In the early '80s she was offered two jobs: one a promotion at Warners, the other a post at the Sea Org – Hubbard's Florida headquarters. I urged her to take the record company job but she dropped me a line to say goodbye, she was off to Clearwater (LRH chose the site of his HQ for the name). I haven't seen her since.

chapter 31

FREDDY WEINTRAUB'S OFFICE was my favourite stop on the executive floor at Warner Brothers Studios. Freddy is a New Yorker and, like me, was a refugee from the music business. His qualifications as production vice-president were two: he had brought the *Woodstock* film to Warner; and when Ted Ashley used to come to New York on business, Freddy got him laid. He had a full Isro, and sported the occasional dashiki. After my first Friday executive committee meeting, he invited me in for a chat. I was curious about John Calley, the erudite head of production. 'Oh, he was a top producer,' said Freddy, 'he made *Ice Station Zebra*.'

I had been reading up on the financial side of the film business. '*Ice Station Zebra*? Didn't that lose more money than any film in history?'

'Yeah, that's the one!' I didn't get it. How did you go from producing an expensive flop to running a studio?

'Joe, Joe, Joe! You have to understand Hollywood! Here, it's not how much money you *make*, it's how much money you *handle*!'

Freddy and I saw a lot of each other. There was a large editing room next to the Music Bungalow filled with film cans. Soon after I arrived, the young Martin Scorsese began opening those endless rolls of film in an effort to rescue a project known around the lot as 'Freddy's Folly'.

Its official title was *Medicine Ball Caravan*, a 'high-concept' documentary by French film-maker François Reichenbach, winner of an Oscar for a film about pianist Artur Rubinstein. He had been dazzled by *Easy Rider* and thrilled by Tom Wolfe's *Electric Kool-Aid Acid Test*. Out of the conjunction of these facts came a project: to film the Grateful Dead in Ken Kesey's Merry Prankster bus 'Further' driving across America and putting on concerts in out-of-the-way places for the awestruck locals. If luck was on Reichenbach's side, someone resembling one of the drooling killers in *Deliverance* would attempt to murder Jerry Garcia and Reichenbach would be there to film it. Freddy and Ted Ashley, in their wisdom, decided this would be the perfect sequel to *Woodstock*.

No sooner was the project green-lighted than problems began. Kesey wanted no part of it, and no, they couldn't use his bus. The Grateful Dead were signed to Warner Brothers Records so they pretended to take it seriously for a while until – just as logistics and contracts were being finalized – they revealed how ludicrous they found the whole idea. In desperation, a yellow school bus was daubed with psychedelic designs and filled with a minor San Francisco band called Stoneground plus their girlfriends, hangers-on and dope dealers and they all set off to explore 'fly-over land', followed at a safe distance by the all-French crew. Joni Mitchell, the Youngbloods, BB King and Alice Cooper were booked to perform with Stoneground at such glamorous points in the American landscape as Gallup, New Mexico, Sioux City, Iowa, and Moline, Illinois, to give the film some star power.

The *Caravan*'s first night in the wilderness found everyone seated round a campfire in the Sierra Nevadas.

The French cameramen were so beguiled by the hippy girls that they consumed whatever beverages they were offered. Soon they were all having their first LSD trips.

Warner Brothers had set ways of doing things. Each day, every foot of film shot for a Warner-financed film anywhere in the world was flown back to Burbank, developed, printed and screened for senior studio executives. When the first *Caravan* dailies arrived, heads were scratched and anxious (pre-mobile phone) messages left at hotel desks.

Much of the early footage consisted of lingering shots of leaves, children playing in mud, clouds drifting by and occasionally a face. Sound was rarely synched to film. Every time they turned around – breakfast eggs, a canteen of water on a hot day, cocoa before bedtime, the American beer they found so insipid – the Frenchmen were being dosed. The project started to come unglued. Freddy flew frantically back and forth from LA to obscure destinations in Nevada and Utah. He sent the Frenchmen packing and hired a more savvy American crew. *Medicine Ball Caravan* turned into a mundane rock concert film with some barely watchable *cinéma vérité* of hippies daubing face-paint on each other. Assaults by outraged Bible-thumpers failed to materialize.

Scorsese, who had met Weintraub in New York while working as an editor on *Woodstock*, struggled heroically to rescue the useless film, but to little effect. A sign of desperation was how important one synchronization licence became. Jesse Colin Young had written alternative lyrics to Merle Haggard's classic 'Okie From Muskogee', a patriotic anti-hippy anthem. The Youngblood version was called 'Hippy From Olema' and mocked everything Merle felt was good and true and Umerkin. It fell to me to obtain permission for putting Haggard's classic to this nefarious use.

The rights were controlled by the king of Bakersfield country music, Buck Owens. Buck is a genial huckster and a great singer who built an empire around *Hee-Haw*, a syndicated TV programme celebrating Okie culture and mocking Nashville's Grand Ol' Opry. Bakersfield C&W was jauntier and more 'manly' than the Nashville variety and much beloved of truck drivers. I had a pretty good collection of Buck Owens recordings at home myself and was ambivalent about my mission to hustle him. When I got him on the phone, I started off formally: 'Hello, Mr Owens, this is Joe Boyd from Warner Brothers Films.'

'Mr Owens's ma *daddy*! *Buck*'s m'name,' he bellowed back. The good ol' boy routine was non-stop and quite charming. Nothing would give him greater pleasure, it seemed, than to accommodate the great Warner Brothers. And would I give his best regards to Mo Ostin, while I was at it? When he eventually decided not to grant the licence, he was discretion itself as he explained how *he* had no problem with it, but Merle's mother would not be happy.

Scorsese, meanwhile, settled in among the Young Turks of Hollywood and started dating Freddy's daughter. Albert Grossman's former road manager Jonathan Taplin (who had looked after the Kweskins, Dylan and Janis Joplin) often visited Marty and me on the lot. His uncle ran a bank in Cleveland and he came up with the finance for *Mean Streets*.

Medicine Ball Caravan mercifully closed a week after it opened; there is, as yet, no sign of a DVD release with added footage. Karl Marx observed that history repeats itself first as tragedy and then as farce. Anyone tracing the sixties through its music documentaries, from *Woodstock* to Altamont's *Gimme Shelter* to *Medicine Ball Caravan*, might agree.

chapter 32

JIMI HENDRIX'S MOTHER was a jitterbug champion in Seattle during the Second World War. She married Al Hendrix the day before he shipped out with the merchant marine. By the time VJ Day arrived, she was used to the wild life; the marriage never worked and the kids stayed with Al. She would sneak in through the bedroom window on her way home from a bar to cuddle young Jimi, reeking of booze and cheap perfume and leaving before dawn. She died of TB at twenty-seven, the same age as her son when he took the fatal pills.

The interviews with Jimi's brother and cousins that tell this story were great on paper, but didn't play well enough on screen to make the final cut of the film. My stay at Warner Brothers had become a great deal more interesting since I was commissioned to assemble a feature-length documentary about the recently deceased Hendrix.

Mike Jeffreys always encouraged film-makers to shoot Hendrix's shows. He would grant them access, plug in their lights for them, give them backstage passes and avoid signing the release. Later he would offer them a contract giving him a controlling interest in the film. All refused to sign, with the result that there was a lot of unseen footage gathering dust. After Jimi's death, his father hired a veteran civil rights and show business attorney named Leo Branton (previous clients: Nat 'King' Cole and Dorothy Dandridge) to represent the estate. Jeffreys fumed, but the death of his client put an end to his managerial control. For three months after the fatal night, he was bent double, his back muscles in spasm. Jeffreys' friends said it showed how much he cared; Jimi's claimed it was a combination of guilt and despair over lost earnings.

As Warner Brothers was Jimi's American label, Leo came to meet with Mo. Mo and Leo crossed the road to see Ted Ashley, Ted rang me to join the meeting and an hour later I was a film-maker. Since I was part-owner of some wonderful Hendrix footage myself (the clip of him on a stool with an acoustic twelve-string singing 'Hear My Train A-Comin'), I could talk to other producers as a fellow sufferer at the hands of Jeffreys. I brought on board John Head, an Englishman with production experience who instantly inspired trust. Friends of Jimi's horrified at the idea of a big corporation exploiting its deceased asset were reassured by his understated manner and easy grasp of their feelings.

John introduced me in turn to Gary Weis, a southern Californian who had been a member of the American volleyball team at the Maccabiah Games (the Jewish Olympics). His photo, in full spike a foot above the net, hung behind the bar at the Sorrento Grill on Will Rogers Beach in Santa Monica. He had studied photography at UCLA, then dropped out to do some surfing. One day, a girl gave him a lift as he hitch-hiked up the Pacific Coast Highway. Gary in those days was pretty irresistible, looking both athletic and artistic, plus being one of the funniest men I've ever met. The driver, Sharon Peckinpah (Sam's daughter), fell for him, as did so many others before and since.

Sam was making *The Ballad of Cable Hogue* for Warner Brothers. There was a new fashion for 'featurettes' –

films about making films – so Ted Ashley wanted a crew to follow the director around on the set. Peckinpah loathed the idea, but finally agreed on condition that Gary be the one to make it. He did such a great job that the producer hired him on his next movie, a Gene Hackman dud called *Prime Cut*. The best things about this piece of trash are Gary's featurette and the screen debut of Sissy Spacek (who also fell for Gary). Gary lived in a garage in Santa Monica next door to photographer William Wegman and his immortal Weimaraner, Man Ray, with whom we all had the honour of playing chase-the-tennis-ball.

I tackled the research and rights clearances, John rounded up people we wanted to talk to, Gary filmed the interviews and took charge of the editing and we made all creative decisions collectively. We secured footage from the Woodstock, Monterey Pop, Atlanta and Isle of Wight festivals, a video of the Band of Gypsies from the Fillmore East, the Berkeley concert, guest appearances on the *Dick Cavett Show*, *Ready Steady Go!* and German TV's *Beat Club*, plus my clip with the twelve-string. We found a few filmed interviews of Hendrix, plus some radio material for voice-overs.

Interviewees included his family in Seattle, his army buddy Billy Cox in Nashville, his old friends from Harlem, many of his girlfriends and rock gods Jagger, Clapton, Townshend and Little Richard. Fayne Pridgin, who was living with Jimi in a cold-water walk-up in Harlem when he was scraping by on gigs with the Isley Brothers, told of his return home one day carrying a newly purchased LP. She demanded to know what it was, but he tried to hide it. Finally she grabbed it and looked uncomprehendingly at the cover: 'Bob Dylan? Who the fuck is *Bob Dylan*? You spent our food money on *Bob Dylan*?' Little Richard described watching Jimi play: 'He used to make my *big toe* shoot up in my *boot*!'

The relaxed nature of the interviews was down to John's calm approach in asking the questions and Gary's ability to get the subjects pissing themselves with laughter between takes. Our biggest crisis arrived after the first round of filming in London. We sent the 16mm film to Burbank while we flew to New York for more interviews. The shipping room at Warner Brothers is a very busy place, with hundreds of octagonal metal cans of 35mm film arriving daily. A few cardboard boxes of 16mm must have been an anomaly no one knew what to do with. When we arrived back a week later, they had disappeared.

After some detective work, I concluded that the boxes had been placed near the trash bin and were almost certainly now buried under a layer of dirt in the disused quarry that serves as Burbank's city dump. We hired a bulldozer and a mechanical shovel and, with the help of the dump manager, tried to locate the spot where the trash from seven days previous would be buried. We spent a surreal and fetid afternoon with hoe and pitchfork searching for our interviews. As the sun set, we gave up and booked flights to London to reshoot.

The girlfriends and road managers were happy to do whatever was necessary for their moment in the limelight. But our best interview had been Pete Townshend and I dreaded making that call. As I feared, he was on a family holiday in Wales and did not wish to be disturbed by our crazy problem; he had only done the interview as a favour in the first place. He left me one window: the Who were going to film a promo clip for their next single at the old *Ready Steady Go!* studios in Wembley. That was his one working day all summer. If we were standing by, ready to shoot as soon as the filming finished, he would grant us another interview.

We watched as the indefatigable group played for over

an hour in front of about a hundred kids on a hot August afternoon, promising them *another* hour after the shoot to make sure they all stuck around. Then, during one of his windmill strums, Pete impaled his right palm on the Telecaster's switch. He was rushed to a nearby casualty unit for stitches while everyone held their breath.

He came back looking pale but finished the shoot, then played another hour of furious guitar to reward the kids for their patience. By the end, his bandaged hand was soaked with blood. Pete disappeared into the dressing room as the technicians started dismantling the stage. We bribed the lighting crew to keep a couple of spots lit as the clock ticked away. When I poked my head into the dressing room, Pete looked daggers at me: 'I said I'd do it and I will. I'll be there when I'm ready.'

When he turned up, he looked at the magazine of film and asked how long it was. 'Eleven minutes,' said Gary. 'That's how long you've got. Let's go.' He looked awful, the light was poor, I was in despair. The lost interview had been shot behind Pete's house in Twickenham on a beautiful afternoon by the Thames and had been one of the most insightful we did. He had told a great story about Eric Clapton ringing him up to go to the movies and how, in the darkness, they confessed their mutual intimidation by the new guy in town.

The instant the camera started rolling, Pete was transformed. He did an almost identical interview, told the same anecdotes and acted as if he was vaguely enjoying himself. When it was over, I asked how he did it. He told me that early in his career Kit Lambert had introduced him to a hypnotist who gave him the trance-state suggestion that the minute he stepped onstage, whatever was bothering him would evaporate and he would perform to the maximum of his abilities. I saw The Who many times and there was never a bad show. When Pete came to Sound Techniques to play with Keith Moon and Ronnie Lane on Mike Heron's solo album (under the *nom de guerre* of 'Tommy and the Bijoux'), I never had to monitor his track: we just listened to the drums and bass and stopped when they made a mistake. Pete was always note-perfect.

There were conspicuous absences among the interviewees. One was Jeffreys: every time we tried to pin down a date, he would disappear, or postpone, or say he wanted to think about it some more. He remained cordial but wary, jealous of my power over the footage and worried about what the other interviewees were saying about him. Finally, we went ahead without him.

He was a strange man, a bridge between eras. From owning a nightclub in Newcastle to managing the Animals to dealing with mind-blown stars like Hendrix and the post-Haight–Ashbury Eric Burdon was clearly a journey that had bewildered him. His attempts to control his environment amid the chaos included always changing his plane reservations at the last minute. He had a premonition that he would die in an air crash, so he saw it as a means of outguessing fate. He built a retreat for himself and his artists in Majorca and was constantly flying back and forth from London. Just before our film was released, he switched flights at the last minute in Palma during a French air traffic controllers' strike. His new plane collided with a military jet over Nantes, killing everyone on board.

Hendrix biographers revile Jeffreys's reluctance to let Jimi play with his black American peers instead of the English-boy rhythm section. There were questions over his accounting practices and (unfounded) whispers about dark goings-on connected with Jimi's death, linked to his star's threat to change managers. We interviewed Alan Douglas, the new manager Jimi was flirting with when he died.

Douglas was a friend of Danny Halperin's, an old-school hipster who kept pace. He made some ground-breaking records (the Last Poets, for one) and recorded a number of jam sessions with Jimi. Alan understood Jimi's urge to make more adventurous, soulful music and encouraged it. Jeffreys saw Alan as the Devil incarnate, luring Jimi away into a dark – and uncommercial – world.

Douglas talked to us in his Greenwich Village apartment, the afternoon sun beaming through the skylight like a spotlight. He claimed Jimi had asked him to take over his management and that he was getting ready to board a plane for London with the contracts in his briefcase when he learned of Jimi's death. As we edited the film, trying to get it down under two hours, we dropped first one then another of Alan's soundbites until only one remained. He looks quizzically up at John's question: 'Drugs? Sure, Jimi was into whatever was going around' (pause). 'Of course, I used to' (short, violent nasal inhale) 'check it out for him first.' We were never certain whether Alan meant the snort as a meaningful emphasis or whether he just needed to take a breath at that moment, but it made for good cinema. When I looked at the final cut, I realized that my brief friendship with Alan would probably end when he saw it.

Leo Branton was pondering what to do with the various unreleased Hendrix masters. He wanted nothing to do with Jeffreys – the two were sworn enemies – and Eddie Kramer, engineer on most of Jimi's albums, was tainted by his connection to the past. Branton didn't like the sound of Douglas and was suspicious of his reluctance to give the estate access to his many hours of Hendrix recordings. I resolved to break the logjam, partly as a gesture to Alan prior to his viewing the film, but mainly to help my employers. I invited Leo, Alan and Mo Ostin to lunch in Burbank. There, the three of them sealed the deal that put

Hendrix's posthumous recording career in the hands of Alan Douglas and began the partnership between Leo and Alan that would survive into the '90s. Gratitude has a short memory: it was years after the release of the film before Alan spoke to me again, and he tried on several occasions to have it taken out of circulation.

On my flight to London ahead of our first interview shoot, I saw a tall, striking black girl struggling with a huge clothes bag. I helped her put it in the overhead compartment and we exchanged smiles as I headed for my seat. When we arrived at Heathrow the next morning, I came across her again, still wrestling with her luggage. We divided it up and chatted as we made our way through immigration and customs. I gave her a lift in a taxi and we were almost at her destination when she asked what brought me to London. She nearly fainted when I told her of my mission. She was Devon Wilson, the legendary 'Dolly Dagger', the girl Jimi had left to stay with Monica Dannerman just before he died. She had heard about our documentary and had wanted no part of it. My gallantry seemed to reassure her: we exchanged phone numbers and agreed to arrange an interview.

The first time I called, a guarded and suspicious woman said that Devon couldn't come to the phone. I tried again and finally spoke to her. She sounded completely out of it, complaining of jet lag, but clearly stoned. All that week I tried to get through, but she never returned calls and the atmosphere in the flat whenever someone answered was completely narcotized. Any interview we might have done, of course, would have ended up as San Fernando Valley landfill. By the time we came back for our second try, Devon was dead of an overdose.

Arranging an interview with Monica Dannerman, on the other hand, wasn't hard at all. The difficult part was keeping awake during it. We couldn't see what had drawn Jimi to the gloomy, self-justifying, rather plain German ex-figure-skater.

There was no dozing off around Leo Branton. His work for the Hendrix estate was a minor distraction from his primary task that year as chief defence counsel for Angela Davis. Davis, a radical professor, had befriended a group of imprisoned Black Power activists and was accused of supplying guns for their bloody break-out attempt. She became a hate figure for the Nixon administration and a symbol of everything white America loathed and feared about black radicalism. Leo would visit our editing room on Fridays, the weekly recess day in the trial taking place in Marin County.

Theoretically, as our associate producer, he was there to view our most recent changes to the film. But Leo was from a generation of educated, upwardly mobile blacks for whom 'sophistication' was a key word. He was a friend of Harry Edison and his musical taste was epitomized by Sarah Vaughan, Nat 'King' Cole, Dorothy Dandridge and – on the outer fringe – Miles Davis. He disliked Miles's Hendrix-inspired experiments and found Jimi's influence on music and on the image of black people in general somewhat distasteful.

This conflict between his position and his taste usually led to a quick change of subject. He would give us a blow-by-blow account of the week's events at the trial. He could do wicked impersonations of the judge, the prosecuting attorney and the police witnesses as they twisted like pretzels to try to pin the charge on Davis. We understood why he was such a great defence attorney; Angela Davis was found not guilty.

Many hours in the editing room were spent poring over the Isle of Wight footage. In contrast to the situation with the other Hendrix material, we had secured all five camera rolls (shot by the remarkable 'Tattoist' camera operators collective) and could make our own choice of cuts. We were particularly impressed with Camera 5, Nic Knowland's camera from stage right. During 'Red House', Knowland focuses on the microphone in profile as Jimi leans in to sing a line then resists the temptation to follow as Jimi backs away to play a guitar lick. With the left side of the frame filled with aquamarine light and mist, Jimi's face suddenly darts back in through the haze as he delivers the next line. The shot is so musical, the viewer is pulled into the metre and flow of the song. We stayed on Camera 5 for huge swaths of the Isle of Wight sequence at the end of the film. The mood created by director Murray Lerner and the Tattoist team captured the despair and genius of Jimi's performance. We ended the film with the shot of him dropping his guitar on stage with a thud and walking away, as if he had just tossed an empty cigarette pack into the gutter. Three weeks later, he was dead.

I had little contact with Hendrix during his lifetime. I met him once at UFO and was at the famous Savile Theatre show where he jumped on top of Noel Redding and seemed to be either hitting or humping him. Delving into his short life to assemble the film was fascinating and unbearably sad. Before being discovered, he made pilgrimages to the Greenwich Village clubs I had frequented with Paul Rothchild and became obsessed with Dylan and the folk-rock scene. In the R&B world where he made his living he was surrounded by brilliant talents who dreamed of *The Ed Sullivan Show*, Las Vegas, *American Bandstand* and the Top Forty. Jimi, alone of his Harlem friends, fantasized about being managed by Albert Grossman, playing in London with the Rolling Stones or the Beatles and writing songs about gypsies and space travel. Fayne Pridgin told of the time Jimi brought a 'special present' for her from London. '*Acid?* What the fuck is *acid*?' There were few in Harlem into anything besides grass, coke, booze or smack.

His sophistication was on display in a clip from *The Dick Cavett Show*. The host brings up the 'gimmick' charge over Jimi picking the guitar with his teeth, playing it behind his head and setting it alight at Monterey. (The first two were blues traditions commonly practised by Buddy Guy, but generally unknown to white audiences.) 'Gimmicks! I'm sick and tired of hearing that all the time. People are always accusing me of using gimmicks!' Long pause. Then, *faux* meekly, 'Yes, they're right, we do.'

Our film was a memorial, not a piece of investigative journalism, so it draws no conclusions about his death. We came to feel that he had spent his life torn in different directions: between his mother and his father; his sensitive nature and the toughness of his street buddies; the R&B world and Greenwich Village. He always tried to keep both sides happy. In the final week of his life he promised Alan Douglas that he would leave Jeffreys just as he assured Jeffreys he would stay. He told Bill Cox he was now the permanent holder of the bass chair and sent word to Noel Redding that he wanted to talk to him about coming back. He was, for whatever reason, fascinated with Monica Dannerman and they talked of getting a flat together, but he had phoned Devon that last day saying he couldn't wait to come back to her. Is it any wonder he wanted a good long sleep?

The film – entitled simply *Jimi Hendrix* – did reasonably well but the Hendrix family (Al had remarried, his new wife a middle-class Japanese woman) disliked its references to drugs and sex and the interviews with his friends from the Harlem days. Al grew impatient with the estate's modest income and demanded to be bought out for a million dollars.

Leo found him his million and the rights were turned over to an investment company in the Dutch Antilles. Leo and Alan Douglas became the odd couple, working together for this mysterious firm to make the Hendrix catalogue into something of value. When they started negotiating a hundred-million-dollar sale of the catalogue twenty years later, Al came out of the woodwork, backed by billionaire fan Paul Allen, and sued to regain ownership.

On the face of it, he had no case: a sale, after all, is a sale. But Allen's detectives turned up the awkward fact that Branton was an owner of the Antilles company with whom he had negotiated the deal. Alan and Leo were forced to walk away, missing their big payday, and Leo, one of America's greatest civil rights attorneys, had a question mark hanging over his career as he came to retire. When Al died, he left the estate in the hands of his stepdaughter, a Japanese-American born-again Christian of no blood relation to Jimi. Paul Allen has built a museum in Seattle to memorialize him. *Jimi Hendrix* is now available on DVD.

chapter 33

THE CALL FROM JOHN WOOD didn't come as a complete surprise. Not after that terrible evening in early 1974 when Nick came to see me. He looked far worse than I had ever seen him: his hair was greasy, his hands dirty, his clothes rumpled. More unnervingly, he was angry. I had told him he was a genius, and others had concurred. So, he demanded, why wasn't he famous and rich? This rage must have festered beneath that inexpressive exterior for years. I confessed my own disillusionment – I had thought a great record would open all doors. Some good reviews, a few plays on John Peel – with no live shows, it hadn't been enough.

I proposed starting a new album. I had no idea what would emerge, but it was the only therapy at my disposal. At Sound Techniques he stumbled trying to play and sing at the same time. We decided to record the guitar first, then overdub the vocals. John and I exchanged anguished looks: this was the man who had recorded the guitar and vocal of 'River Man' live with an orchestra. We struggled to get four guitar tracks down on tape the first night, then came back the following evening for the vocals and to do a rough mix. The words of the songs were even more devastating than the way he recorded them:

Why leave me hanging on a star
When you deem me so high
When you deem me so high?

Why leave me sailing in a sea
When you hear me so clear
When you hear me so clear?

And:

Black-eyed dog he called at my door
Black-eyed dog he called for more
Black-eyed dog he knew my name
Black-eyed dog he knew my name

Growing old and I want to go home
Growing old and I don't want to know.

Cerberus and Robert Johnson's 'Hellhound' were never more ominous.

I was in California months later when John rang to tell me Nick was dead. The coroner's inquest returned a verdict of suicide, but I wasn't convinced. The anti-depressants Nick had been taking were different from modern drugs; doses were far stronger and the side effects only beginning to be understood. Nick's parents said he was very positive in the weeks before his death, planning a move back to London and starting to play the guitar again. But the drugs have been known to cause patients to 'roller-coaster'. How would he have responded if, after weeks of feeling good about the future, he suddenly crashed back into despair? Might he, one terrible night, have decided he needed a lot more of those pills that once made him feel so optimistic? Did he know that too many could be fatal? The lyrics of his last songs may support the coroner's view, but I prefer to imagine Nick making a desperate lunge for life rather than a calculated surrender to death.

The months after his death brought anguished thoughts. Would he still be alive if I had stayed in London? Was it my phone call which gave him the reassurance he needed to start the treatment that led to the fatal pills? I kept thinking about 'Fruit Tree', as if those prophetic lyrics somehow made it all OK, that this was his choice. But the angry man I met that evening was not fulfilling some gloomy romantic fantasy, he was in a hell of bitter loneliness and despair. That story was not from 'Fruit Tree' but from another of his early songs, 'Day Is Done':

When the game's been fought
You speed the ball across the court
Lost much sooner than you would have thought
Now the game's been fought.

When the party's through
Seems so very sad for you
Didn't do the things you meant to do
Now there's no time to start anew
Now the party's through.

When the day is done
Down to earth then sinks the sun
Along with everything that was lost and won
When the day is done.

The sale of Witchseason included a provision that Nick's LPs must never be deleted, although I didn't need to argue the point with Blackwell – he loved Nick, too. When he died, his sales were non-existent. Slowly, they began an annual increase that grew steeper year by year. Thoughtful articles by Arthur Lubow, Brian Cullman and Peter Paphides helped. In the late '70s, his family and I started to get an occasional pilgrim from a small town in Ohio, or

Scandinavia, or the north of England. They just wanted to tell us how much his music meant to them and talk to someone who knew him. His parents were so touched by this that some were permitted to spend a night in Nick's room and make copies of his home recordings – hence the bootlegs of recent years.

Then we started getting enquiries about film scripts and biographies. By the time the Volkswagen commercial with 'Pink Moon' arrived on American television in the late '90s, there was an established Nick Drake cult, the records were selling tens of thousands a year and Nick's was a fashionable name for young singers to drop when asked to cite their influences. Is Nick's music, as critics often state, 'timeless'? Or has it been liberated from its period by failing to connect with audiences when it was released? Nick's music was never a soundtrack for their parents' memories, so modern audiences are free to make it their own.

Nick listened carefully to Dylan, to Bert Jansch and Davey Graham, and to genteel bluesmen like Josh White and Brownie McGhee. He enjoyed Delius and Chopin, Miles Davis and Django Reinhardt, and read English poetry. He and his sister Gabrielle used to perform duets inspired by Nina and Frederick. But analyses of his influences have difficulty explaining the originality of his music, particularly the shape of his chords. When I visited the family home in Tanworth-in-Arden, I saw a piano in the hall with music paper scattered on top. His mother Molly, a wonderfully energetic and funny woman, mentioned that she had written 'a few amateur things'. Many years after Nick's and Molly's deaths, Gabrielle gave me a tape of her mother's songs. There, in her piano chords, are the roots of Nick's harmonies. His reinvention of the standard guitar tuning was the only way to match the music he heard as he was growing up. Molly's compositions are of a period but very beautiful and not just because they foreshadow Nick's. Perhaps the core of his musical nature was so strong because his greatest influence had nothing to do with the world outside his home.

Many have speculated about Nick's sexuality. There is certainly a virginal quality about his music and I never saw him behaving in a sexual way with anyone, male or female. Linda Thompson tried to seduce Nick once, but he just sat on the end of the bed, fully clothed, looking at his hands. He assumes the role of onlooker in his songs, yearningly observing girls from a distance, begging them to pay him some attention. He sings of others living fast and exciting lives – 'three hours from London, Jeremy flies, hoping to keep the sun from his eyes'.

English public schools could be devastating places for male sexuality. It was a cliché in the sixties that boys emerged from such places 'inverted' or inhibited while girls left their boarding schools eager for action. Yet Nick's music is supremely sensual: the delicate whisper of his voice, the romantic melodies, the tenderly sad lyrics, the intricate dexterity of his fingers on the guitar – all fascinate and attract female listeners.

Gabrielle Drake has had a successful career as an actor in the theatre and on television. Her characterizations often take on the classic sexiness of the husky-voiced upper-middle-class English rose, like a Joan Greenwood or Glynis Johns. She seems to have suffered none of Nick's isolation or loneliness. In person, she is self-contained but direct and seems very comfortable in her physicality and her femininity with none of Nick's apologetic stoop or hesitant speech.

Gabrielle now administers the estate with great determination and concern for Nick's legacy. As the sixties drew to a close, who would have predicted that the end of the millennium would see Nick's music so much more prominent than that of the Incredible String Band, Fairport Convention, John Martyn or Sandy Denny? Perhaps even Leonard Cohen's? I might have said 'Don't bet against it', but only under my breath.

The smart money then would have been on Sandy. Despite the problems with Fotheringay, she entered the '70s with her career in full sail. John Wood, Richard Thompson and husband Trevor all worked with her as producers and came up with powerful versions of great songs, but there was no single classic album. She and I restored friendly relations when I returned to London in the mid-'70s but were never again as close. A song she wrote soon after the breakup of Fotheringay seemed directed at me:

I've just gone solo
Do you play solo?
Ain't life a solo?

Solitude was something she was determined to avoid, throwing herself into relationships with needy urgency:

When the music's playing
That's when it changes
And no longer do we seem like total strangers
It's all those words which always get in the way
Of what you want to say

When I wake up
In the morning
I think it only fair to give you warning
I probably won't go away
I'll more than likely stay.

After years of increasing problems with drink and occasional white powders, she became pregnant – possibly to save her crumbling marriage. But the birth of her daughter Georgia in 1977 failed to provide the cure, and when Trevor left for Australia with their child – ostensibly to show her to his parents – she despaired of seeing either of them again. The last of a series of bad falls – first at her home, then her parents' house, finally at a friend's flat in London – left her with a cerebral haemorrhage. She never regained consciousness and died on 21 April, 1978. Trevor remarried, moved back to Australia and died in his sleep eleven years later. Georgia was raised by Trevor's second wife and still lives in Australia.

Sandy and Nick regarded each other with respect but from a distance. Sandy couldn't relate to Nick, and Nick was as reticent towards her as he was towards most people. They were both English to the core, but what might seem a nuance of difference between suburban middle class and rural/colonial upper middle class is actually a chasm; it was easier for the working-class Bob Squire or Danny Thompson to communicate with either than for them to relate to each other.

Both benefited from an upbringing and education that steeped in them a sense of history. Sandy had a solid grounding in English literature and adored the relationship between the history she learned at school and the ancient ballads she taught Fairport. Nick grew up inhaling the air of an elite education: the Romantic and Elizabethan poets were omnipresent in his school years. Nick's emulators rarely have the cultural context to grasp how remote their lyrics are from his.

Another gap between Nick and Sandy was drugs. She never liked cannabis much – it was too introspective. For her, drink was the way to relax, and when her life began to spiral downhill, cocaine briefly boosted her confidence. Nick never, to my knowledge, ventured much beyond hashish. But he shared with Sandy an instinctive rejection of moderation and his endless spliffs played a large part in his isolation.

I listened in the studio control room as musicians' modes of consciousness-alteration proceeded from grass, hash and acid to heroin and cocaine by the 1970s. All but the latter could, on occasion, provide benefits, at least to the music. I never knew cocaine to improve anything. When the white lines came out, it was time to call it a night: the music could only get worse. If I joined in, the next day's playback would provide clear evidence of the deterioration of both the performances and of my critical ability to judge them. I suspect that the surge in cocaine's popularity explains – at least in part – why so many great sixties artists made such bad records in the following decade.

Psychologists Timothy Leary and Richard Alpert were dismissed from Harvard for failing to maintain a professional distance: they used to trip along with the students. When I was at Harvard and a girlfriend started having a bad trip, I rang Alpert's home at 3 a.m. and he calmly advised me to put her into a warm bath to relax her. By the time millions of kids were re-creating those Harvard experiments, Alpert had decided he wanted something else. He set off for India where he met a Californian hitch-hiker who seemed calmer than anyone he had ever met. He followed him to the remote cave where his guru lived on a diet of moss. The holy man recounted all Alpert's dreams since he had met the hitch-hiker and, among the aspirins, anti-diarrhoea pills and Valiums in Alpert's pillbox, picked out the twelve tabs of Owsley acid. After swallowing them, he proceeded to discuss spiritual paths for the next eight hours as if nothing had happened. In that cave, Alpert was transformed into Baba Ram Dass and never took drugs again.

Is this one legacy of the sixties? That after flinging

open the doors to a world previously known only at the margins of society, the pioneers would move on, leaving the masses to add drugs to the myriad forces pulling our society towards chaos and mediocrity? As to the sixties' musical bequest, other generations will decide whether it proves more durable than that of the later decades of the century. I wouldn't bet against it.

The atmosphere in which music flourished then had a lot to do with economics. It was a time of unprecedented prosperity. People are supposedly wealthier now, yet most feel they haven't enough money and time is at an even greater premium. The prediction that our biggest dilemma in the new millennium would be how to use the endless hours of leisure time freed up by computers has proved to be futurology's least amusing joke. In the sixties, we had surpluses of both money and time.

Friends of mine lived comfortably in Greenwich Village, Harvard Square, Bayswater, Santa Monica and on the Left Bank and were, by current standards, broke. Yet they survived easily on occasional coffee-house gigs or part-time work. Today, urbanites must feverishly maximize their economic potential just to maintain a small flat in Hoboken, Somerville, Hackney, Korea Town or Belleville. The economy of the sixties cut us a lot of slack, leaving time to travel, take drugs, write songs and rethink the universe. There was a feeling that nothing was nailed down, that an assumption held was one worth challenging. The meek regularly took on the mighty and often won – or at least drew. Debt-free students with time on their hands forced the Pentagon to stop using drafted American kids as cannon fodder and altered the political landscape of France.

The tightening of fiscal screws that began with the 1973 oil crisis may not have been a conspiracy to rein in this dangerous laxness, but it has certainly worked out to the advantage of the powerful. Ever since, prices have ratcheted upwards in relation to hours worked and the results of this squeeze can be seen everywhere. Protesters today seem like peasants outside the castle gates compared to the fiercely determined and unified crowds I joined in the sixties. Our confidence grew out of a feeling that large sections of the population – and the media – were with us and from what we saw as the inexorable power of our music and our convictions. In our glorious optimism, we believed that 'when the mode of music changes, the walls of the city shake'. And we achieved a great deal before the authorities figured out how to capitalize on our self-destructiveness. Right-wing commentators still spit with anger when they contemplate how fundamentally the sixties altered society. The environmental and human rights movements and the theoretical equality of races and sexes are only the tip of a huge iceberg. Ideals that remain our source of hope for the future took root in the sixties.

Part of our strength came from our sense of connection with the past. I remember feeling in my teens that the past was so close I could touch it. I heard my grandmother talk about Vienna at the turn of the century and play Brahms in a long-forgotten style as I sat next to her on the piano bench, watching her long veiny fingers. She told me that as a teenager she could rest the heel of her left hand on a pane of glass, raise her fourth finger, bring it down and crack the glass. I could hear the sound of that violent impact in my mind, a feat of undistracted discipline almost impossible to imagine, yet as close as her mesmerizing hands.

Sitting in Princeton listening to old records, we became obsessed with the past. We tried to pierce the veil of time and grasp what it sounded, felt, looked and smelled like. In Harvard Square and London I met many with similar preoccupations; they didn't seem unusual at all. When old blues singers began to reappear, it delivered a rush of excitement and adrenalin. Meeting and travelling with Gary Davis and Lonnie Johnson – even Coleman Hawkins – armoured me against a host of disappointments.

History today seems more like a postmodern collage; we are surrounded by two-dimensional representations of our heritage. Access via amazon.com or iPod to all those boxed sets of old blues singers – or Nick Drake, for that matter – doesn't equate with the sense of discovery and connection we experienced. The very existence of such a wealth of information creates an overload that can drown out vivid moments of revelation.

We fuelled ourselves with inspiration from our cultural heritage, and in so doing helped turn it into smoke. The roots of today's digitized and sampled culture lie in those years of genuine enquiry and enthusiasm. Much of the sixties is mirrored in that Sunday night at Newport, when Dylan sent Pete Seeger fleeing into the night with the jubilant aggression of his music – music originally inspired by Seeger himself.

What followed in the wake of that night swept up most of the potential young fans of Thelonious Monk or Skip James, propelled them into the Fillmores and blew their minds with the simplistic sounds of the Grateful Dead. Few took time to mourn, as we did backstage at Newport, for what was so heedlessly tossed aside.

Before the turn of the century – the nineteenth century, that is – there was an underground craze that swept through black America. Someone came up with a catchy AAB twelve-bar structure with melancholy melodic intervals which provided the perfect frame on which to hang lyrics about heartbreak, natural disasters, evil white bosses and every other aspect of life at the end of a century that had falsely promised a road to freedom. Blues itself was an innovative craze that swept away decades – perhaps centuries – of folk traditions. We hear echoes of what disappeared in the recordings of Henry Thomas and Charlie Patton, but it is like trying to reconstruct a Cherokee city from a few arrowheads and beads unearthed at a construction site in downtown Atlanta. The destructiveness that comes with innovation is a process as old as history.

The England that awaited me when I moved to London a few months after Newport was only just emerging from a long class-ridden slumber. In the '80s, when I developed a film project with screenwriter Michael Thomas about Christine Keeler, Stephen Ward and the Profumo affair, I learned just how momentous had been the upheaval in the year prior to my arrival. Released as *Scandal* in 1988, our film helped England rewrite a bit of its own history: the movie's success placed Ward and Keeler in the roles of victims of the Establishment rather than the irresponsible upstarts the press had made them out to be at the time. The story helped explain the sense of adventure and excitement I found in so many people in 1964; it was as if a great weight had been lifted off their shoulders. But the sense of delight at new possibilities lasted only a few years before the return of Conservative government and 1973's three-day week put an end to it. But like the rest of the world, Britain would never return to its pre-sixties assumptions about life and society.

At the height of the decade, we remained optimistic in a way that today – as we watch our world being consumed from under us – is impossible to imagine. For me, the contrast between spring and autumn '67 in London planted the first doubts. The violence at Altamont eroded optimism for many; Charles Manson and the descent of Haight–Ashbury into squalor relieved us of a lot more. The discovery – thanks to Michael Herr's *Dispatches* – that

American fighter pilots could machine-gun Vietnamese farmers for sport while listening to Dylan and Hendrix on cockpit headphones finished off what remained for me. As my time at Warner Brothers drew to a close, I stood on a hilltop in Laurel Canyon watching the smoke on the southern horizon as members of the Symbionese Liberation Army were incinerated by an LA SWAT team. By then, the ideals of the sixties were visible mostly in fun-house-mirror form. Today, when the mode of music changes, the walls of the city are covered in corporate ads sponsoring superficially subversive artists.

I limit my regrets to friends and peers whose lives were consumed by the intensity of the times. I think of Nick and Sandy, of Martin Lamble and Jeannie Taylor, of Bob Squire (who broke his own rule against heroin and died of it). I mourn Chris McGregor, Dudu Pukwana, Mongezi Feza and Johnny Dyani, who, lured by the false promise of our rhetoric, died so young and so far from home.

I think of Jimi Hendrix, whom I knew only on film but about whom I learned so much, a man whose dreams led him into a life surrounded by pressures and people who meant him little good. Devon Wilson haunts me: her charisma and intelligence flashed so brightly in the course of one taxi ride that I couldn't forget her. Sentimentally, I wished he had made it back to her; perhaps they could have saved each other.

Roy Guest, who died a sad and lonely death in the '90s, was, like Stephen Ward, someone for whom the sixties came too late to undo the damage inflicted by aristocratic snobbery and cruelty.

I mourn Don Simpson; the man I knew bore little resemblance to the bloated cartoon character found dead beside his pool in 1996, still pursuing the Hollywood dreams we shared for a time.

I miss the pre-Scientology Mike Heron and Robin Williamson and wish I had never left them alone with David Simons or let them duck for cover out of the Woodstock rain.

I wonder what might have happened had I stayed in London in 1971.

Tony Howard and Paul Rothchild were not casualties of the era but died far too soon, and I miss them; where would I have been without them? I think also of Hoppy, who, though he shines today as brightly as ever, left behind him in prison the optimism and confidence that were a beacon for so many of us.

But I think happily of those friends who continue to perform with the same spirit that delighted me when first I heard them more than thirty years ago – Norma Waterson, Richard Thompson, Geoff Muldaur and Danny Thompson foremost among them.

And as for me, I cheated. I never got too stoned. I became the *éminence grise* I aspired to be, and disproved at least one sixties myth: I *was* there, and I *do* remember.

joe boyd

productions and co-productions 1966–1974

1966

Sydney Carter	Lord Of The Dance	EP	Elektra EPK 801
Alasdair Clayre	Alasdair Clayre	LP	Elektra EUK 255
The Incredible String Band	The Incredible String Band	LP	Elektra EUK 251
Various artists	A Cold Wind Blows	LP	Elektra EUK 253
Various artists	What's Shakin' – *3 tracks by Eric Clapton & the Powerhouse*	LP	Elektra EUK 250

1967

Shirley Collins	The Power Of The True Love Knot	LP	Polydor 583 025
The Incredible String Band	The 5000 Spirits Or The Layers Of The Onion	LP	Elektra EUK 257
Pink Floyd	Arnold Layne / Candy and A Currant Bun	S	Columbia DB 8156
The Purple Gang	Granny Takes A Trip / Bootleg Whiskey	S	Transatlantic BIG T 111
The Purple Gang	Strikes! – *only Granny Takes A Trip*	LP	Transatlantic TRA 174
Dave Swarbrick, Martin Carthy & Diz Disley	Rags Reels & Airs	LP	Bounty BY 6030

1968

Fairport Convention	If I Had A Ribbon Bow / If (Stomp)	S	Track 604 020
Fairport Convention	Fairport Convention	LP	Polydor 583 035
The Incredible String Band	The Hangman's Beautiful Daughter	LP	Elektra EUK 258
The Incredible String Band	Wee Tam & The Big Huge	2LP	Elektra EKS 74036/7
Chris McGregor Group	Very Urgent	LP	Polydor 184 137
Various artists	Kalpana – instrumental and dance music of India	LP	Nonsuch 72022 (US)
Various artists	Tonite Let's All Make Love In London – *2 tracks by Pink Floyd*	LP	Instant INLP 002

1969			
Nick Drake	Five Leaves Left	LP	Island ILPS 9105
Fairport Convention	What We Did On Our Holidays	LP	Island ILPS 9092
Fairport Convention	Si Tu Dois Partir / Genesis Hall	S	Island WIP 6064
Fairport Convention	Unhalfbricking	LP	Island ILPS 9102
Fairport Convention	Liege & Lief	LP	Island ILPS 9115
The Incredible String Band	Changing Horses	LP	Elektra EKS 75047
Dr Strangely Strange	Kip Of The Serenes	LP	Island ILPS 9106

1970			
Vashti Bunyan	Just Another Diamond Day	LP	Phillips 6308 019
Nick Drake	Bryter Layter	LP	Island ILPS 9134
Fairport Convention	Full House	LP	Island ILPS 9130
Fairport Convention	Now Be Thankful / Sir B McKenzie's…	S	Island WIP 6089
Fotheringay	Fotheringay	LP	Island ILPS 9125
The Incredible String Band	I Looked Up	LP	Elektra 2460 002
The Incredible String Band	'U'	2LP	Elektra 2409 001/2
The Incredible String Band	Be Glad For The Song Has No Ending	LP	Island ILPS 9140
Chris McGregor's Brotherhood of Breath	Brotherhood Of Breath	LP	RCA Neon NE2
John & Beverley Martyn	Stormbringer!	LP	Island ILPS 911
Geoff & Maria Muldaur	Pottery Pie	LP	Reprise RS 6350 (US)

1971			
Mike Heron	Smiling Men With Bad Reputations	LP	Island ILPS 9146
John & Beverley Martyn	The Road To Ruin	LP	Island ILPS 9133
Nico	Desertshore	LP	Reprise K 46065
Dr Strangely Strange	Heavy Petting	LP	Vertigo 6360 009

1973			
Maria Muldaur	Maria Muldaur	LP	Reprise K 44255
Maria Muldaur	Midnight At The Oasis / Any Old Time	S	Reprise K 17532
Eric Weisberg & Steve Mandel	Duelling Banjos / Reuben's Train	S	Warner Bros K 16223

1974			
Maria Muldaur	Waitress In A Donut Shop	LP	Reprise K 54025
Muleskinner	Muleskinner	LP	Warner Bros BS 2787

index